KU-176-160

Ukrainian

PHRASEBOOK & DICTIONARY

Acknowledgments
Associate Publisher Mina Patria
Associate Product Director Angela Tinson
Product Editor Elizabeth Jones, Amanda Williamson
Series Designer James Hardy
Language Writer Marko Pavlyshyn
Cover Image Researcher Naomi Parker

Thanks

Larissa Frost, Carol Jackson, Chris Love, Wayne Murphy

Published by Lonely Planet Global Limited
CRN 554153

4th Edition – April 2014
ISBN 978 1 74321 185 4
Text © Lonely Planet 2014
Cover Image St Michael's Monastery, Kyiv, Ukraine, Aldo Pavan /
4CORNERS ©

Printed in Malaysia   10 9 8 7 6 5 4

Contact lonelyplanet.com/contact

Although the authors and Lonely Planet try to make the information
as accurate as possible, we accept no responsibility for any loss, injury
or inconvenience sustained by anyone using this book.

Paper in this book is certified against the Forest Stewardship Council™
standards. FSC™ promotes environmentally responsible, socially
beneficial and economically viable management of the world's forests.

MIX
Paper from
responsible sources
FSC™ C021741

acknowledgments

about the author

Marko Pavlyshyn heads the Mykola Zerov Program in Ukrainian Studies at Monash University, Melbourne, where he is also Director of the Centre for European Studies. He is the author of *Canon and Iconostasis* (Kyiv, 1997) and numerous studies on modern Ukrainian literature.

from the author

Thanks to Olya Pavlyshyn for all her help, our son Damian for his patience, my Monash students for their suggestions, and our family and friends in Ukraine for their information and advice.

from the publisher

Thanks to James Dingley and Olena Bekh who wrote the first edition of the Lonely Planet *Ukrainian Phrasebook*, from which this edition developed. Many thanks also to Marko Kandybko for his work on the Sustainable Travel section and Solomiya Buk for her eagle eye and insightful suggestions in proofing and revising this edition.

In Lonely Planet's Melbourne office, Associate Publisher Ben Handicott, Project Manager, Jane Atkin and Commissioning Editors, Quentin Frayne and Karin Vidstrup Monk, all put in the hard yards to help bring the new edition to life.

CONTENTS

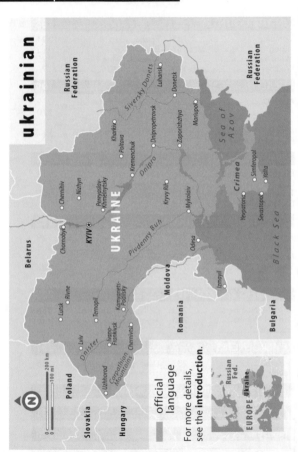

ukrainian

Russian Federation

Belarus

Russian Federation

Poland

Slovakia

Hungary

Romania

Moldova

Bulgaria

Uzhhorod

Lviv

Lutsk

Rivne

Ternopil

Ivano-Frankivsk

Kamyanets-Podilsky

Chernivtsi

Carpathian Mountains

Dnister

Pivdenny Buh

Chornobyl

★ KYIV

Chernihiv

Nizhyn

Pereyaslav-Khmelnytsky

UKRAINE

Kharkiv

Poltava

Kremenchuk

Dnipro

Dnipropetrovsk

Kryvy Rih

Mykolaiv

Siversky Donets

Luhansk

Donetsk

Zaporizhzhya

Mariupol

Sea of Azov

Odesa

Izmayil

Crimea

Yevpatoria

Sevastopol

Simferopol

Yalta

Black Sea

N

0   200 km
0   100 mi

official language

For more details,
see the **introduction**.

EUROPE

Russian Fed.

Ukraine

INTRODUCTION

Ukrainian is the official language of Ukraine, the second-largest country in Europe (603,700 sq km). It's the native language of the great majority of Ukraine's 45 million people and is also spoken in Eastern Europe (Russia, Poland, Belarus, Slovakia, Romania, Hungary and Moldova) and Central Asia (Kazakhstan, Uzbekistan and Kyrgyzstan). There are Ukrainian-speaking communities in Canada, the United States, South America and Australia.

Ukrainians refer to their country as 'Ukraine' rather than 'the Ukraine', as many feel that the latter implies a region, not an independent country. Ukraine's history is rooted in Kyivan Rus', the powerful Slavic state from the 10th and 11th centuries. Another famous page in Ukrainian history is the time of the Cossack Hetmanate during the 17th and 18th centuries. After a short-lived period of independence in 1917–20, Ukraine became part of the Soviet Union, and finally recovered its independence in 1991. Famous for the fabulously fertile black soil of its steppes, Ukraine today is also highly urbanised and industrialised. Its economic potential and strategic importance ensure that it has an important role to play on the world stage.

Ukrainian belongs to the Slavic group of the Indo-European family of languages and is most closely related to Russian and Belarusian. Its development has been turbulent: the written form was banned by the Russian tsars in the 19th century, and after a short revival at the beginning of the 20th century came Stalin's policy of 'Russification', which meant that Ukrainian was significantly supplanted by Russian in most domains. Political factors were largely responsible for the development of what was regarded as 'proper' Ukrainian. The Ukrainian used in this book is the standard literary language.

Ukrainian uses the Cyrillic alphabet (so called after St Cyril, who is credited with inventing it in the 9th century to help spread Orthodox Christianity among the 'pagan' Slavs). This alphabet is easier to master than it may first appear. You will be able to recognise many words, eg музика is 'music', театр is 'theatre' and автобус is 'autobus'.

INTRODUCTION

Other Ukrainian words are related to their English counterparts, thanks to the Indo-European origin that they share, but sometimes this relationship is a little harder to spot – хліб, 'bread', is the same in origin as the English 'loaf' or, even more fantastic, верблюд, 'camel', actually comes from the Greek word for 'elephant'. With a bit of practice, though, you'll be able to recognise and read these words too without any difficulties.

Anyone visiting Ukraine who shows even a slight familiarity with the language will be sure of a very warm welcome. By showing that you know some Ukrainian you are sharing in the adventure of freedom that the Ukrainian people themselves are now experiencing. We wish you good luck on your journey to Ukraine and with the Ukrainian language. ba-*zha*-ye-mo shcha-*sly*-vo-yi do-*ro*-hy!(Бажаємо щасливої дороги!), 'Bon voyage!'

ABBREVIATIONS USED IN THIS BOOK

adj	adjective	n	noun
adv	adverb	neut	neuter
conj	conjunction	pl	plural
f	feminine	pol	polite
inf	informal	prep	preposition
lit	literal translation	sg	singular
m	masculine	v	verb

GETTING STARTED

The most common greeting in Ukrainian is *do*-bry den' (добрий день), corresponding to our 'Good day; Hello'. Try to memorise the small – but important – words like tak (так) for 'Yes' and ni (ні) for 'No'. You'll hear *dya*-ku-yu (дякую) for 'Thank you' and 'Please' is bud' *la*-ska (будь ласка) or *pro*-shu (прошу).

When you're meeting people you'll find the phrases on page 46 useful and, if you want to join in the conversation, turn to page 53 for some handy conversation fillers. The phrases on page 65 will help if you're having trouble making yourself understood and, in case of emergencies, turn to page 237.

LEGEND

The following notation is used throughout this phrasebook:

( ) parentheses

- enclosing text within a phrase is optional:

> I'm trying to give up (smoking).
> ya na-ma-*ha*-yu-sya
> *ky*-nu-ty (pa-*ly*-ty)
>
> Я намагаюся
> кинути (палити).

- enclosing text not within a phrase (but following it or in a list) indicates one of the following:
  - meaning, eg, demonstration (protest)
  - usage, eg, date (time)
  - part of speech, eg, human (adj), near (prep)
  - singular versus plural form, eg, footstep(s)
  - literal translation, eg, (lit: driver not saw us)

/ forward slash

- indicates when single words on either side of the slash are interchangeable:

> I need ...
> me-*ni tre*-ba/po-*trib*-no ...   Мені треба/потрібно ...

> denotes:
>
> I need ...   me-*ni tre*-ba ...   Мені треба ...
> and I need ...   me-*ni* po-*trib*-no ...   Мені потрібно ...

- separates two (or more) alternatives where they consist of <u>one</u> word only. These could be synonyms or different forms of the same word (typically masculine, feminine or neuter, singular or plural, informal or polite):

> flower(s)   *kvi*-tka/*kvi*-ty (sg/pl)   квітка/квіти
> I stopped the car.   ya zu-py-*nyw*/   Я зупинив/
>   zu-py-*ny*-la   зупинила
>   ma-*shy*-nu (m/f)   машину.

> The last example denotes:
>
> I stopped the car. ya zu-py-*nyw*   Я зупинив
> and   ma-*shy*-nu (m)   машину.
> I stopped the car. ya zu-py-*ny*-la   Я зупинила
>   ma-*shy*-nu (f)   машину.

INTRODUCTION

; **semicolon**
• separates two (or more) alternatives where one (or more) consists of <u>more</u> than one word:

to change (trains)	ro-*by*-ty	робити
	pe-re-*sad*-ku;	пересадку;
	pe-re-si-*da*-ty	пересідати

denotes:

	to change (trains)	ro-*by*-ty	робити
		pe-re-*sad*-ku	пересадку
and	to change (trains)	pe-re-si-*da*-ty	пересідати

[] **square brackets**
• contain two (or more) different constructions, separated by a semicolon. Depending on context, one construction is compulsory in the phrase:

I'd like to get Internet access.	
ya [kho-*tiw* by; kho-*ti*-la b]	Я [хотів би; хотіла б]
di-*sta*-ty *do*-stup	дістати доступ
do in-ter-*ne*-tu (m/f)	до інтернету.
[What time; Where] shall we meet?	
ko-*ly*/de nam	Коли/Де нам
zu-*stri*-ty-sya?	зустрітися?

• **bullet points**
• are used in the dictionary only (in transliteration and script) to separate the alternatives (synonyms) in the foreign language:

suitcase	che-mo-*dan* •	чемодан •
	va-*li*-za • va-*liz*-ka	валіза • валізка

If it is necessary to clarify the difference between alternatives, this is indicated in parentheses after each.

PRONUNCIATION

Unlike English, where one letter may be pronounced in many different ways, each letter in Ukrainian usually stands for only one sound. This means that even as a beginner you should be able to read aloud from unfamiliar texts and be easily understood by speakers of Ukrainian. Beware, however, of the letters that look like English ones, but in fact stand for quite different sounds (see list on page 18).

VOWELS
Ukrainian has six pure vowels. All are short.

Script	Transliteration	Pronunciation
А а	a	as the 'a' in the Italian *pasta*
Е е	e	as the 'e' in 'end'
И и	y	as the 'i' in 'still', short; it never precedes or follows a proper vowel
І і	i	as the 'ee' in 'see'; it softens the preceding consonant
О о	o	as the 'o' in 'pot', but with the jaws slightly more closed and the lips a little more pursed
У у	u	as the 'u' in 'put'

There is one semivowel:

Й й	y	as the 'y' in 'yellow'; it almost always precedes or follows a pure vowel

PRONUNCIATION

There are four iotated vowels. This means that they begin with a sound like the 'y' in yellow and continue with a pure vowel.

Я	я	ya	as the 'y' in 'yellow' followed by the 'a' as in the Italian *pasta*
Є	є	ye	as the 'y' in 'yellow' followed by the 'e' as in 'end'
Ї	ї	yi	as the 'y' in 'yellow' followed by the 'ee' as in 'see'
Ю	ю	yu	as the 'y' in 'yellow' followed by the 'u' as in 'put'

ADVENTURES OF THE LETTER Ґ

The letter ґ has had a chequered career in Ukrainian alphabets in the 20th century. In 1929 it was included in the alphabet agreed upon by the orthographic conference held in Kharkiv and convened by Soviet Ukrainian authorities, but with the participation of non-Soviet Ukrainian scholars. *Ukrainian Orthography*, published in Kyiv in 1946, excluded the letter ґ. The sound g, wherever it appeared, was now to be represented by the letter г.

Ukrainians outside Ukraine and the Soviet sphere of influence retained the 1929 orthography. Many argued that the 1946 version was designed to bring Ukrainian orthography closer to Russian, especially in the rendering of foreign words. Ukrainians in Western countries staunchly continued writing 'Hegel' and 'Hemingway' as Геґель and Гемінґвей, while the spelling accepted in Ukraine was Гегель and Хемінгуей.

In 1990, on the eve of the fall of the USSR, the letter ґ was reintroduced into the Ukrainian alphabet. In 1993 it was incorporated into a new edition of *Ukrainian Orthography*.

CONSONANTS

Б	б	b	as the 'b' in 'box'
В	в	v	as the 'v' in 'van' before a vowel;
		w	as the in 'w' in 'wood' before a consonant or at the end of a word or syllable
Г	г	h	as the 'h' in 'hat', but stronger (the transliteration becomes <u>h</u> when directly after z (з); together they become <u>zh</u> and are pronounced as a 'z' and 'h' separately; see page 19)
Ґ	ґ	g	as the 'g' in 'good'
Д	д	d	as the 'd' in 'dog'
Ж	ж	zh	as the 's' in 'treasure'
З	з	z	as the 'z' in 'zoo' (the transliteration becomes <u>z</u> when directly before h (г); together they become <u>zh</u> and are pronounced as a 'z' and 'h' separately; see page 19)
К	к	k	as the 'k' in 'king'
Л	л	l	as the 'l' in 'land'
М	м	m	as the 'm' in 'much'
Н	н	n	as the 'n' in 'note'
П	п	p	as the 'p' in 'pet'
Р	р	r	as a trilled 'r'
С	с	s	as the 's' in 'sin'
Т	т	t	as the 't' in 'tame'
Ф	ф	f	as the 'f' in 'fun'
Х	х	kh	as the 'ch' in the Scottish *loch*
Ц	ц	ts	as the 'ts' in 'bits'
Ч	ч	ch	as the 'ch' in 'chew'
Ш	ш	sh	as the 'sh' in 'ship'
Щ	щ	shch	as the 'shch' in 'fresh cheese'
Ь	ь	'	indicates the preceding consonant is a 'soft consonant'; see page 16

Soft Consonants

Some consonants – d (д), z (з), l (л), n (н), s (с), t (т), and ts (ц) – are sometimes 'softened'. The 'soft' consonant is pronounced with the tongue closer to the palate than in the case of its 'hard' counterpart. If a consonant is pronounced as a soft consonant, this is indicated by the soft sign ' (ь) following it. The difference between n (н) and n' (нь) is like the difference between the 'n' in 'canoe' and the 'n' in 'sinew'. Similarly, d (д) is pronounced like the 'd' in 'do', while d' (дь) is like the 'd' in 'dew'.

THE UKRAINIAN ALPHABET

Capital	Lower case	Capital	Lower case
А	а	Н	н
Б	б	О	о
В	в	П	п
Г	г	Р	р
Ґ	ґ	С	с
Д	д	Т	т
Е	е	У	у
Є	є	Ф	ф
Ж	ж	Х	х
З	з	Ц	ц
И	и	Ч	ч
І	і	Ш	ш
Ї	ї	Щ	щ
Й	й	Ю	ю
К	к	Я	я
Л	л	Ь	ь
М	m		

TRANSLITERATION SYSTEM

Several different systems of transliterating Ukrainian into English are used for various purposes. In library catalogues and formal English versions of personal and place names, the Library of Congress (LC) system of transliteration is commonly used. While the LC system is designed to provide a uniform method of spelling Ukrainian words in Roman script, the system of transliteration (or transcription) to be used in this book aims to help the user to pronounce the words correctly by reproducing each Ukrainian sound with a Roman letter or letters corresponding to a similar English sound.

PRONUNCIATION

THE POLITICS OF TRANSLITERATION

The issue of transliteration has political significance. Since their country became independent, Ukrainians have become increasingly aware of the need to bring the Ukrainian forms of place names into international circulation. Ukraine's capital city is still sometimes referred to in English as Kiev, but this is a transliteration of the Russian form of its name. The Ukrainian Government decreed on 14 October 1995 that the name of the city was to be spelled Kyiv in Roman script. Then, in 1996, the Ukrainian Commission on Legal Terminology approved a system for transliterating personal and place names that follows the LC system in most respects. This is the system we'll be using for Ukrainian names in our English-language text. Thus, the major Ukrainian port on the Black Sea, Одеса, appears in our English text as Odesa – not Odessa, which is the transliteration from Russian.

Mostly, but not always, this official transliteration will be identical with the transliteration we use in this book for showing how a word is pronounced. Odesa remains o-de-sa, but Kyiv (Київ) and Chernihiv (Чернігів) will appear as ky-iw and cher-ni-hiw.

Generally, the transliteration system used here endeavours to represent each Ukrainian letter with one English equivalent. However, this is not always possible. For example, as you can see from the list of Ukrainian consonants on page 15, the letter в has two possible pronunciations, 'v' (v) and 'w' (w), depending on its position. It has a 'v' sound (v) when it precedes a vowel, and a 'w' sound (w) when it precedes a consonant or is at the end of a word or syllable. So вода, 'water', is pronounced vo-*da* and слово, 'word', is pronounced *slo*-vo, whereas втрата, 'loss', is pronounced *wtra*-ta and the name of Ukraine's capital, Київ, becomes *ky*-iw. On the other hand, the Roman letter y is used to represent two letters – и and й. The vowel и corresponds to the sound 'ir' in 'birch' (but pronounced short) while the semivowel й is like the 'y' in 'yellow'.

Sometimes it seems sensible to sacrifice complete consistency in order to avoid awkward combinations of letters. For example, Київ, the capital of Ukraine, if transliterated strictly according to the transliteration system devised in this book, would appear as *ky*-yiw, and the common greeting добрий день would be *do*-bryy den'. As *ky*-iw and *do*-bry den' look much less strange to an eye accustomed to English, a single y is used in transliterations wherever a yy would otherwise appear.

LETTERS IN DISGUISE

Here's a list of the Cyrillic characters that resemble Roman characters, but are pronounced differently:

В	в	pronounced as v or w in English (not as b)
Г	г	pronounced as h in English (not as r)
Ґ	ґ	pronounced as g in English (not as r)
И	и	pronounced as i in 'still' in English (not as n)
Й	й	pronounced as y in English (not as n)
Н	н	pronounced as n in English (not as h)
Р	р	pronounced as r in English (not as p)
С	с	pronounced as s in English (not as c)
У	у	pronounced as u in English (not as y)
Я	я	pronounced as ya in English (not as r)
Ь	ь	indicates a soft consonant in Ukrainian (not a b)

As you can see in the pronunciation guide on page 15 the letter ж is zh in the transliterations. There are also some words in Ukrainian where the two letters з (represented in the transliterations by z) and г (represented by h) come together, for example in Згода!, 'Agreed!'. The corresponding sounds are 'z' (z) followed by 'h' (h). If this word were transcribed as *zho-*da, confusion could arise, as ж is pronounced like the 's' in 'treasure'. For this reason, wherever the two letters зг come together in a word, they will appear underlined in the transliterations (zh). Therefore, журнал is transliterated as zhur-*nal*, 'journal', but згода! is <u>zho</u>-da, 'Agreed!'.

You may also see a few Ukrainian words spelt in Cyrillic with an apostrophe. This does not represent a sound. It means that the 'y' sound following the apostrophe should be strongly pronounced. For example, п'явка, 'leech', від'їзд, 'departure', and комп'ютер, 'computer', are pronounced *pyaw*-ka, vid-*yizd* and kom-*pyu*-ter respectively, all with the 'y' sound strongly pronounced.

Note that in this book the Ukrainian apostrophe is not transliterated; the apostrophe that appears in some transliterations corresponds to the Ukrainian letter ь, the 'soft sign' (see page 16):

учитель	u-*chy*-tel'	teacher
Львів	l'viw	Lviv

Finally, you will find that there are words which are sometimes spelt with в at the beginning, and at other times with у, as in вдома/удома (*wdo*-ma/u-*do*-ma), 'at home'. If the previous word ends in a vowel, then в will be used; if it ends in a consonant, у will be used.

Similarly, some words sometimes begin with й and at other times with i, like the verb йти/iти (yty/i-*ty*) meaning 'to go'. As in the above example, preceding word endings determine which letter is to start the word; here й comes after a vowel and i after a consonant.

PRONUNCIATION

INTONATION

Intonation is much the same as in English. It falls at the end of a sentence denoting a statement, but rises towards the end for a question.

STRESS

Where a word has two syllables or more, stressed syllables are indicated by *italics* in the transliterations.

TO STRESS OR NOT TO STRESS?

There is no rule which allows a learner to predict where the stress falls in an unfamiliar Ukrainian word. Words which are written identically, but have stress on different syllables, can have quite different meanings. Do not confuse the following:

дорога	do-*ro*-ha	road
	do-ro-*ha*	dear (adj)
замок	*za*-mok	castle
	za-*mok*	lock
орган	*or*-han	organ (part of the body)
	or-*han*	organ (musical instrument)
брати	bra-*ty*	brothers
	bra-ty	to take

WORD ORDER

The word order for Ukrainian sentences is the same as in English (subject-verb-object):

I live in London.
> ya zhy-*vu* w *lon*-do-ni   Я живу в Лондоні.
> (lit: I live in London)

Sometimes the subject is placed last to put special emphasis on it:

The President of Ukraine
lives in this building.
> u *ts'o*-mu bu-*dyn*-ku zhy-*ve*   У цьому будинку живе
> pre-zy-*dent* u-kra-*yi*-ny   президент України.
> (lit: in this building lives
>   president of Ukraine)

ARTICLES

Ukrainian uses neither the definite article ('the' in English), nor an indefinite article ('a' or 'an'); so dim (дім) can mean 'house', 'a house' or 'the house', according to the context.

NOUNS
Gender

Nouns in Ukrainian can be masculine, feminine or neuter.

Nouns that are masculine usually end in a consonant. In the majority of the cases this consonant is 'hard', ie not -y (-й) and not followed by the soft sign ' (-ь):

table	stil	стіл
exit	*vy*-khid	вихід

'Soft' masculine nouns end in the soft sign ' (-ь), or in -y (-й):

boy	*khlo*-pets'	хлопець
day	den'	день
tram	tram-*vay*	трамвай

Most feminine nouns end in -a (-а) or -ya (-я):

girl	*diw*-chy-na	дівчина
book	*knyzh*-ka	книжка
poetry	po-*e*-zi-ya	поезія
Olya	*o*-lya	Оля

GRAMMATICAL TERMS

A number of basic grammatical terms are used in this chapter:

adjective	adds information about a noun *red* wine
adverb	adds information about a verb or adjective He runs *quickly.* *very* big
case	when the form of a word expresses its function in the sentence (not as common in English as in many other languages) *Lisa's* book. (possessive) *She* runs. (subject) You like *her.* (object)
conjunction	joins together sentences or parts of a sentence Wash the car *and* walk the dog.
noun	a person (*John*), thing (*book*), place (*beach*) or idea (*happiness*)
object	refers to the noun or pronoun that is affected by the verb Paul washes the *dog.*
preposition	introduces information about location, place or direction *at* the market
pronoun	usually takes the place of a noun *he* sings instead of Paul sings
subject	refers to the noun or pronoun that is performing an action *The man* washes the dog.
verb	an action or doing word He *runs* fast.

GRAMMAR

Some feminine nouns end in a consonant:

night	nich	ніч
thing	rich	річ
salt	sil'	сіль
pleasure	pry-*em*-nist'	приємність

Most neuter nouns end in -o (**-o**) or -e (**-e**), but some end in -ya (**-я**):

apple	*ya*-blu-ko	яблуко
sea	*mo*-re	море
name	i-*mya*	ім'я
question	py-*tan*-nya	питання

Plurals

Forming the plural in Ukrainian is not as straightforward as in English. In general, to pluralise a masculine noun, add -y (**-и**) or, if the noun ends in the soft sign ' (**-ь**), replace ' (**-ь**) with -i (**-і**):

garden/gardens	sad/sa-*dy*	сад/сади
teacher/teachers	u-*chy*-tel'/	учитель/
	u-chy-te-*li*	учителі

The plural of feminine nouns is formed by dropping the final -a (**-а**) or -ya (**-я**) of the singular form and adding, respectively, -y (**-и**) or -i (**-і**):

book/books	*knyzh*-ka/	книжка/
	knyzh-*ky*	книжки
Sunday/Sundays	ne-*di*-lya/ne-*di*-li	неділя/неділі

Neuter nouns in the plural change -o (**-o**) to -a (**-а**) and -e (**-e**) to -a (**-а**) or -ya (**-я**) or, after zh (**ж**), ch (**ч**), sh (**ш**) and shch (**щ**), to -a (**-а**):

tree/trees	*de*-re-vo/de-*re*-va	дерево/дерева
field/fields	*po*-le/po-*lya*	поле/поля
surname/	*pri*-zvy-shche/	прізвище/
surnames	*pri*-zvy-shcha	прізвища

Neuter nouns ending in -ya (-я) generally do not change in the plural (like py-*tan*-nya (**питання**) meaning 'question/questions'), although there are a few important exceptions such as:

name/names   i-*mya*/i-me-*na*   ім'я/імена

Note that some Ukrainian nouns in the singular correspond to an English plural:

biscuits   *pe*-chy-vo (sg)   печиво

and vice versa:

door   *dve*-ri (pl)   двері

Cases

In English, we can work out the function of a noun in a sentence by looking at its position in the sentence or, sometimes, by looking at the preposition that precedes it. This is how we distinguish if a particular noun is the subject, object, indirect object etc of the sentence. Ukrainian, however, uses cases to indicate the function of nouns and some other classes of words like adjectives and pronouns. This means Ukrainian nouns change their endings according to their function in the sentence, ie whether they're the subject, object, indirect object etc. There are seven cases in Ukrainian, but the following notes on three main cases may help you sort out the structure of some of the phrases in this book.

Nominative – this is the form you'll find in a dictionary. All nouns used in the examples so far are in the nominative. A noun in the nominative case is the **subject** of a sentence. It tells us who or what is performing the action to which the verb refers.

The taxi driver works every day.
   tak-*syst* pra-*tsyu*-ye   Таксист працює
   shcho-*dnya*   щодня.
                                   (lit: taxi-driver works
                                       every-day)

Accusative – a noun in the accusative case is the **object** of a sentence. The object is on the 'receiving end' of the action expressed in a verb. Generally, masculine and neuter nouns have the same endings in the accusative case as they do in the nominative case. A feminine noun in the accusative changes the -a (**-a**) ending of its nominative form to -u (**-y**) in the singular. Generally, for plural it remains the same as in the nominative case.

I want to buy **a car**.
  ya *kho*-chu ku-*py*-ty
  ma-*shy*-nu

Я хочу купити
машину.
(lit: I want to-buy car)

Dative – a noun in the dative case is the **indirect object** of a sentence. An indirect object is usually the 'beneficiary' of the action expressed by the verb. In the sentence 'Give the money to me', 'money' is the direct object (and is therefore in the accusative case) and 'me' is the indirect object (and in the dative case). In English, the preposition 'for' is often used in instances where Ukrainian uses the dative, as in 'I want to buy a present for my wife'. There will probably be little need to be concerned with the endings of nouns – you'll be understood anyway.

She bought **us** a present.
  vo-*na* ku-*py*-la nam
  po-da-*ru*-nok

Вона купила нам
подарунок.
(lit: she bought us
    present)

Ivan showed **the tourist** a map.
  i-*van* po-ka-*zaw*
  tu-*ry*-sto-vi *kar*-tu

Іван показав
туристові карту.
(lit: Ivan showed
    tourist map)

ADJECTIVES

Adjectives in Ukrainian precede the noun they refer to and change their form according to the gender, number and case of this noun. Adjectives are listed in dictionaries in the masculine nominative singular form. The ending is -yy (-ий) (reduced in this phrasebook to a single -y, see page 18) or -iy (-ій). This ending changes to -a (-а) or -ya (-я) before feminine nouns, and to -e (-е) or -ye (-є) before neuter nouns. The plural ending for adjectives before nouns of all genders is -i (-і).

beautiful	*har*-ny	гарний
beautiful	*har*-ny	гарний
building	bu-*dy*-nok (m)	будинок
beautiful girl	*har*-na *di*-wchy-na (f)	гарна дівчина
beautiful city	*har*-ne *mi*-sto (neut)	гарне місто
beautiful	*har*-ni bu-*dyn*-ky (pl)	гарні будинки
buildings		

Comparatives & Superlatives

Many adjectives form the comparative by adding -sh- (-ш-) or -ish- (-іш-) before the ending. The superlative is created by adding the prefix nay- (най-) to the comparative form.

new	no-*vy*	новий
newer	no-*vi*-shy	новіший
newest	nay-no-*vi*-shy	найновіший
cheap	de-*she*-vy	дешевий
cheaper	de-*shew*-shy	дешевший
cheapest	nay-de-*shew*-shy	найдешевший

(See page 15 for the transliteration of в as v or w.)

Many important adjectives, however, do not follow this pattern, or follow it only approximately:

big	ve-*ly*-ky	великий
bigger	*bil'*-shy	більший
biggest	nay-*bil'*-shy	найбільший
expensive	do-ro-*hy*	дорогий
more expensive	do-*rozh*-chy	дорожчий
most expensive	nay-do-*rozh*-chy	найдорожчий

'Y' LONELY?

Remember that in the transcriptions used in this book, a single y is used wherever a yy would otherwise appear. For example, Київ, the capital of Ukraine, if transliterated strictly according to the transliteration rules, would appear as *ky-yiw*, and the common greeting добрий день, 'hello', would be *do-bryy den'*. In this book they will appear as *ky*-iw and *do-bry den'*.

ADVERBS

Adverbs in Ukrainian are formed by replacing the endings of the adjectives with -e (-e) or -o (-o). The adjective *do*-bry (добрий) meaning 'good', changes to *do*-bre (добре) to become the adverb 'well':

a good man
  do-bry cho-lo-*vik*   добрий чоловік
                             (lit: good man)

He speaks Ukrainian well.
  vin *do*-bre roz-mow-*lya*-ye   Він добре розмовляє
  u-kra-*yin*-s'ko-yu *mo*-vo-yu   українською мовою.
                             (lit: he well speaks
                             in-Ukrainian language)

Adverbs usually come second in a Ukrainian sentence, as shown in the example above.

GRAMMAR

Here are a few commonly used adjectives and adverbs:

wonderful (adj)	chu-*do*-vy	чудовий
Wonderful! (adv)	chu-*do*-vo!	Чудово!
good/kind (adj)	*do*-bry	добрий
Good/Fine! (adv)	*do*-bre!	Добре!
well (adv)	*do*-bre	добре
cold (adj)	kho-*lo*-dny	холодний
coldly (adv)	*kho*-lo-dno	холодно

Note that the adverb itself can stand for a complete English sentence:

It's cold.	*kho*-lo-dno	Холодно.

PRONOUNS
Personal Pronouns
As happens sometimes in English, personal pronouns in Ukrainian have different forms for the different cases – just think about the difference between 'I', 'me' and 'mine' – but you'll get by using only the nominative, the case normally used when the pronoun is the subject of the sentence. People will find this a bit odd, but you'll be understood. It's useful, however, to be able to recognise the pronouns when they appear as a direct object (accusative case) or as an indirect object (dative case).

Nominative Case				
	Singular		Plural	
1st person	I	ya (я)	we	my (ми)
2nd person	you	ty (ти) (inf)	you	vy (ви) (inf/pol)
		vy (ви) (pol)		
3rd person	he	vin (він)	they	vo-*ny* (вони)
	she	vo-*na* (вона)		
	it	vo-*no* (воно)		

They have already arrived.
vo-*ny* wzhe pry-*i*-kha-ly

Вони вже приїхали.
(lit: they already arrived)

Do **you** know Barcelona?
vy *zna*-ye-te bar-se-*lo*-nu?

Ви знаєте Барселону?
(lit: you know Barcelona?)

Accusative Case			
	Singular		Plural
1st person	me	me-*ne* (мене)	us nas (нас)
2nd person	you	te-*be* (тебе) (inf)	you vas (вас) (inf/pol)
		vas (вас) (pol)	
3rd person	him	yo-*ho* (його)	them yikh (їх)
	her	yi-*yi* (її)	
	it	yo-*ho* (його)	

The driver didn't see **us**.
vo-*diy* ne *ba*-chyw nas

Водій не бачив нас.
(lit: driver not saw us)

I'll wait for **you**.
ya che-*ka*-ty-mu vas/te-*be*
(pol/inf)

Я чекатиму вас/тебе.
(lit: I shall-wait for-you)

Dative Case			
	Singular		Plural
1st person	me	me-*ni* (мені)	us nam (нам)
2nd person	you	to-*bi* (тобі) (inf)	you vam (вам)(inf/pol)
		vam (вам) (pol)	
3rd person	him	yo-*mu* (йому)	them yim (їм)
	her	yiy (їй)	
	it	yo-*mu* (йому)	

Please give **me** the menu.
bud' *la*-ska, *day*-te
me-*ni* me-*nyu*

Будь ласка, дайте
мені меню.
(lit: please, give me menu)

Do **you** need help?
vam po-*trib*-na
do-po-*mo*-ha?

Вам потрібна
допомога?
(lit: for-you is-necessary assistance?)

Informal & Polite Pronouns

The second person singular, ty (ти), is the familiar form of 'you' in the nominative case and should only be used when speaking to someone you know well or when you're invited to use it. Otherwise always address an adult person with vy (Ви). This is not only the plural form of 'you' (not capitalised in this case), but also the polite singular form of 'you'.

When addressing a person in a letter, write the pronoun Ty (Ти) or Vy (Ви) with a capital letter (also see Writing Letters on page 137). The same distinction between informal and polite forms and the same capitalisation rule also apply to the accusative and dative forms of 'you' in the singular and plural.

Possessive Pronouns

The following pronouns change their form according to the gender, number and case of the noun they refer to, but you will be understood using the nominative form outlined below.

referring to	singular noun			plural
	M	F	NEUT	M/F/NEUT
my/mine	miy (мій)	mo-ya (моя)	mo-ye (моє)	mo-yi (мої)
your/yours	tviy (твій)	tvo-ya (твоя)	tvo-ye (твоє)	tvo-yi (твої)
his hers it/its	yo-ho (його) yi-yi (її) yo-ho (його)			
our/ours	nash (наш)	na-sha (наша)	na-she (наше)	na-shi (наші)
your/yours	vash (ваш)	va-sha (ваша)	va-she (ваше)	va-shi (ваші)
their/theirs	yikh (їх)			

Note that, in Ukrainian, the same form of the pronoun is used for 'my' and 'mine', for 'your' and 'yours', etc:

This is my place.
  tse mo-*ye* mi-stse   Це моє місце.
                         (lit: this my place)

This place is mine.
  tse *mi*-stse mo-*ye*   Це місце моє.
                         (lit: this place mine)

Remember to use tviy (твій), 'your, yours', only in situations when you would use the familiar personal pronoun ty (ти), 'you'.

Demonstrative Pronouns

The demonstrative pronouns in English are 'this', 'these', 'that' and 'those'. The most useful demonstrative pronoun in Ukrainian is tse (це), which means 'this/that' or 'these/those':

This is my passport.
tse miy *pa*-sport

Це мій паспорт.
(lit: this my passport)

These are her suitcases.
tse yi-*yi* va-*li*-zy

Це її валізи.
(lit: these her suitcases)

Reflexive Pronouns

The words 'myself', 'himself', 'themselves' etc, as in 'I'm washing myself', 'He can see himself in the mirror' and 'They are fooling themselves', are called reflexive pronouns. The single Ukrainian reflexive pronoun se-*be* (себе) corresponds to all the English reflexive pronouns. Often, however, the suffix -sya (-ся) is added to the verb to indicate a reflexive:

I'm getting dressed.
ya o-dya-*ha*-yu-sya

Я одягаюся.
(lit: I am-dressing-myself)

She is putting her shoes on.
vo-*na* wzu-*va*-yet'-sya

Вона взувається.
(lit: she is-shoeing-herself)

Some verbs are reflexive in Ukrainian that are not reflexive in English, for example smi-*ya*-ty-sya (сміятися), 'to laugh'.

VERBS

In Ukrainian, verbs take on different endings depending on the
tense of the verb (present, past or future) and on whether the
subject of the sentence is in the first, second or third person and
in the singular or plural. In the past tense, endings also differ
depending on the gender of the subject.

The dictionary form of a verb is called an infinitive. In English
infinitives are indicated by the word 'to': 'to see', 'to write' etc.
In Ukrainian the infinitive form ends in -ty (-ти).

Present

An infinitive which has the letter -a (-a) before the ending -ty (-ти)
usually takes the following endings in the present tense:

to read	chy-ta-ty	читати
I read	ya chy-ta-yu	я читаю
you read	ty chy-ta-yesh	ти читаєш
he/she/it reads	vin/vo-na/vo-no chy-ta-ye	він/вона/воно читає
we read	my chy-ta-ye-mo	ми читаємо
you read	vy chy-ta-ye-te	ви читаєте
they read	vo-ny chy-ta-yut'	вони читають

With -y (-и) before the infinitive ending, the verb will usually
take the following endings in the present tense:

to see	ba-chy-ty	бачити
I see	ya ba-chu	я бачу
you see	ty ba-chysh	ти бачиш
he/she/it sees	vin/vo-na/vo-no ba-chyt'	він/вона/воно бачить
we see	my ba-chy-mo	ми бачимо
you see	vy ba-chy-te	ви бачите
they see	vo-ny ba-chat'	вони бачать

As usual, there are exceptions, so don't worry if you come across
some verbs which do not correspond to these patterns.

Past

To form the past tense, drop the ending -ty (-ти) from the infinitive of the verb and add -w (-в) for a masculine singular subject, -la (-ла) for a feminine singular subject and -lo (-ло) for a neuter singular subject. If the subject is plural, the ending changes to -ly (-ли) for all genders.

I (m) saw the university.
  ya *ba*-chyw u-ni-ver-sy-*tet*

Я бачив університет.
(lit: I saw university)

I (f) saw the church.
  ya *ba*-chy-la *tser*-kvu

Я бачила церкву.
(lit: I saw church)

The chicken (n) saw the grain.
  kur-*cha* ba-chy-lo zer-*no*

Курча бачило зерно.
(lit: chicken saw grain)

We saw a good restaurant.
  my *ba*-chy-ly *do*-bry
  re-sto-*ran*

Ми бачили добрий
ресторан.
(lit: we saw good restaurant)

GRAMMAR

Future

To form the future tense, it is important to understand that each Ukrainian verb actually has two forms, called 'aspects', which reflect different degrees of completion of the action described by a verb. But before we go into explaining the details of this – and before you read on – you might want to know that there's no need for you to really know the different forms for the future tense. You could simply use the present tense endings for all verbs – you'll still be understood! You could also add words that refer to the future, like *zaw*-tra (завтра), 'tomorrow', and na-*stup*-no-ho *tyzh*-nya (наступного тижня), 'next week'. These time markers can be placed anywhere in the sentence. (Also see Time, Dates & Festivals on page 223.)

Unless you want to know all the forms for the future tense and start making the distinction between the imperfective and perfective aspects of verbs, we recommend you skip the following paragraphs and continue with the verb 'to be' on page 36.

'Imperfective aspect' refers to action in progress, repeated action or action thought of in general terms. 'Perfective aspect' refers to action that has been or will be completed. Often the perfective aspect of a verb can be formed by adding a prefix to the imperfective. For example, the infinitive of the verb 'to write' (in such senses as 'to be writing' or 'to write repeatedly') is py-*sa*-ty (писати). This is the imperfective aspect. On the other hand, the infinitive of the same verb 'to write' in the sense 'to finish writing a particular text' is na-py-*sa*-ty (написати). This is the perfective.

Imperfective Aspect

There are two ways of constructing the future tense of the imperfective forms of verbs. You can either use the forms of the verb *bu*-ty (бути), 'to be', together with the infinitive, or you can add a particular set of endings to the infinitive. The two forms of the verb chy-*ta*-ty (читати), 'to read', in the future tense will be as follows:

to read	chy-*ta*-ty	читати
I will read	ya *bu*-du chy-*ta*-ty	я буду читати
you will read	ty *bu*-desh chy-*ta*-ty	ти будеш читати
he/she/it will read	vin/vo-*na*/vo-*no* *bu*-de chy-*ta*-ty	він/вона/воно буде читати
we will read	my *bu*-de-mo chy-*ta*-ty	ми будемо читати
you will read	vy *bu*-de-te chy-*ta*-ty	ви будете читати
they will read	vo-*ny* bu-dut' chy-*ta*-ty	вони будуть читати

(Also see the verb 'to be' on page 36.)

or:

to read	chy-*ta*-ty	читати
I will read	ya chy-*ta*-ty-mu	я читатиму
you will read	ty chy-*ta*-ty-mesh	ти читатимеш
he/she/it will read	vin/vo-*na*/vo-*no* chy-*ta*-ty-me	він/вона/воно читатиме
we will read	my chy-*ta*-ty-me-mo	ми читатимемо
you will read	vy chy-*ta*-ty-me-te	ви читатимете
they will read	vo-*ny* chy-*ta*-ty-mut'	вони читатимуть

Perfective Aspect

The future tense of the perfective forms of a verb is formed by using the same endings as for the imperfective forms of the present tense: ya chy-*ta*-yu (Я читаю) means 'I'm reading' (imperfective), but ya pro-chy-*ta*-yu (Я прочитаю) means 'I will read (something to the end)' (perfective).

TO BE

The verb corresponding to the English 'to be', *bu*-ty (бути), is seldom used in Ukrainian in the present tense. It's understood from the context.

I'm from Australia.
ya z aw-*stra*-li-yi   Я з Австралії.
                             (lit: I from Australia)

This is an interesting museum.
tse tsi-*ka*-vy mu-*zey*   Це цікавий музей.
                             (lit: this interesting museum)

You can use the word ye (є) to mean 'am', 'are' or 'is', but it's not essential. It's often used to mean 'there is/are':

There's a good restaurant
in Poltava.
u pol-*ta*-vi ye *do*-bry   У Полтаві є добрий
re-sto-*ran*   ресторан.
                              (lit: in Poltava there-is
                                  good restaurant)

The negative form 'there is/are not' is ne-*ma*-ye (немає) or ne-*ma* (нема):

There's no restaurant here.
tut ne-*ma*-ye re-sto-*ra*-nu Тут немає ресторану.
                               (lit: here there-is-not restaurant)

In the past tense, the forms of the verb *bu*-ty (бути), 'to be', are:

buw (m)	був
bu-*la* (f)	була
bu-*lo* (neut)	було
bu-*ly* (pl)	були

We have already encountered the forms of the verb *bu*-ty (бути), 'to be', on page 35.

on page 35.

GRAMMAR

TO HAVE

There are two ways of saying 'to have' and both are in regular use. The first way is simply to use the verb *ma*-ty (мати), 'to have'. It takes the same endings as the verb chy-*ta*-ty (читати), 'to read'. (See page 35 for the conjugation of this verb.)

I have a visa.
    ya *ma*-yu *vi*-zu   Я маю візу.
                           (lit: I have visa)

The second way is a little more complex. You use the preposition w (в) or u (у), 'to', then the appropriate pronoun, then a form of the verb *bu*-ty (бути), 'to be':

I have a visa.
    u *me*-ne ye *vi*-za   У мене є віза.
                           (lit: to me there-is visa)

We have ...
    u nas ye ...   У нас є ...
                           (lit: to us there-is/are ...)

She had a visa.
    u *ne*-yi bu-*la vi*-za   У неї була віза.
                           (lit: to her was visa)

NEGATIVES

To make a sentence negative, put the word ne (не) in front of the verb:

I don't know.
    ya ne *zna*-yu   Я не знаю.
                           (lit: I not know)

IMPERATIVES

Ukrainian verbs have special endings to express commands. A command may be in the second person singular, in the second person plural (which is also the polite form, singular and plural) or in the first person plural. The rules governing these endings are quite complex. Below are a few phrases using imperatives that travellers might want to use frequently. Note that, when using a second person imperative, you should use bud' *la*-ska (будь ласка), 'please', in the sentence, otherwise you might be perceived as being rude.

Could you please tell me
where the post office is?
  ska-*zhy*/ska-*zhit'*,
  bud' *la*-ska,
  de *po*-shta? (inf/pol)

Скажи/Скажіть,
будь ласка,
де пошта?
(lit: say, please,
    where post office?)

Show me on the map, please.
  po-ka-*zhy*/po-ka-*zhit'*, bud'
  la-ska, na *kar*-ti (inf/pol)

Покажи/Покажіть, будь
ласка, на карті.
(lit: show, please, on map)

Give me three tickets, please.
  day/*day*-te, bud' *la*-ska,
  try kvyt-*ky* (inf/pol)

Дай/Дайте, будь ласка,
три квитки.
(lit: give, please, three tickets)

Let's go to the hotel.
  kho-*di*-mo do ho-*te*-lyu

Ходімо до готелю.
(lit: let-us-go to hotel)

MODALS

Modals are verbs that modify the meaning of another verb. They express an ability, necessity, desire or need, as in 'can read', 'need to go' and 'want to drink'. The English verbs 'to be able to', 'may', 'must', 'should', 'to want' and 'to need' are all modals.

To Be Able To; May

The Ukrainian equivalent of 'to be able to' is the verb moh-*ty* (могти), which agrees in number and person with the subject of the sentence:

Can you read?
   chy ty *mo*-zhesh   Чи ти можеш
   chy-*ta*-ty?   читати?
                        (lit: is-it-that you can read?)

He can eat and drink a lot.
   vin *mo*-zhe *yi*-sty y   Він може їсти й
   py-ty ba-*ha*-to   пити багато.
                        (lit: he can eat and
                          drink much)

When 'can' has the meaning 'may; to have permission', however, Ukrainian uses just one word, *mo*-zhna (можна), regardless of the subject:

May I take photographs here?
   mo-zhna (me-*ni*) tut   Можна (мені) тут
   fo-to-hra-fu-*va*-ty?   фотографувати?
                        (lit: is-it-permitted (for-me)
                        here to-take-photographs?)

Yes, you may.
   tak, *mo*-zhna   Так, можна.
                        (lit: yes, it-is-permitted)

No, you may not.
   ni, ne *mo*-zhna   Ні, не можна.
                        (lit: no, not it-is-permitted)

GRAMMAR

Must; Have To

The easiest way to say that you have to do something is to translate
the English expression word for word into Ukrainian: first the
pronoun for the subject, then the verb *ma*-ty (**мати**), 'to have',
followed by an infinitive:

I have to go.
    ya *ma*-yu yty   **Я маю йти.**
                              (lit: I have to-go)

The word *tre*-ba (**треба**) is also used to mean 'must; have to'
but is used with a dative form of the personal pronoun (see
Personal Pronouns, page 28):

I must ...
    me-*ni tre*-ba ...   **Мені треба ...**
                          (lit: to-me is-needed ...)

Do you have to ...?
    vam *tre*-ba ...?   **Вам треба ...?**
                          (lit: to-you is-needed ...?)

Should; Ought To

The Ukrainian equivalent is not actually a verb, but an adjective:
po-*vy*-nen (**повинен**) (m); po-*vyn*-na (**повинна**) (f); po-*vyn*-ne
(**повинне**) (neut); and po-*vyn*-ni (**повинні**) (pl).

You (pl) should know
where the museum is.
    vy po-*vyn*-ni *zna*-ty,   **Ви повинні знати,**
    de mu-*zey*   **де музей.**
                          (lit: you should know,
                             where museum)

GRAMMAR

Want; Would Like

The infinitive is kho-*ti*-ty (хотіти):

I want ...
ya *kho*-chu ...   Я хочу ...
                                 (lit: I want ...)

What do you want?
shcho vy *kho*-che-te?   Що ви хочете?
                                 (lit: what you want?)

I would like to buy ...
ya [kho-*tiw* by;   Я [хотів би;
kho-*ti*-la b] ku-*py*-ty ...   хотіла б] купити ...
(m/f)   (lit: I [want by; want b]
                                 to-buy ...)

Would you like ...?
vy kho-*ti*-ly b ...?   Ви хотіли б ...?
                                 (lit: you want b ...?)

Need

The Ukrainian word to use here is the adjective po-*tri*-ben (потрібен) (m), po-*trib*-na (потрібна) (f), po-*trib*-ne (потрібне) (n) or po-*trib*-ni (потрібні) (pl), which literally means 'necessary'. The form of this word depends upon what's needed, not on who does the needing, that is, on the object, not the subject of the sentence:

I need a dictionary.
me-*ni* po-*tri*-ben   Мені потрібен
slow-*nyk*   словник.
                                 (lit: to-me necessary dictionary)

Do you need help?
vam po-*trib*-na   Вам потрібна
do-po-*mo*-ha?   допомога?
                                 (lit: to-you necessary help?)

In the first example po-*tri*-ben (потрібен) is used since the object needed is slow-*nyk* (словник), 'dictionary', a singular masculine noun. In the second example po-*trib*-na (потрібна) refers to do-po-*mo*-ha (допомога), 'help', which is a singular feminine noun.

GRAMMAR

PREPOSITIONS

Ukrainian prepositions are tied up very closely with the case system of nouns. When using a preposition in conjunction with a noun, the noun has to appear in the case that the specific preposition governs. Some prepositions can govern more than one case; their meaning will differ according to the case of the noun.

This means that the use of prepositions in Ukrainian is not as straightforward as in English. However, if you combine the following prepositions with the nominative – or dictionary – form of the noun, you'll still be understood.

above/over	nad	над
across	che-rez	через
after	pi-slya	після
at (time)	o	о
before (time)	pe-red	перед
during	pid chas	під час
for	za/dlya	за/для
from	z/vid	з/від
in (place)	u; w or v	у/в
in (time)	che-rez/za	через/за
in front of	pe-red	перед
near	bi-lya/ko-lo	біля/коло
next to	bi-lya	біля
on	na	на
through	che-rez	через
to	do; u; w or v	до/у/в
under	pid	під
with (together with)	z	з
without	bez	без

Note that the preposition 'with' (by means of) does not require a preposition in Ukrainian. This meaning is conveyed by the case of the noun, in this example the instrumental case (not described in this book):

Can we pay with dollars?

mozh-na pla-*ty*-ty
do-la-ra-my?

Можна платити
доларами?
(lit: is-it-permitted
to-pay with-dollars?)

QUESTIONS

Using intonation is enough to form a question – just raise the tone towards the end of the sentence. You can also precede your question with the little word chy? (чи?) or follow it with tak? (так?). These are the equivalent of the English tag questions 'isn't it?', 'aren't you?', 'don't they?', etc.

Do you live in London?

vy zhy-ve-*te* w *lon*-do-ni?	Ви живете в Лондоні? (lit: you live in London?)
chy vy zhy-ve-*te* w *lon*-do-ni?	Чи ви живете в Лондоні? (lit: is-it-that you live in London?)
vy zhy-ve-*te* w *lon*-do-ni, tak?	Ви живете в Лондоні, так? (lit: you live in London, yes?)

QUESTION WORDS

How?	yak?	Як?
How much?	*skil'*-ky?	Скільки?
What?	shcho?	Що?
When?	ko-*ly*?	Коли?
Where?	de?	Де?
Where from?	*zvid*-ky?	Звідки?
Where (to)?	ku-*dy*?	Куди?
Which?	ko-*try*? (m)	Котрий?
	ko-*tra*? (f)	Котра?
	ko-*tre*? (n)	Котре?
	ko-*tri*? (pl)	Котрі?
Who?	khto?	Хто?
Why?	cho-*mu*?	Чому?

Note that Ukrainian makes a clear distinction between 'where' and 'where (to)':

Where do you live?
de vy zhy-ve-*te*?

Де ви живете?
(lit: where you live?)

Where are you going?
ku-dy vy yde-*te*?

Куди ви йдете?
(lit: where-to you go?)

CONJUNCTIONS

although	khoch	хоч
and	i/y/ta	і/й/та
because	to-*mu* shcho	тому що
but	a-*le*	але
if	yak-*shcho*	якщо
or	a-*bo*	або
since ... (from the time that)	vid-ko-*ly*; z to-*ho* cha-su, yak ...	відколи; з того часу, як ...
since (because, in so far as)	to-*mu* shcho; o-*skil'*-ky	тому що; оскільки
so that	shchob	щоб
therefore	to-*mu*	тому
to; in order to	shchob	щоб
when	ko-*ly*	коли
while ... (at the same time as)	u toy chas, yak ...	у той час, як ...
while (whereas)	khoch	хоч

Note that the form used for 'and' depends on the surrounding sounds. However, it's always safe to use i (і).

ЗНАЙОМСТВА

MEETING PEOPLE

The experience of most travellers is that Ukrainians are friendly and easy to talk to. You are likely to find that people are interested in finding out about you, your life and your interests, and ready to engage in conversation and be open about themselves. On the whole, people will be forgiving of your lack of knowledge of local customs and will give credit for all efforts on your part to communicate and to behave according to Ukrainian ways. Your efforts to express yourself in Ukrainian, especially, will earn you high marks.

YOU SHOULD KNOW

ТРЕБА ЗНАТИ

These are the phrases that you'll need most frequently:

Yes.	tak	Так.
No.	ni	Ні.
Please.	bud' *la*-ska; *pro*-shu	Будь ласка; Прошу.
Thank you.	*dya*-ku-yu	Дякую.
Good day!	*do*-bry den'!	Добрий день!
Hello!	do-*bry*-den'/ pry-*vit*! (inf)	Добридень/ Привіт!
Goodbye.	do po-*ba*-chen-nya; do *zu*-stri-chi	До побачення; До зустрічі.

GREETINGS & GOODBYES		**ЗУСТРІЧІ Й ПРОЩАННЯ**

In Ukrainian the standard greetings corresponding to 'Good day' and 'Good evening' will be acceptable in all social situations.

Good day!	*do*-bry den'!	Добрий день!
Good evening!	*do*-bry *ve*-chir!	Добрий вечір!

Also common is:

Good morning!	*do*-bro-ho *ran*-ku!	Доброго ранку!

It is best to combine these with the person's name in the socially appropriate form (see also Forms of Address on page 52):

Good day, Olenka. *do*-bry den', o-*len*-ko	Добрий день, Оленко.
Good evening, Mr Yaroslav. *do*-bry *ve*-chir, *pa*-ne ya-ro-*sla*-ve	Добрий вечір, пане Ярославе.
Good morning, Ms Ivanenko. *do*-bro-ho *ran*-ku, *pa*-ni i-va-*nen*-ko	Доброго ранку, пані Іваненко.
Good day, Viktor Mykhailovych. *do*-bry den', *vik*-to-re my-*khay*-lo-vy-chu	Добрий день, Вікторе Михайловичу.

Goodbye;	do po-*ba*-chen-nya;	До побачення;
See you.	do *zu*-stri-chi	До зустрічі.
Good night.	do-*bra*-nich	Добраніч.

More informal goodbyes include:

Cheerio!	shcha-*sly*-vo	Щасливо!
Bye! (inf)	bu-*vay*/ bu-*vay*-te! (sg/pl)	Бувай/ Бувайте!
Bye! (very inf)	pa!/pa-*pa*!	Па!/Па-па!

MEETING PEOPLE

CIVILITIES БУДЬМО ВВІЧЛИВІ

Outside of formal situations, and when speaking with a person you have met before, it's common to follow the greeting with a question about the person's general state:

How are you?
yak *spra*-vy? Як справи?

A question about the person's health is normal only if you know that the person has been unwell:

How's your health?
yak *va*-she zdo-*ro*-v'ya? Як Ваше здоров'я?
How are you feeling?
yak vy po-chu-*va*-ye-te-sya? Як Ви почуваєтеся?

The following informal expressions are suitable when talking to people who you know well and who are of your own age group:

Hi!	pry-*vit*!	Привіт!
How's life?	yak zhyt-*tya*?	Як життя?
What's new?	shcho no-*vo*-ho?	Що нового?

And here are some common responses:

Fine, thanks.	*do*-bre, *dya*-ku-yu	Добре, дякую.
OK, thanks.	*dya*-ku-yu, nor-*mal'*-no	Дякую, нормально.
Not too bad, thanks.	*dya*-ku-yu, ne-po-*ha*-no	Дякую, непогано.
There's nothing new.	ni-*cho*-ho no-*vo*-ho	Нічого нового.
What about you?	a u vas; a w *te*-be? (pol/inf)	А у Вас; А в тебе?

GIVE THE KISS A MISS!

Despite the stereotypical image of Slavs energetically kissing one another on the cheek three times when they meet, this custom is practically defunct in Ukraine. Only relatives and very good friends will embrace or kiss on meeting. An attempt to do so outside these intimate circles is likely to cause embarrassment.

For men it's usual, though not compulsory, to shake hands when meeting. When joining a group, a man will often shake hands with each of its members, both women and men. It's less usual for a woman to initiate a handshake.

Occasionally, and especially in Western Ukraine, a man will kiss a woman's hand when greeting her, but the practice carries a distinctly Old World flavour and is best avoided by the tourist. Usually, a handshake will do.

MEETING PEOPLE

When parting, you could say:

It was very nice meeting you.
    bu-*lo du*-zhe pry-*em*-no   Було дуже приємно
    po-zna-*yo*-my-ty-sya z *va*-my   познайомитися з Вами.

I hope we'll see each
other again soon.
    spo-di-*va*-yu-sya, shcho *my*   Сподіваюся, що ми
    ne-za-*ba*-rom shche raz   незабаром ще раз
    po-*ba*-chy-mo-sya   побачимося.

I'm sorry, but I must be going.
    pe-re-*pro*-shu-yu, a-*le* ya   Перепрошую, але я
    wzhe *mu*-shu yty   вже мушу йти.

Please give my regards to
your husband/wife.
    bud' *la*-ska, pe-re-*day*-te   Будь ласка, передайте
    pry-*vit* [*va*-sho-mu   привіт [Вашому
    cho-lo-*vi*-ko-vi;   чоловікові;
    va-shiy dru-*zhy*-ni]   Вашій дружині].

APOLOGIES   ВИБАЧЕННЯ

Excuse me.
    vy-bach-te/   Вибачте/
    pro-*bach*-te (me-*ni*)   Пробачте (мені).

I'm (very) sorry.
    (*du*-zhe) pe-re-*pro*-shu-yu   (Дуже) перепрошую.

Excuse me. (when squeezing
through a crowd)
    bud' *la*-ska,   Будь ласка,
    do-*zvol'*-te pro-*yty*   дозвольте пройти.

It's OK; Never mind.
    ni-*cho*-ho   Нічого.

Don't worry.
    ne tur-*buy*-te-sya   Не турбуйтеся.

MEETING PEOPLE

VISITING & DINING

One of the best ways of getting a feel for Ukrainians' values, concerns and way of life is to accept an invitation to visit a family at home. Ukrainians are famously hospitable and go to great lengths to make the visit a festive event at which the guest is the centre of attention.

When invited, especially for the first time, assume that you can be expected to stay for a number of hours and that a sumptuous meal will be served. It's a good idea to bring some appropriate gifts; care will certainly be lavished upon you. As in the West, flowers, chocolates and alcohol are the staples. You can combine these with more personal items or souvenirs. Find out in advance if your hosts have children, and if they do, equip yourself with a gift for each child.

If there are any foods that you do not eat, explain this when you are invited. Refusing food at the table will be awkward, as the hosts will have gone to considerable trouble to shop for, and prepare, every dish.

There's a popular superstition that shaking hands across a threshold brings bad luck, so reserve your handshakes until you've entered the premises.

In the entrance hall you'll be helped to divest yourself of bags and coats. In Ukraine people remove their street shoes when they come into a residence, and you should do this too. Ignore your hosts' pleas to keep your shoes on unless they make a real fuss. You may be offered a pair of slippers to put on, and it's equally all right to accept these or not.

There's no need to
take your shoes off.
   ne *tre*-ba [*zni*-ma-ty   Не треба [знімати
   vzut-*tya*; roz-zu-*va*-ty-sya]   взуття; роззуватися].

No, I'll feel better if I do.
   ni, ya tak *kra*-shche   Ні, я так краще
   po-chu-*va*-yu-sya   почуваюся.

VISITING & DINING

Apartments are generally fairly small, so you're likely to be asked to sit down at the table straight away. If you're single, you're very unlikely to be placed at a corner of the table – there used to be a popular superstition that if you sat at the corner you would not marry for several years. The hostess, sometimes assisted by the host, will soon begin bringing food from the kitchen – first cold dishes, then hot ones. There will be many different foods rather than a progression from appetiser to main course to dessert, and you should at least attempt to try everything.

The hosts are not going to believe any claims that you've had enough. There can be pressure to eat more, and it's quite likely that food will be put on your plate without your asking for it.

Nonalcoholic and alcoholic drinks will be served and toasts will play an important part in structuring the meal (see Making a Toast on page 179).

Tea or coffee will be served at the end, probably with delicious pastries. Your hosts may offer to see you to the nearest public transport stop or taxi stand. Don't hesitate to accept such an offer if you feel at all uncertain about finding your way.

MEETING PEOPLE

FORMS OF ADDRESS   ЗВЕРТАННЯ

In formal situations, men shake hands when being introduced or when they introduce themselves. Women may also shake hands if they choose. It was obligatory in Soviet times to address people formally by their first name and patronymic (a name derived from the first name of the father). This is still the most widely used formal address. For men, patronymics end in -ovych (-ович), for women in -iwna (iвна). Thus, examples of full formal names might be:

Petro Stepanovych Hrinchenko
    pe-*tro* ste-*pa*-no-vych   Петро Степанович
    hrin-*chen*-ko   Грінченко
Marta Stepanivna Kravchuk
    mar-ta ste-*pa*-ni-wna   Марта Степанівна
    kraw-*chuk*   Кравчук

When you address people, the endings of their name(s) change – Ukrainian uses a separate case to address people – and the surname is not used if you use the patronymic:

Good day, Petro Stepanovych.
    do-bry den', *pe*-tre   Добрий день, Петре
    ste-*pa*-no-vy-chu   Степановичу.
Good evening, Marta Stepanivna.
    do-bry *ve*-chir, *mar*-to   Добрий вечір, Марто
    ste-*pa*-niw-no   Степанівно.

In independent Ukraine it's becoming increasingly common to use the equivalents of 'Mr' and 'Ms' with a person's surname or, in slightly less formal circumstances, his or her first name. Pan, 'Mr', changes to *pa*-ne when you address a man, whereas *pa*-ni, 'Ms', does not change. There's no separate word for 'Mrs', and the word for 'Miss' is obsolete.

Hello, Mr Kravchenko.
    do-*bry*-den', *pa*-ne   Добридень, пане
    kraw-chen-ko   Кравченко.

See also Greetings & Goodbyes on page 46.

MEETING PEOPLE

What's your name?
yak vas zvut'/*zva*-ty?   Як Вас звуть/звати?
My name is ...
me-*ne* zvut'/*zva*-ty ...   Мене звуть/звати ...
Here's my business card.
os' mo-*ya* vi-*zyt*-na   Ось моя візитна
kar-tka   картка.
Pleased to meet you.
du-zhe pry-*em*-no   Дуже приємно.

I'd like to   po-zna-*yom*-te-sya,   Познайомтеся,
introduce   tse ...   це ...
you to my ...
  colleague   miy ko-*le*-ha   мій колега
  friend   miy druh   мій друг
  girlfriend   mo-*ya po*-dru-ha   моя подруга
  husband   miy cho-lo-*vik*   мій чоловік
  wife   mo-*ya* dru-*zhy*-na   моя дружина

MAKING CONVERSATION   РОЗМОВА

You'll find it easy to meet and talk with locals. Ukrainians enjoy lively conversation, especially with foreigners. The following questions could spark off interaction between yourself and the people you meet:

Do you live here?
vy tut zhy-ve-*te*?   Ви тут живете?
Where are you going?
ku-*dy* vy yde-*te*?   Куди Ви йдете?

What are you doing?
   shcho vy *ro*-by-te?   Що Ви робите?

Great day, isn't it?
   pre-*kras*-ny den',   Прекрасний день,
   pra-wda?   правда?

It's cold/warm today, isn't it?
   kho-lo-dno/*te*-plo   Холодно/Тепло
   s'o-*ho*-dni, *pra*-wda?   сьогодні, правда?

The following openers are equally useful:

| How's the family? | yak si-*mya*? | Як сім'я? |
| How's work? | yak ro-*bo*-ta? | Як робота? |

Here are some possible replies:

Great!	chu-*do*-vo!	Чудово!
Fine!	*do*-bre!	Добре!
OK.	nor-*mal'*-no	Нормально.
So-so.	po-ma-*len'*-ku	Помаленьку.
Rotten.	po-*ha*-no	Погано.

Things couldn't be better!
   kra-shche ne bu-*va*-ye!   Краще не буває!
Things can't get worse!
   hir-she *ni*-ku-dy!   Гірше нікуди!

TACK A TAK

To turn a sentence into a question, just use the intonation of your voice or tack the word tak? (Так) onto the end of the sentence.

NATIONALITIES   НАЦІОНАЛЬНІСТЬ

You'll find that the names of many countries are similar to their English equivalents. Some are quite different though, eg ky-*tay* (Китай) for China and ni-*mech*-chy-na (Німеччина) for Germany. If you're still unable to explain, simply try pointing at the script in the third column below.

Where are you from?
    zvid-ky vy?   Звідки ви?

We come from ...	my z ...	Ми з ...
I'm from ...	ya z ...	Я з ...
Australia	aw-*stra*-li-yi	Австралії
Canada	ka-*na*-dy	Канади
China	ky-*ta*-yu	Китаю
England	*an*-hli-yi	Англії
France	*fran*-tsi-yi	Франції
Germany	ni-*mech*-chy-ny	Німеччини
Ireland	ir-*lan*-di-yi	Ірландії
Italy	i-*ta*-li-yi	Італії
Japan	ya-*po*-ni-yi	Японії
the Middle East	blyz'-*ko*-ho	Близького
	skho-du	Сходу
New Zealand	no-*vo*-yi	Нової
	ze-*lan*-di-yi	Зеландії
Scandinavia	skan-dy-*na*-vi-yi	Скандинавії
Scotland	sho-*tlan*-di-yi	Шотландії
South Africa	piw-*den*-no-yi	Південної
	a-fry-ky	Африки
Spain	i-*spa*-ni-yi	Іспанії
the United States	spo-*lu*-che-nykh	Сполучених
	shta-tiw	Штатів
	a-*me*-ry-ky	Америки
Wales	u-*el*'-su	Уельсу

MEETING PEOPLE

I live in/at the/a ...	ya zhy-*vu* ...	Я живу ...
city	w *mi*-sti	в місті
countryside	za *mi*-stom	за містом
mountains	w *ho*-rakh	в горах
seaside	*bi*-lya *mo*-rya	біля моря
village	w se-*li*	в селі

MR ONE-AND-A-HALF-FUR-COATS

Ukrainian surnames have a number of suffixes that mean 'son of'. The most familiar of these is -enko (-енко), but -uk, -yuk, -chuk, -iw and -yn (-ук, -юк, -чук, -ів and -ин) are also very common. Some surnames are based on Christian names, eg, i-va-*nen*-ko (Іваненко), i-*va*-niw (Іванів), i-va-*nyuk* (Іванюк) and i-van-*chuk* (Іванчук). Some derive from trades or professions. The word for shoemaker, shvets' (швець), is related to the surnames shvets', shew-*chuk* and shew-*chen*-ko (Швець, Шевчук and Шевченко). Some refer to ethnic origin, like ta-*ta*-ryn (Татарин), 'the Tatar', and others to the place of origin: po-li-*shchuk* (Поліщук), 'from Polissya' and don-chyk (Дончик), 'from the Don'.

One type of surname that has few counterparts in other traditions is the surname based on the nicknames that the Zaporozhian Cossacks gave each other. These would sometimes refer to an adventure or comic event: piw-to-ra-ko-*zhu*-kha (Півторакожуха), 'One-and-a-half-fur-coats'; ne-py-*py*-vo (Непийпиво), 'Drink-no-beer' and za-hu-by-ko-le-so (Загубиколесо), which literally means 'Lose-a-wheel'.

CULTURAL DIFFERENCES

КУЛЬТУРНІ ОСОБЛИВОСТІ

How do you do this
in your country?
  yak tse *ro*-byt'-sya/*ro*-blyat'
  u *va*-shiy kra-*yi*-ni?

Як це робиться/роблять
у вашій країні?

Is this a local or a
national custom?
  tse mi-*stse*-vy chy
  za-*hal*'-ny *zvy*-chay?

Це місцевий чи
загальний звичай?

I don't want to offend you.
  ya ne *kho*-chu vas
  o-*bra*-zy-ty

Я не хочу вас
образити.

I'm sorry, I'm not
accustomed to this.
  vy-bach-te, ya ne zvyk/
  zvy-kla do *ts'o*-ho (m/f)

Вибачте, я не звик/
звикла до цього.

I don't mind watching,
but I prefer not to participate.
  ya *mo*-zhu po-dy-*vy*-ty-sya,
  a-*le* ne *bra*-ty-mu *u*-cha-sti

Я можу подивитися,
але не братиму участі.

I'm sorry, it's against my ...	*vy*-bach-te, a-*le* tse su-pe-*re*-chyt' ...	Вибачте, але це суперечить ...
beliefs	*mo*-*yim* pe-re-ko-*nan*-nyam	моїм переконанням
culture	mo-*yiy* kul'-*tu*-ri	моїй культурі
religion	mo-*yiy* re-*li*-hi-yi	моїй релігії

MEETING PEOPLE

MONEY TALKS

Do not be alarmed or offended if a person asks how much you earn. This used to be a completely standard inquiry, though it has become less so as the gap between the wealthy and the poor has increased.

AGE   ВІК

How old are you?
    skil'-ky vam *ro*-kiw?   Скільки Вам років?
How old is your child?
    skil'-ky *ro*-kiw *va*-shiy   Скільки років вашій
    dy-*ty*-ni?   дитині?
I'm 24 (years old).
    me-*ni dva*-tsyat'   Мені двадцять
    cho-*ty*-ry (*ro*-ky)   чотири (роки).
He/She is 10 (years old).
    yo-*mu*/yiy *de*-syat'   Йому/їй десять
    (*ro*-kiw) (m/f)   (років).
When's your birthday?
    ko-*ly* vash den'   Коли Ваш день
    na-*ro*-dzhen-nya?   народження?

(See Numbers & Amounts, page 233, for your age.)

OCCUPATIONS   ПРОФЕСІЇ

What's your occupation?
    kym vy pra-*tsyu*-ye-te?   Ким Ви працюєте?

In the following list the masculine form appears first, the feminine second.

I'm (a/an) ...	ya ...	Я ...
accountant	bu-*khal*-ter	бухгалтер
actor	ak-*tor*/ak-*try*-sa	актор/актриса
architect	ar-khi-*tek*-tor	архітектор
artist	khu-*do*-zhnyk/	художник/
	khu-*do*-zhny-tsya	художниця
businessperson	bi-zne-*smen*;	бізнесмен;
	di-lo-*va zhin*-ka	ділова жінка
carpenter	te-*slyar*	тесляр
chef	*ku*-khar	кухар
doctor	*li*-kar	лікар
driver	vo-*diy*	водій
engineer	in-zhe-*ner*	інженер

farmer	*fer*-mer	фермер
journalist	zhur-na-*list*/	журналіст/
	zhur-na-*lis*-tka	журналістка
lawyer	yu-*ryst*	юрист
musician	mu-zy-*kant*	музикант
nurse	med-*brat*/	медбрат/
	med-se-*stra*	медсестра
office worker	pra-tsi-*wnyk*	працівник
	o-fi-su;	офісу;
	pra-tsi-*wny*-tsya	працівниця
	o-fi-su	офісу
police officer (in Ukraine)	mi-li-tsi-o-*ner*	міліціонер
police officer (in some other countries)	po-li-*tseys*'-ky	поліцейський
postman	ly-sto-*no*-sha	листоноша
retired	pen-si-o-*ner*/	пенсіонер/
	pen-si-o-*ner*-ka	пенсіонерка
sailor	mo-*ryak*	моряк
scientist	na-u-*ko*-vets'	науковець
secretary	se-kre-*tar*/	секретар/
	se-kre-*tar*-ka	секретарка
soldier	viys'-ko-*vy*	військовий
student	stu-*dent*/	студент/
	stu-*den*-tka	студентка
teacher	u-*chy*-tel'/	учитель/
	u-*chy*-tel'-ka	учителька
translator/ interpreter	pe-re-kla-*dach*/	перекладач/
	pe-re-kla-*da*-chka	перекладачка
unemployed	be-zro-*bi*-tny/	безробітний/
	be-zro-*bi*-tna	безробітна
waiter	o-fi-tsi-*ant*/	офіціант/
	o-fi-tsi-*an*-tka	офіціантка
writer	pys'-*men*-nyk/	письменник/
	pys'-*men*-ny-tsya	письменниця

Where do you work?
de vy pra-*tsyu*-ye-te?　　　Де Ви працюєте?

I work in/at　　　ya pra-*tsyu*-yu w ...　　　Я працюю в ...
a/an/the ...
　　bank　　　　　*ban*-ku　　　　　　банку
　　company '...'　kom-*pa*-ni-yi '...'　компанії '...'
　　embassy　　　po-*sol*'-stvi　　　посольстві
　　hospital　　　li-*kar*-ni　　　　лікарні
　　newspaper　　ha-*ze*-ti　　　　газеті
　　restaurant　　re-sto-*ra*-ni　　ресторані
　　theatre　　　te-*a*-tri　　　　театрі
　　university　　u-ni-ver-sy-*te*-ti　університеті

What do you study?
shcho [vy vy-*wcha*-ye-te;　Що [Ви вивчаєте;
ty vy-*wcha*-yesh]? (pol/inf)　ти вивчаєш]?

I study ...　　　ya vy-*wcha*-yu ...　　Я вивчаю ...
　　art　　　　　my-*stets*-tvo　　мистецтво
　　arts/　　　　hu-ma-ni-*tar*-ni　гуманітарні
　　　humanities　na-*u*-ky　　　　науки
　　business　　　*bi*-znes　　　　бізнес
　　teaching　　　pe-da-*ho*-hi-ku　педагогіку
　　engineering　　in-zhe-*ner*-nu　інженерну
　　　　　　　　spra-*vu*　　　　справу
　　English　　　an-*hliys*'-ku　англійську
　　　　　　　　mo-vu　　　　　мову
　　foreign　　　i-no-*zem*-ni　іноземні
　　　languages　　*mo*-vy　　　　мови
　　law　　　　　*pra*-vo　　　　право
　　medicine　　　me-dy-*tsy*-nu　медицину
　　Ukrainian　　u-kra-*yins*'-ku　українську
　　　　　　　　mo-vu　　　　мову
　　science　　　*toch*-ni　　　точні
　　　　　　　　na-*u*-ky　　　науки

FEELINGS

ПОЧУТТЯ

Are you ...; Do you feel ...?	vam ...?	Вам ...?

I am/feel ...	me-*ni* ...	Мені ...
afraid	*stra*-shno	страшно
ashamed	*so*-rom-no	соромно
bored	*nu*-dno	нудно
cold	*kho*-lo-dno	холодно
comfortable	*zruch*-no	зручно
happy	*ve*-se-lo	весело
hot	*zhar*-ko	жарко
pleased	pry-*em*-no	приємно
sad	*sum*-no	сумно
sorry (regret)	*shko*-da	шкода
uncomfortable	ne-*zruch*-no	незручно
warm	*te*-plo	тепло

SPACE INVADERS

Though there are situations, eg on public transport, when you're packed so tightly that body contact with strangers is unavoidable, Ukrainians generally have the same sense of private space that Westerners have.

It's not usual to touch the person to whom you're speaking, though a man may sometimes take another man by the arm, elbow or shoulder to make a point. Children accompanied by their parents, on the other hand, are frequently touched by visitors or family friends. A pat on the head, putting an arm around a child's shoulders or sitting the child on your knee is quite acceptable and the child will not usually protest.

As a rule, Ukrainians do not gesticulate all that much when speaking.

MEETING PEOPLE

I am/feel …	ya …	Я …
angry	ser-*dy*-ty/	сердитий/
	ser-*dy*-ta (m/f)	сердита
grateful	*vdyach*-ny/	вдячний/
	vdyach-na (m/f)	вдячна
tired	*wtom*-le-ny/	втомлений/
	wtom-le-na (m/f)	втомлена
well	zdo-*ro*-vy/	здоровий/
	zdo-*ro*-va (m/f)	здорова
worried	stur-*bo*-va-ny	стурбований/
	stur-*bo*-va-na (m/f)	стурбована

I'm in a hurry.
   ya po-spi-*sha*-yu   Я поспішаю.
I'm hungry.
   ya *kho*-chu *yi*-sty   Я хочу їсти.
I'm thirsty.
   ya *kho*-chu *py*-ty   Я хочу пити.
I feel sleepy.
   ya *kho*-chu *spa*-ty   Я хочу спати.
I want to have a rest.
   ya *kho*-chu vid-po-*chy*-ty   Я хочу відпочити.
I want to have a wash.
   ya *kho*-chu po-*my*-ty-sya   Я хочу помитися.

TELL ME, PLEASE …

If you want to attract someone's attention in order to ask a question, you should say ska-*zhit'*, bud' *la*-ska (Скажіть, будь ласка, …) which means 'Tell me, please …'. If you wish to enter someone's room or ask permission to do something, you should ask *mozh*-na? (Можна?) which means 'May I?'.

EXPRESSING OPINIONS

НА МОЮ ДУМКУ...

Ukrainian uses two verbs to express the idea of liking something: lyu-*by*-ty (любити) and po-*do*-ba-ty-sya (подобатися). Generally lyu-*by*-ty expresses a greater intensity of feeling than po-*do*-ba-ty-sya, but this is not always the case, as can be seen from the examples below:

Do you like ...?	vam po-*do*-ba-yet'-sya ...?	Вам подобається ...?
I (don't) like ...	me-*ni* (ne) po-*do*-ba-yet'-sya ...	Мені (не) подобається ...
playing sport	za-*yma*-ty-sya *spor*-tom	займатися спортом
playing the piano	*hra*-ty na for-te-pi-*a*-no	грати на фортепіано
reading books	chy-*ta*-ty knyzh-*ky*	читати книжки
singing	spi-*va*-ty	співати
the theatre	te-*atr*	театр
your country	*va*-sha kra-*yi*-na	ваша країна

I (don't) like ...	ya (ne) lyu-*blyu* ...	Я (не) люблю ...
humour	*hu*-mor	гумор
the cinema	ki-*no*	кіно
the summer	*li*-to	літо
travelling	po-do-ro-zhu-*va*-ty	подорожувати

English	Pronunciation	Ukrainian
I think ...	ya *du*-ma-yu ...	Я думаю ...
In my opinion ...	na mo-*yu dum*-ku ...	На мою думку ...
Yes, (it is).	tak, (*pra*-vyl'-no)	Так, (правильно).
No, (it isn't).	ni, (ne *pra*-vyl'-no)	Ні, (не правильно).
I (dis)agree.	ya (ne) *zho*-den/ *zho*-dna (m/f)	Я (не) згоден/ згодна.
I'm not against it.	ya ne *pro*-ty	Я не проти.
Is that correct?	*pra*-vyl'-no?	Правильно?
You're right.	vy *ma*-ye-te *ra*-tsi-yu	Ви маєте рацію.
Is that true?	(tse) *praw*-da?	(Це) правда?
We'll see.	po-*ba*-chy-mo	Побачимо.
Agreed!	*zho*-da!	Згода!
Of course!	zvy-*chay*-no!	Звичайно!
Without doubt!	bez-pe-*rech*-no!	Безперечно!
No problem!	ne-*ma*(-ye) pro-*blem*!	Нема(є) проблем!

English	Pronunciation	Ukrainian
That's impossible!	tse ne-mo-*zhly*-vo!	Це неможливо!
That's (not) right/true!	(ne) *praw*-da!	(Не) правда!
You're mistaken.	vy po-my-*lya*-ye-te-sya	Ви помиляєтеся.
That's going too far!	tse za-*nad*-to!	Це занадто!

BREAKING THE LANGUAGE BARRIER

ДОЛАЙМО МОВНИЙ БАР'ЄР!

I'm a foreigner.
    ya i-no-*ze*-mets'/
    i-no-*zem*-ka (m/f)

Я іноземець/
іноземка.

I understand.
    ya ro-zu-*mi*-yu

Я розумію.

I don't understand (you).
    ya (vas) ne ro-zu-*mi*-yu

Я (Вас) не розумію.

I didn't understand
what you said.
    ya ne zro-zu-*miw*/
    zro-zu-*mi*-la,
    shcho vy ska-*za*-ly (m/f)

Я не зрозумів/
зрозуміла,
що Ви сказали.

I'm sorry, what did you say?
    pe-re-*pro*-shu-yu, shcho
    vy ska-*za*-ly?

Перепрошую, що
Ви сказали?

I (don't) know how to say this.
    ya (ne) *zna*-yu,
    yak tse ska-*za*-ty

Я (не) знаю,
як це сказати.

I (don't) know what this is called.
    ya (ne) *zna*-yu, yak tse
    na-zy-*va*-yet'-sya

Я (не) знаю, як це
називається.

I don't speak Ukrainian very well yet.
    ya shche ne *du*-zhe *do*-bre
    roz-mow-*lya*-yu
    u-kra-*yins*'-ko-yu *mo*-vo-yu

Я ще не дуже добре
розмовляю
українською мовою.

I speak ...	ya roz-mow-*lya*-yu ...	Я розмовляю ...
Do you speak ...?	vy roz-mow-*lya*-ye-te	Ви розмовляєте
... (*mo*-vo-yu)?	... (мовою)?	
English	an-*hliy*-s'ko-yu	англійською
French	fran-*tsuz*'-ko-yu	французькою
German	ni-*me*-ts'ko-yu	німецькою
Russian	ro-*siy*-s'ko-yu	російською
Spanish	i-*span*-s'ko-yu	іспанською

What does this mean?
| shcho tse o-zna-*cha*-ye? | Що це означає? |

What does ... mean?
| shcho o-zna-*cha*-ye ...? | Що означає ...? |

What's this called?
| yak tse na-zy-*va*-yet'-sya? | Як це називається? |

Could you please ...?	vy ne mo-*hly* b ...?	Ви не могли б ...?
speak slowly	ho-vo-*ry*-ty	говорити
	po-*vil*'-no	повільно
repeat the	po-wto-*ry*-ty	повторити
question	za-py-*tan*-nya	запитання
repeat the	po-wto-*ry*-ty	повторити
last word	o-*stan*-nye *slo*-vo	останнє слово

ПОДОРОЖІ

GETTING AROUND

Public transport in Ukraine is cheap and easy to use, but be prepared for crowded conditions in rush hours. Don't be afraid to push – everyone else does! It's a good idea to learn some Cyrillic so you can recognise signs at a glance. Trolleybuses, trams and buses will get you around the cities. Kyiv, Kharkiv and Dnipropetrovsk have metro systems, and there is the so-called 'light metro' in Kryvy Rih. Taxis are fairly plentiful, but be sure to negotiate a price before starting your journey, especially when hailing a car.

FINDING YOUR WAY

Excuse me, where am I?
vy-ba-chte, de ya
zna-*kho*-dzhu-sya?

I'm looking for ...
ya shu-*ka*-yu ...

What's this place/street called?
yak na-zy-*va*-yet'-sya
[tse *mi*-stse;
tsya *vu*-ly-tsya]?

ЯК ДІЙТИ ДО ...?

Вибачте, де я
знаходжуся?

Я шукаю ...

як називається
[це місце;
ця вулиця]?

Щасливо!

Бувай!

Where's the ...?	de ...?	Де ...?
airport	a-e-ro-*port*	аеропорт
bus station	aw-to-vog-*zal*/	автовокзал/
	aw-to-*stan*-tsi-ya	автостанція
metro station	*stan*-tsi-ya me-*tro*	станція метро
nearest bus/tram/	nay-*blyzh*-cha	найближча
trolleybus stop	zu-*pyn*-ka	зупинка
	a-*wto*-bu-sa/	автобуса/
	tram-*va*-ya/	трамвая/
	tro-*ley*-bu-sa	тролейбуса
taxi stand	zu-*pyn*-ka tak-*si*	зупинка таксі
ticket office	(kvy-*tko*-va) *ka*-sa	(квиткова) каса
train station	(za-li-*znych*-ny)	(залізничний)
	vog-*zal*)	вокзал
port	port	порт

Where's (Khreshchatyk Street)?
de *vu*-ly-tsya (khre-*shcha*-tyk)?   Де вулиця (Хрещатик)?

What ... is this?	ya-*ky* tse ...?	Який це ...?
alley	pro-*vu*-lok	провулок
avenue	pro-*spekt*	проспект
boulevard	bul'-*var*	бульвар
square	may-*dan*	майдан

What ... is this?	ya-*ka* tse ...?	Яка це ...?
square	*plo*-shcha	площа
street	*vu*-ly-tsya	вулиця

(Also see Writing Letters, page 137, for some common abbreviations.)

DE TU-A-*LET*?

To ask where something is, simply say de ...? (Де ...?), followed by whatever it is you're looking for. For example, de zu-*pyn*-ka tak-*si*? (Де зупинка таксі?), 'Where's the taxi stand?, de tu-a-*let*? (Де туалет?), 'Where's the toilet?' and de *po*-shta? (Де пошта?), 'Where's the post office?'.

Ukrainian has a number of words for the verb 'to go'. Which verb you use depends on *how* you are going! If you're going on foot the verb is i-*ty* (іти), which you may also hear as di-*yty* (дійти), 'to get to', or pry-*ty* (прийти), 'to arrive'. If you're travelling by some means of wheeled transport, the verb is *yi*-kha-ty (їхати), which may appear as do-*yi*-kha-ty (доїхати), 'to get to', or pry-*i*-kha-ty (приїхати), 'to arrive'.

How do I get to the ...?	yak di-*sta*-ty-sya do ...?; (general term)	Як дістатися до ...?;
	yak do-*yi*-kha-ty do ...?; (by some means of transport)	Як доїхати до ...?;
	yak ya *mo*-zhu di-*yty* do ...?(on foot)	Як я можу дійти до ...?
metro	me-*tro*	метро
museum	mu-*ze*-yu	музею
park	*par*-ku	парку
theatre	te-*a*-tru	театру

Is it nearby/far?
tse *blyz*'-ko/da-*le*-ko? Це близько/далеко?

How far is it to (Desiatynna Street)?
chy da-*le*-ko (*vu*-ly-tsya de-sya-*tyn*-na)? Чи далеко (вулиця Десятинна)?

Can I walk there?
ya *mo*-zhu di-*yty* tu-*dy* pi-shky? Я можу дійти туди пішки?

Can you show me on the map?
vy *mo*-zhe-te po-ka-*za*-ty (me-*ni*) na *kar*-ti? Ви можете показати (мені) на карті?

How many minutes' walk?
skil'-ky khvy-*lyn* i-*ty*? Скільки хвилин іти?

GETTING AROUND

Directions

Вказівки

Go straight ahead.	i-*dit' prya*-mo	Ідіть прямо.
Turn left.	po-ver-*nit'*	Поверніть
	na-*li*-vo/li-*vo*-ruch	наліво/ліворуч.
Turn right.	po-ver-*nit'*	Поверніть
	na-*pra*-vo/	направо/
	pra-*vo*-ruch	праворуч.
at the corner	na *ro*-zi	на розі
at the traffic lights	*bi*-lya svi-tlo-*fo*-ra	біля світлофора
at the square	na *plo*-shchi	на площі
at the crossing	na pe-re-*kho*-di	на переході
through the	*che*-rez	через
underpass	pid-*ze*-mny	підземний
	pe-re-*khid*	перехід
north	*piw*-nich	північ
south	*piw*-den'	південь
east	skhid	схід
west	*za*-khid	захід

ADDRESSES

АДРЕСА

When giving an address, do as the Ukrainians do: give the name of the street first, then the building number, then the number of the apartment:

> Zelena Street, No 56, Apt 13
> *vu*-ly-tsya ze-*le*-na,   вулиця Зелена,
> bu-*dy*-nok   будинок п'ятдесят
> pya-de-*syat* shist',   шість (56),
> kvar-*ty*-ra try-*na*-tsyat' квартира тринадцять (13)

When writing down an address, make sure you have both building number and flat number. The number of the building you're looking for may not always be clearly marked, so be ready to ask a passer-by.

Most apartment buildings have several entrance foyers, each of which gives access to a particular group of apartments. If you're invited to someone's home, be sure to ask how to find the right entrance, pid-*yizd* (під'їзд). Some apartment buildings have security doors at the entrances, so you should also ask for the code.

What's your address?
| ya-*ka va*-sha a-*dre*-sa? | Яка ваша адреса? |

What's the number of this building?
| ya-*ky* tse *no*-mer bu-*dyn*-ku? | Який це номер будинку? |

What's the number of your building?
| ya-*ky no*-mer *va*-sho-ho bu-*dyn*-ku? | Який номер вашого будинку? |

What's the number of your apartment?
| ya-*ky no*-mer *va*-sho-yi kvar-*ty*-ry? | Який номер вашої квартири? |

Which is your entrance?
| ya-*ky* vash pid-*yizd*? | Який ваш під'їзд? |

What's the code for the security lock?
| ya-*ky* u vas kod zam-*ka* na *dve*-ryakh? | Який у вас код замка на дверях? |

For instructions on addressing mail, see Writing Letters, page 137.

A STREET BY ANOTHER NAME

буд.	будинок	bu-*dy*-nok	building
бул.	бульвар	bul'-*var*	boulevard
вул.	вулиця	*vu*-ly-tsya	street
кв.	квартира	kvar-*ty*-ra	apartment
м.	місто	*mi*-sto	city
пл.	площа	*plo*-shcha	square
пров.	провулок	pro-*vu*-lok	lane
просп.	проспект	pro-*spekt*	avenue
с.	село	se-*lo*	village

GETTING AROUND

BUYING TICKETS   КУПІВЛЯ КВИТКІВ

The rules for buying public transport tickets differ from city to city. In some cases, it's possible to pay inside a vehicle, while in other situations you can buy your tickets for buses, trams and trolleybuses in advance from kiosks near most stops. When required, insert your ticket in the punching machine, kom-*po*-ster (компостер), on board the vehicle. If you're going to be in a city for two weeks or more it's probably worthwhile buying a travel card, pro-yi-*zny* kvy-*tok* (проїзний квиток). These last for one calendar month and they're available for different combinations of public transport modes, eg metro and trolleybus, or bus and tram, or the system as a whole.

Excuse me, where's
the ticket office?
   vy-ba-chte, bud' *la*-ska,
   de kvy-*tko*-vi *ka*-sy?

Вибачте, будь ласка,
де квиткові каси?

Where's the information desk?
   de do-vid-*ko*-ve byu-*ro*?

Де довідкове бюро?

Where can I buy a bus ticket?
   de *mo*-zhna ku-*py*-ty
   kvy-*tok* na a-*wto*-bus?

Де можна купити
квиток на автобус?

We want to go to ...
   my *kho*-che-mo
   po-*yi*-kha-ty do ...

Ми хочемо
поїхати до ...

How much does a ticket cost?
   skil'-ky *ko*-shtu-ye
   kvy-*tok*?

Скільки коштує
квиток?

Do you have student/
seniors'/children's discounts?
   vy da-*ye*-te *znyzh*-ky
   stu-*den*-tam/
   pen-si-o-*ne*-ram/*di*-tyam?

Ви даєте знижки
студентам/
пенсіонерам/дітям?

Do I need to book?
   chy *tre*-ba
   za-mow-*lya*-ty na-pe-*red*?

Чи треба
замовляти наперед?

Please give me (10) tickets.
   da-yte, bud' *la*-ska,
   (*de*-syat') kvy-*tkiw*

Дайте, будь ласка,
(десять) квитків.

I'd like ...	ya b kho-*tiw*/ kho-*ti*-la ... (m/f)	Я б хотів/ хотіла ...
one ticket to ...	o-*dyn* kvy-*tok* do ...	один квиток до ...
two tickets to ...	dva kvy-*tky* do ...	два квитки до ...
a reservation	*bro*-nyu	броню
a one way (ticket)	kvy-*tok* v o-*dyn* bik	квиток в один бік
a return (ticket)	kvy-*tok* tu-*dy* i na-*zad*; zvo-*ro*-tny kvy-*tok*	квиток туди і назад; зворотний квиток

SIGNS

ДОВІДКОВЕ БЮРО	INFORMATION
КАМЕРА СХОВУ	LEFT LUGGAGE
КОМПОСТЕР	PUNCHING MACHINE
КАСИ ПОПЕРЕДНЬОГО ПРОДАЖУ КВИТКІВ	PURCHASE OF ADVANCE TICKETS
КВИТКИ	TICKETS
КАСА/КАСИ	TICKET OFFICE
ПРОЇЗНИЙ КВИТОК	TRAVEL CARD
ЗАЛ ЧЕКАННЯ	WAITING ROOM

Can I make a reservation
for ... {date}?

mo-zhna za-bro-nyu-*va*-ty/
za-*mo*-vy-ty kvy-*tok* na ...?

Можна забронювати/
замовити квиток на ...?

A second-class/
third-class ticket, please.

da-yte, bud' *la*-ska,
ku-*pey*-ny/
plats-*kar*-tny
kvy-*tok*

Дайте, будь ласка,
купейний/
плацкартний
квиток.

GETTING AROUND

AIR   У ПОВІТРІ

International flights to Kyiv land at Boryspil International Airport, 40km east of the city centre. There are regular bus connections into town. Take standard precautions when accepting a ride in a private car. In Kyiv, Zhuliany airport is closer to town but is for domestic flights only.

Air travel within Ukraine has traditionally been quite expensive and train travel was the preferred option, but low-cost airlines have begun emerging on several domestic lines. International flights to Kyiv, Odesa, Dnipropetrovsk, Lviv and other major cities, mainly from European ports, are fairly plentiful. There are a couple of domestic flights daily between Kyiv and the other major cities. It's generally fairly easy to obtain tickets. These are bought at airline offices or at the airport itself. *mya*-ko-yi po-*sad*-ky! (М'якої посадки!), 'Happy landing!' (literally: 'soft landing').

Is there a flight to ...?
   chy ye reys do ...?   Чи є рейс до ...?
When's the next flight to ...?
   ko-*ly* na-*stu*-pny   Коли наступний
   reys do ...?   рейс до...?
What's the flight number?
   ya-*ky no*-mer *rey*-su?   Який номер рейсу?
Where do we check in?
   de re-ye-*stra*-tsi-ya?   Де реєстрація?
When do we have to check in?
   ko-*ly* po-chy-*na*-yet'-sya   Коли починається
   re-ye-*stra*-tsi-ya na reys?   реєстрація на рейс?
[One hour; Two hours]
before departure.
   [za ho-*dy*-nu;   [За годину;
   za dvi ho-*dy*-ny]   за дві години]
   do vid-*l'o*-tu   до відльоту.
Where do I check in luggage?
   de *mo*-zhna   Де можна
   zda-ty ba-*hazh*?   здати багаж?

Where do I pick up luggage?
de *mo*-zhna o-*der*-zha-ty
ba-*hazh*?

Де можна одержати
багаж?

My luggage hasn't arrived.
ne-*ma*-ye mo-*ho* ba-ha-*zhu*

Немає мого багажу.

SIGNS

ПРИБУТТЯ	**ARRIVALS**
ВИДАЧА БАГАЖУ	**BAGGAGE CLAIM**
РЕЄСТРАЦІЯ	**CHECK-IN**
МИТНИЦЯ	**CUSTOMS**
ВІДПРАВЛЕННЯ	**DEPARTURES**
БЮРО ЗНАХІДОК	**LOST PROPERTY**
ОБМІН ВАЛЮТИ	**MONEY EXCHANGE**
ПАСПОРТНИЙ	**PASSPORT**
КОНТРОЛЬ	**CONTROL**

At Customs

На митниці

I have nothing to declare.
u *me*-ne ne-*ma*-ye ni-*cho*-ho
dlya de-kla-*ra*-tsi-yi

У мене немає нічого
для декларації.

I have something to declare.
ya *kho*-chu shchos'
za-de-kla-ru-*va*-ty

Я хочу щось
задекларувати.

Do I have to declare this?
tse *tre*-ba
za-de-kla-ru-*va*-ty?

Це треба
задекларувати?

This is all my luggage.
tse ves' miy ba-*hazh*

Це весь мій багаж.

That's not mine.
tse ne mo-*ye*

Це не моє.

I didn't know I had to declare it.
ya ne znaw/*zna*-la (m/f),
shcho tse *tre*-ba bu-*lo*
za-de-kla-ru-*va*-ty

Я не знав/знала,
що це треба було
задекларувати.

GETTING AROUND

TRAIN   ПОЇЗД

The train is still the cheapest and most convenient way to get around Ukraine, and it's a good way to meet people. Almost all long-distance journeys in Ukraine are overnight, and some cities are connected with Kyiv by faster express trains for a daytime journey. All trains around the country run on Kyiv time. On trains, you'll find the following types of carriages:

es-*ve* (СВ) – an abbreviation for *spal'*-ny va-*hon* (спальний вагон), 'sleeping car'. This is the most luxurious and expensive way to travel: two berths to a compartment. These carriages may not be available on all long-distance trains. The prices for these cars are comparable with airfares.

OVERNIGHT TRACKIES

Reserved train tickets show the number of the train, the carriage number and the seat number.

Retiring for the night follows a ritual. When the time is ripe either the men or the women leave the compartment for the corridor, while those remaining inside change for the night. Then the parties change places and the procedure is repeated. The dress code calls for a tracksuit rather than pyjamas.

Each carriage has its own supervisor, pro-vi-*dnyk* (провідник), who distributes bed linen at the start of the trip. In most cases, the charge for it is included in the ticket price. You can also order a cup of coffee, a glass of tea or a bottle of beer. A more substantial meal can be arranged in the va-*hon*-re-sto-*ran* (вагон-ресторан), 'restaurant car', available on most long-distance trains. You can also take some food and drink with you.

People are very sociable on trains and will almost always engage in conversation. Passengers in the one compartment will often share snacks and drinks.

ku-*pey*-ny va-*hon* (купейний вагон) – literally 'car with compartments'. This is probably closest to a second-class sleeper: four berths to a compartment.

plats-*kart*-ny va-*hon* (плацкартний вагон) – an open-plan car with reserved bunks. This is the closest to third class.

za-*hal'*-ny va-*hon* (загальний вагон) – literally 'common car'. You cannot reserve these seats. First come, first seated! These carriages are cheap and good for local colour, but do not expect to get any sleep. They're better for short journeys.

YOU MAY HEAR ...

u-va-*ha*!	Attention!
vash kvy-*tok*, bud' *la*-ska	Your ticket, please.
mists' ne-ma-ye	It's full.
po-yizd za-*pi*-znyu-yet'-sya	The train is delayed.
po-yizd vi-*dmi*-ne-no	The train is cancelled.
de-vya-no-sto	Train No 92
dru-hy po-yizd	is arriving
pry-bu-*va*-ye na	on track 1.
per-shu ko-li-yu	

I'd like a first-class sleeper.
  ya b kho-*tiw*/
  kho-*ti*-la es-*ve* (m/f)

Я б хотів/
хотіла 'СВ'.

When's the next train to ...?
  ko-*ly* na-*stup*-ny
  po-yizd do ...?

Коли наступний
поїзд до ...?

Do I need to change trains?
  chy po-*trib*-no ro-*by*-ty
  pe-re-*sad*-ku?

Чи потрібно робити
пересадку?

What time does the train leave?
  ko-*ly* vid-praw-*lya*-yet'-sya
  po-yizd?

Коли відправляється
поїзд?

What time does the train arrive?
  ko-*ly* po-yizd pry-bu-*va*-ye?   Коли поїзд прибуває?
What station is this?
  ya-*ka* tse *stan*-tsi-ya?   Яка це станція?
What's the next station?
  ya-*ka* na-*stup*-na *stan*-tsi-ya?   Яка наступна станція?
How long does the trip take?
  yak *dow*-ho *tre*-ba *yi*-kha-ty?   Як довго треба їхати?
No smoking!
  ne pa-*ly*-ty!   Не палити!

berth	po-*ly*-tsya	полиця
lower	*ny*-zhnya	нижня
upper	*verkh*-nya	верхня
car/carriage	va-*hon*	вагон
compartment	ku-*pe*	купе
express train	shvyd-*ky* po-*yizd*	швидкий поїзд
kiosk	ki-*osk*	кіоск
local train	pry-mis'-*ky* po-yizd	приміський поїзд
local electric train	e-lek-*try*-chka	електричка
platform	plat-*for*-ma/pe-*ron*	платформа/перон
railway station	za-li-*znych*-na *stan*-tsi-ya/vog-*zal*	залізнична станція/вокзал
timetable	*roz*-klad (*ru*-khu po-yi-*zdiw*)	розклад (руху поїздів)
track	*ko*-li-ya	колія
train	po-*yizd*/po-*tyah*	поїзд/потяг

BUS, TRAM & TROLLEYBUS

АВТОБУС, ТРАМВАЙ І ТРОЛЕЙБУС

Trams, buses and trolleybuses run frequent services between early morning and about midnight. They can become extremely crowded, but people are accustomed to this. Often there's no way of getting on except by pushing, and you should not hesitate to do so.

bus	aw-*to*-bus	автобус
tram	tram-*vay*	трамвай
trolleybus	tro-*ley*-bus	тролейбус

Does this bus go to ...?
tsey aw-*to*-bus *yi*-de do ...?   Цей автобус їде до ...?

How often do buses come?
yak *cha*-sto *kho*-dyt'
aw-*to*-bus?   Як часто ходить автобус?

What time's the ... bus?	o ko-*triy* ho-*dy*-ni ... aw-*to*-bus?	О котрій годині ... автобус?
next	na-*stup*-ny	наступний
first	*per*-shy	перший
last	o-*stan*-niy	останній

Where's the nearest bus stop?
de nay-*blyzh*-cha
aw-*to*-bu-sna
zu-*pyn*-ka?   Де найближча автобусна зупинка?

Which bus goes to ...?
ya-*ky* aw-*to*-bus *i*-de do ...?   Який автобус іде до ...?

Can you tell me where to get off?
vy *mo*-zhe-te me-*ni*
ska-*za*-ty, de
vy-*kho*-dy-ty?   Ви можете мені казати, де виходити?

Can you tell me when we
get to ...?
   vy *mo*-zhe-te
   me-*ni* ska-*za*-ty, ko-*ly*
   my do-*yi*-de-mo do ...?

Ви можете
мені казати, коли
ми доїдемо до ...?

Can you tell me
where we are?
   ska-*zhit'*, bud' *la*-ska,
   de my *za*-raz?

Скажіть, будь ласка,
де ми зараз?

What stop is this?
   ya-*ka* tse zu-*pyn*-ka?

Яка це зупинка?

JUST LIKE SARDINES

If you find yourself on a crowded vehicle, the following
phrases will be useful:

Excuse me, I'd like to get off!
   do-*zvol'*-te
   (pro-*yty*)

Дозвольте
(пройти).

Are you getting off now?
   vy za-raz
   vy-*kho*-dy-te?

Ви зараз
виходите?

Are you getting off
at the next stop?
   vy vy-*kho*-dy-te
   na na-*stup*-niy
   (zu-*pyn*-tsi)?

Ви виходите
на наступній
(зупинці)?

Please pass this ticket
to be punched.
   pe-re-*day*-te na
   kom-*pos*-ter

Передайте на
компостер.

Please tell the driver to stop.
   po-pro-*sit'* vo-di-*ya*
   zu-py-*ny*-ty-sya

Попросіть водія
зупинитися.

SHUTTLE BUS   МАРШРУТНЕ ТАКСІ
In the larger cities there are minibuses that follow various
routes. This service is known as mar-*shrut*-ne tak-*si* (маршрутне
таксі), literally 'transport route taxi', or just as marsh-*rut*-ka
(маршрутка). The fare is somewhat higher than on other types of
public transport. You pay the driver in cash. So as not to hold up
the vehicle, passengers can enter first, then pass the fare forward
to the driver. Don't be afraid to give more money than what the
fare is – the change will be given back to you! The shuttle stops
on request anywhere along the route.

shuttle bus   mar-*shrut*-ne tak-*si*   маршрутне таксі

Please, pass the money
forward.
     pe-re-*day*-te *hro*-shi,   Передайте гроші,
     bud' *la*-ska   будь ласка.
Stop at the lights, please.
     zu-py-*nit*'-sya na   Зупиніться на
     svi-tlo-*fo*-ri, bud' *la*-ska   світлофорі, будь ласка.

METRO   МЕТРО
Kyiv, Kharkiv and Dnipropetrovsk have metro systems. A flat
fare system operates; simply buy your token, zhe-*ton* (жетон),
at the booth in the station and insert it into the slot on the
entrance gate.

Where's the nearest metro station?
     de nay-*blyzh*-cha   Де найближча
     stan-tsi-ya me-*tro*?   станція метро?
Where do I purchase
tokens for the metro?
     de *mo*-zhna ku-*py*-ty   Де можна купити
     zhe-*to*-nyna me-*tro*?   жетони на метро?
How much does a token cost?
     skil'-ky *ko*-shtu-ye   Скільки коштує
     zhe-*ton*?   жетон?

GETTING AROUND

Does this train go to ...?
tsey *po*-yizd i-*de* do ...?   Цей поїзд іде до ...?
What station is this?
ya-*ka* tse *stan*-tsi-ya?   Яка це станція?
What metro line is this?
ya-*ka* tse *li*-ni-ya me-*tro*?   Яка це лінія метро?

SIGNS

A	BUS STOP	TP	TROLLEYBUS STOP
T	TRAM STOP	M	METRO

TAXI   ТАКСІ
There are a few taxi ranks, and taxis can be ordered by phone or
hailed. Note that in the vicinity of airports, train and bus stations,
the drivers usually charge enormous prices, so it's probably best
to order a taxi in such situations. Some taxis are metered, but
even so it's wise to agree on a price before you board.

A word of warning: many drivers of private cars supplement
their income by cruising the streets in search of people wanting
to get somewhere in a hurry. It's always best to use official taxis
only. If you do use a private car, think twice about getting in if
there's anyone else in the car besides the driver.

taxi   tak-*si*   таксі

I want to go to ...
me-*ni tre*-ba *yi*-kha-ty do ...   Мені треба їхати до ...
How much is it to ...?
skil'-ky do ...?   Скільки до ...?
How much (do I owe you)?
skil'-ky (z me-ne)?   Скільки (з мене)?
Do we pay extra for luggage?
chy *tre*-ba do-*pla*-chu-va-ty   Чи треба доплачувати
za ba-*hazh*?   за багаж?

Please, take me ...	pi-dve-*zit'* me-*ne*, bud' *la*-ska ...	Підвезіть мене, будь ласка ...
to the airport	v a-e-ro-*port*	в аеропорт
to the port	u port	у порт
to the station	na *stan*-tsi-yu/ vog-*zal*	на станцію/ вокзал
to a cheap hotel	u de-*she*-vy ho-*tel'*	у дешевий готель

Instructions   Вказівки

Continue!

yid'-te *da*-li, bud' *la*-ska!   Ідьте далі, будь ласка!

Slow down!

pry-hal'-*mu*-yte!   Пригальмуйте!

A little further.

tro-khy *da*-li   Трохи далі.

Turn left.

po-ver-*nit'* li-*vo*-ruch   Поверніть ліворуч.

Turn right.

po-ver-*nit'* pra-*vo*-ruch   Поверніть праворуч.

Into this street.

u tsyu *vu*-ly-tsyu   У цю вулицю.

Round the corner.

za po-vo-*ro*-tom   За поворотом.

Please stop here.

(zu-py-*nit'*-sya) tut, bud' *la*-ska   (Зупиніться) тут, будь ласка.

Please wait for a minute.

za-che-*kay*-te, bud' *la*-ska, khvy-*lyn*-ku   Зачекайте, будь ласка, хвилинку.

ON THE WATER   ПА ВОДІ

There's substantial tourist traffic on the Dnipro River as well as along the Crimean coastline. Popular cruises sail from Kyiv to Odesa. There's little passenger navigation during the colder months of the year. Passenger ferryboats sail on international routes on the Black Sea from Odesa or Illichivsk to Bulgaria, Turkey and Georgia.

When's the next boat to (Odesa)?
ko-*ly* na-*stup*-ny
pa-ro-*plaw* do (o-*de*-sy)?

Коли наступний
пароплав до (Одеси)?

How many hours is it to (Zaporizhzhya)?
skil'-ky ho-*dyn* do
(za-po-*rizh*-zhya)?

Скільки годин до
(Запоріжжя)?

Does the boat stop at (Kaniv)?
chy pa-ro-*plaw* ro-byt'
zu-*pyn*-ku w (*ka*-ne-vi)?

Чи пароплав робить
зупинку в (Каневі)?

What time does the boat depart/arrive?
o ko-*triy* ho-*dy*-ni
pa-ro-*plaw* vid-ply-*va*-ye/
pry-ply-*va*-ye?

О котрій годині
пароплав відпливає/
припливає?

Where does the boat depart from?
zvid-ky pa-ro-*plaw*
vid-ply-*va*-ye?

Звідки пароплав
відпливає?

CAR   МАШИНА/АВТОМОБІЛЬ

You can hire just about any make of car in Ukraine, with or without a driver, especially in Kyiv. Taking your own car is also possible. Most petrol stations in Ukraine use grade based on octane ratings. Occasionally, you can find stations selling petrol of Euro-3 or Euro-4 standards. When driving, note that finding a parking place close to the city centre can be difficult in some cities. Traffic jams are also frequent in larger cities. The roads in Ukraine are in rather bad conditions, especially beyond the main highways, and driving standards are quite low.

Where can I hire a car?
de *mo*-zhna *vy*-nay-nya-ty
ma-*shy*-nu/a-wto-mo-*bil*'?

Де можна винайняти
машину/автомобіль?

How much does it cost per day?
skil'-ky *ko*-shtu-ye
pro-*kat* za den'?

Скільки коштує
прокат за день?

How much does it cost per week?
skil'-ky pla-*ty*-ty za
tyzh-den'?

Скільки платити за
тиждень?

Is insurance included?
chy tse wklyu-*cha*-ye
stra-khu-*van*-nya?

Чи це включає
страхування?

Is mileage included?
ki-lo-me-*trazh*
vklyu-che-no w tsi-*nu*?

Кілометраж
включено в ціну?

Please, give me ...
litres of petrol/gasoline.
da-yte, bud' *la*-ska, ...
li-triw/*li*-try ben-*zy*-nu

Дайте, будь ласка, ...
літрів/літри бензину.

Fill it up.
za-*pow*-nit'/za-*ly*-te

Заповніть/залийте.

Please check the ...   pe-re-*vir*-te,
                       bud' *la*-ska, ...
  oil   *ma*-slo
  water   *vo*-du
  tyre pressure   tysk u *ka*-me-ri

Перевірте,
будь ласка, ...
  масло
  воду
  тиск у камері

Can you tell me the way to ...?
vy ne *ska*-zhe-te, yak
do-*yi*-kha-ty do ...?

Ви не скажете, як
доїхати до ...?

How far is it to ...?
chy da-*le*-ko do ...?

Чи далеко до ...?

GETTING AROUND

air	po-*vi*-trya	повітря
battery	a-ku-mu-*lya*-tor	акумулятор
brakes	*hal'*-ma	гальма
car	ma-*shy*-na/aw-*tol*/	машина/авто/
	aw-to-mo-*bil'*	автомобіль
diesel oil	dyz-*pa*-ly-vo	дизпаливо
drivers licence	pra-*va* vo-di-*ya*	права водія
engine	dvy-*hun*	двигун
lights	*fa*-ry	фари
oil	*ma*-slo	масло
parking	sto-*yan*-ka/	стоянка/
	par-kinh	паркінг
petrol station	za-*praw*-ka/	заправка/
	ben-zo-ko-*lon*-ka	бензоколонка
petrol (gas)	ben-*zyn*	бензин
super	de-vya-*no*-sto	дев'яносто
	pya-ty	п'ятий (95)
premium	de-vya-*no*-sto	дев'яносто
	vo-s'my	восьмий (98)
puncture	pro-*ko*-ly-na	проколина
radiator	ra-di-*a*-tor	радіатор
roadmap	*kar*-ta	карта
tyre(s)	*shy*-na/*shy*-ny (sg/pl)	шина/шини
windscreen	pe-*re*-dnye sklo	переднє скло

Car Problems

Проблеми з машиною

Where's the nearest
petrol/gas station?
   de nay-*blyzh*-cha
   za-*praw*-ka?

Де найближча
заправка?

Please help me.
   do-po-mo-*zhit'*,
   bud' *la*-ska

Допоможіть,
будь ласка.

My car has broken down.
   u *me*-ne po-la-*ma*-la-sya
   ma-*shy*-na

У мене поламалася
машина.

We need a mechanic.
    nam po-*tri*-ben me-*kha*-nik   Нам потрібен механік.
I have a flat tyre.
    w *me*-ne spu-*sty*-la *shy*-na   В мене спустила шина.
The battery's flat.
    u nas siw a-ku-mu-*lya*-tor   У нас сів акумулятор.
The radiator's leaking.
    ra-di-*a*-tor te-*che*   Радіатор тече.
The engine's overheating.
    dvy-*hun* pe-re-hri-*va*-yet'-sya   Двигун перегрівається.
I've lost my car keys.
    ya za-hu-*byw* klyu-*chi*
    vid ma-*shy*-ny   Я загубив ключі
                            від машини.
I've run out of petrol.
    u *me*-ne za-kin-*chyw*-sya   У мене закінчився
    ben-*zyn*   бензин.

BICYCLE   ВЕЛОСИПЕД

Cycling is popular among children in Ukraine. In country areas, where the public transport network is thin, many people use bicycles for short-distance travel and even for transporting goods. With traffic jams becoming frequent in the cities, the number of bicycles and scooters in the streets increases. In recent years there has been an increase in recreational cycling in the cities as well. There's some organised bicycle tourism, and Ukrainian cyclists do well in international competitions.

Is it within cycling distance?
    chy *mo*-zhna tu-*dy*
    do-*yi*-kha-ty na
    ve-lo-sy-*pe*-di   Чи можна туди
                           доїхати на
                           велосипеді?
Where can I hire a bicycle?
    de *mo*-zhna *wzya*-ty
    ve-lo-sy-*ped* na pro-*kat*?   Де можна взяти
                           велосипед на прокат?
Where can I find second-hand bikes for sale?
    de *mo*-zhna ku-*py*-ty
    ne-no-*vy* ve-lo-sy-*ped*?   Де можна купити
                           неновий велосипед?

How much is it per hour/day?
    skil'-ky *ko*-shtu-ye pro-*kat*
    [na ho-*dy*-nu; za den']?

Скільки коштує прокат
[на годину; за день]?

I have a flat tyre.
    w *me*-ne spus-*ty*-la *shy*-na

В мене спустила шина.

Where's a good bicycle
repair shop?
    de tut *do*-bra
    may-*ster*-nya dlya
    re-*mon*-tu ve-lo-sy-*pe*-diw?

Де тут добра
майстерня для
ремонту велосипедів?

Can you repair the bike
by tomorrow?
    chy miy ve-lo-sy-*ped bu*-de
    ho-*to*-vy do *za*-wtra?

Чи мій велосипед буде
готовий до завтра?

bicycle	ve-lo-sy-*ped*	велосипед
bike chain	lan-*tsyuh*	ланцюг
frame	*ra*-ma	рама
front light	pe-*red*-nya *fa*-ra	передня фара
gears	pe-re-*da*-chi	передачі
handlebars	ker-*mo*	кермо
helmet	sho-*lom*	шолом
pedal	pe-*dal'*	педаль
pump	na-*sos*	насос
puncture	pro-*ko*-ly-na	проколина
rear light	*za*-dnye *svi*-tlo	заднє світло
seat	si-*dlo*	сідло
spokes	*spy*-tsi	спиці
tyre(s)	*shy*-na / *shy*-ny	шина/шини
wheel	*ko*-le-so	колесо

ЖИТЛО
ACCOMMODATION

Ukraine is only now discovering its potential as a tourist destination. Since the country achieved independence there has been little investment in the development of cheap hotels with high standards. There are a few four- and five-star hotels in the major cities, but these are expensive. Still, a growing number of hotels charge what in Western countries would be regarded as moderate prices for clean, recently renovated rooms. Both hotels and hostels advertisements can be found on the Internet, and in most cases you can book a room online.

If you're not staying with relatives or friends, there are a few alternatives to hotels. Many people rent rooms or apartments, but it's hard to get information about these before you arrive. Bed and breakfast style accommodation is now plentiful in the picturesque Carpathian Mountains in Western Ukraine. Motels are becoming more common, especially along main roads on the outskirts of major cities. Although they provide parking for cars, they can still be called hotels. Caravan parks are quite rare.

If you're planning to stay in one place for a long period, particularly in larger cities, it might be worth considering renting a flat or a room in a private home. There are agencies that can make these arrangements for you.

ACCOMMODATION

FINDING ACCOMMODATION

ПОШУКИ ЖИТЛА

Can you tell me where a/the ... is?
ska-*zhit'*, bud' *la*-ska, de ...?
Скажіть, будь ласка, де ... ?

camp site	*kem*-pinh	кемпінг
cheap hotel	de-*she*-vy ho-*tel'*	дешевий готель
decent (clean) hotel	pry-*stoy*-ny ho-*tel'*	пристойний готель
good hotel	*har*-ny ho-*tel'*	гарний готель
tourist office	tu-ry-*stych*-ne byu-*ro*	туристичне бюро
nearest hotel	nay-*blyzh*-chy ho-*tel'*	найближчий готель
youth hostel	mo-lo-*dizh*-ny hur-*to*-zhy-tok; *kho*-stel	молодіжний гуртожиток; хостел

BOOKING AHEAD

БРОНЮВАННЯ

Do you have any free rooms?
u vas ye *vil'*-ni no-me-*ry*?
У вас є вільні номери?

I want to book a room.
ya *kho*-chu za-bro-nyu-*va*-ty *no*-mer
Я хочу забронювати номер.

How much is the room ...?
skil'-ky *ko*-shtu-ye *no*-mer ...?
Скільки коштує номер ...?

per night	za nich	за ніч
for ... nights	za ... *no*-chi/ no-*chey*	за ... ночі/ночей
per week	za *tyzh*-den'	за тиждень

I'll/We'll be arriving at (3 pm).
[ya pry-*i*-du; my pry-*i*-de-mo] o (*tre*-tiy dnya)
[Я приїду; Ми приїдемо] о (третій дня).

My name's ...
mo-*ye pri*-zvy-shche ...
Моє прізвище ...

Can I pay by credit card?
mo-zhna pla-*ty*-ty kre-*dy*-tno-yu *kart*-ko-yu?
Можиа платити кредитною карткою?

CHECKING IN

РЕЄСТРАЦІЯ

When you check in you're likely to be asked for your passport. This is a police requirement for registration purposes. It should be returned to you within 24 hours. If it isn't, ask for it. Make sure that it contains official proof of registration with the Department of Visas and Registration. You'll also have to fill out an information form. (Also see Paperwork, page 99.)

I need a room.
me-*ni* po-*tri*-ben *no*-mer
Мені потрібен номер.

> **HELLO!**
>
> Remember to use *do-bry den'* (Добрий день) as a general 'Hello'.

You should have a
reservation in the name of ...
u vas *ma*-ye *bu*-ty
za-*mow*-len-nya na
pri-zvy-shche ...

У вас має бути
замовлення на
прізвище ...

I'd like a ...	ya b kho-*tiw*/kho-*ti*-la ... (m/f)	Я б хотів/хотіла ...
single room	*no*-mer na o-dno-*ho*	номер на одного
double room	*no*-mer na dvokh	номер на двох
shared room	*mi*-stse	місце

I'd like a room with a ...	ya b kho-*tiw*/kho-*ti*-la *no*-mer z ... (m/f)	Я б хотів/хотіла номер з ...
balcony	bal-*ko*-nom	балконом
bathroom	*van*-no-yu	ванною
refrigerator	kho-lo-*dyl'*-ny-kom	холодильником
shower and toilet	*du*-shem i tu-a-*le*-tom	душем і туалетом
telephone	te-le-*fo*-nom	телефоном
TV	te-le-*vi*-zo-rom	телевізором
window	vi-*knom*	вікном

ACCOMMODATION

ACCOMMODATION

RED TAPE

Visa regulations change frequently, so be sure to check with your travel agent or the Ukrainian embassy what these are. At present, the citizens of the European countries, Canada, Japan and USA can enter Ukraine without a visa for a short period of time (up to three months). It's likely that you will need a visa to obtain a working permit, however. The registration of visitors is made at the border entrance points, where you'll be given an 'immigration card' to fill in your personal information as well as the destination of your travel. Make sure you keep this card until you leave Ukraine. (Also see Paperwork on page 99.)

Can I see the room?
   mo-zhna po-dy-*vy*-ty-sya na *no*-mer?

Можна подивитися на номер?

Where's the toilet/bathroom?
   de tu-a-*let*/*van*-na?

Де туалет/ванна?

Is there hot water all day?
   ha-*rya*-cha vo-*da* po-da-*yet*'-sya ves' den'?

Гаряча вода подається весь день?

Is breakfast included?
   chy tse wklyu-*cha*-ye *var*-tist' sni-*dan*-ku?

Чи це включає вартість сніданку?

What time do I have to check out?
   ko-*ly* ya po-*vy*-nen/ po-*vyn*-na zvil'-*ny*-ty *no*-mer? (m/f)

Коли я повинен/ повинна звільнити номер?

What's the room number?
   ya-*ky no*-mer kim-*na*-ty?

Який номер кімнати?

What floor is that?
   ya-*ky* tse *po*-verkh?

Який це поверх?

I'll take it.
   ya be-*ru*

Я беру.

REQUESTS & QUERIES

Can I leave my valuables here?
  chy ya *mo*-zhu za-ly-*shy*-ty
  svo-*yi* ko-*shtow*-ni *re*-chi
  tut?

Чи я можу залишити
свої коштовні речі
тут?

I'd like to make a phone call.
  ya b kho-*tiw*/kho-*ti*-la
  po-dzvo-*ny*-ty (m/f)

Я б хотів/хотіла
подзвонити.

Is there English-language
TV/radio?
  chy ye an-hlo-*mow*-ni
  pro-*hra*-my
  te-le-*ba*-chen-nya/*ra*-di-o?

Чи є англомовні
програми
телебачення/радіо?

Please wake us at seven.
  roz-bu-*dit'* nas o *s'o*-miy,
  bud' *la*-ska

Розбудіть нас о сьомій,
будь ласка.

Could you call me a taxi?
  vy *mo*-zhe-te *vy*-kly-ka-ty
  dlya *me*-ne tak-*si*?

Ви можете викликати
для мене таксі?

IMPERATIVE PLEASE!

The following requests are all in the imperative form
(command form) of the verb. You should use the polite
bud' *la*-ska (будь ласка), meaning 'Please', before the
request.

Come in.	za-*khod'*-te	Заходьте.
Give me ...	*day*-te ...	Дайте ...
Pass me ...	pe-re-*day*-te ...	Передайте ...
Show me ...	po-ka-*zhit'* ...	Покажіть ...
Sit down.	si-*day*-te	Сідайте.
Take ...	viz'-*mit'* ...	Візьміть ...
Tell me.	ska-*zhit'*	Скажіть.
Translate.	pe-re-kla-*dit'*	Перекладіть.

ACCOMMODATION

adaptor	pe-re-khi-*dnyk*	перехідник
alarm clock	bu-*dyl'*-nyk	будильник
bed	*lizh*-ko	ліжко
blanket	*kow*-dra	ковдра
chair	sti-*lets'*	стілець
clean	*chy*-sty	чистий
dirty	brud-ny	брудний
door	dve-ri	двері
electrical	e-lek-*trych*-na	електрична
socket	ro-zet-ka	розетка
fan	ven-ty-*lya*-tor	вентилятор
heating	o-*pa*-len-nya	опалення
light	*svi*-tlo	світло
light switch	vy-my-*kach*	вимикач
lock	za-*mok*	замок
mirror	*dzer*-ka-lo	дзеркало
pillow	po-*dush*-ka	подушка
pillowcase	na-vo-lo-chka	наволочка
sleeping bag	*spal'*-ny mi-*shok*;	спальний мішок;
	spal'-nyk	спальник
suitcase	va-li-za/va-liz-ka/	валіза/валізка/
	che-mo-*dan*	чемодан
table	stil	стіл
shelf	po-*ly*-tsya	полиця
sheets	pro-sty-*ra*-dla	простирадла
soap	*my*-lo	мило
tap/faucet	kran	кран
toilet	tu-a-*let*	туалет
toilet paper	tu-a-*let*-ny	туалетний
	pa-*pir*	папір
towel	rush-*nyk*	рушник
washbasin	u-my-*val'*-nyk	умивальник
window	vik-*no*	вікно

Is there somewhere
to wash clothes?
   chy *mo*-zhna des'
   po-*pra*-ty *o*-dyah?

Чи можна десь
попрати одяг?

Where's there a
laundry/drycleaners?
   de zna-*kho*-dyt'-sya
   pral'-nya/
   khim-*chys*-tka?

Де знаходиться
пральня/
хімчистка?

Where can I do some ironing?
   de *mo*-zhna pra-su-*va*-ty?

Де можна прасувати?

When's the restaurant open?
   ko-*ly* pra-*tsyu*-ye re-sto-*ran*?　Коли працює ресторан?

ACCOMMODATION

Я хочу
забронювати
номер...

ACCOMMODATION

At what time is the
room cleaned?
   o ko-*triy* ho-*dy*-ni   О котрій годині
   pry-by-*ran*-nya?   прибирання?

The room needs to be cleaned.
   no-mer *tre*-ba pry-*bra*-ty   Номер треба прибрати.

Please change the sheets.
   zmi-*nit'*, bud'   Змініть, будь
   la-ska, po-*stil'*   ласка, постіль.

Can I have my passport, please?
   chy ya *mo*-zhu *wzya*-ty   Чи я можу взяти
   sviy *pa*-sport?   свій паспорт?

Can I have ...? *mo*-zhna *wzya*-ty ...?; Можна взяти ...?;
              day-te, bud' *la*-ska, ... Дайте, будь ласка, ...

my key	miy klyuch	мій ключ
my luggage	miy ba-*hazh*	мій багаж
the bill	ra-*khu*-nok	рахунок

NO PROBLEM!

The simplest way of asking permission to do something
is to say:

May I?   *mo*-zhna?   Можна?

You can also ask vy do-zvo-*ly*-te? (Ви дозволите?) which
literally means 'Do you permit?' or, if you prefer, vy ne
za-pe-re-chu-*ye*-te? (Ви не заперечуєте?) which means
'You don't object, do you?'.

You could answer with:

Please do.	tak, *pro*-shu	Так, прошу.
Of course.	zvy-*chay*-no	Звичайно.
Unfortunately not.	na zhal', ni	На жаль, ні.
I don't want to.	ya ne *kho*-chu	Я не хочу.
I can't.	ya ne *mo*-zhu	Я не можу.
I won't.	ya ne *bu*-du	Я не буду.

COMPLAINTS

СКАРГИ

Do you have another room?
    u vas ye *in*-shy *no*-mer?

У вас є інший номер?

The shower/tap doesn't work.
    dush/kran ne pra-*tsyu*-ye

Душ/кран не працює.

There's no hot water.
    ne-*ma*-ye
    ha-*rya*-cho-yi vo-*dy*

Немає
гарячої води.

There's a broken ...	u *no*-me-ri	У номері
in my room.	po-*la*-ma-ne ...	поламане ...
bed	*lizh*-ko (neut)	ліжко
radio	*ra*-di-o (neut)	радіо

There's a broken ...	u *no*-me-ri	У номері
in my room.	po-*la*-ma-ny ...	поламаний ...
light switch	vy-my-*kach* (m)	вимикач
television	te-le-*vi*-zor (m)	телевізор

There's no toilet
paper in my room.
    u mo-*ye*-mu *no*-me-ri ne-*ma*
    tu-a-*let*-no-ho pa-*pe*-ru

У моєму номері нема
туалетного паперу.

I can't open/close
the window.
    vik-*no* ne
    vid-chy-*nya*-yet'-sya/
    za-chy-*nya*-yet'-sya

Вікно не
відчиняється/
зачиняється.

It's very cold/hot here.
    tut *du*-zhe *kho*-lod-no/
    zhar-ko

Тут дуже холодно/
жарко.

It's very noisy here.
    tut *du*-zhe *shum*-no

Тут дуже шумно.

The room is dirty.
    u *no*-me-ri *brud*-no

У номері брудно.

ACCOMMODATION

ACCOMMODATION

CHECKING OUT

ВИСЕЛЯЄМОСЯ З ГОТЕЛЮ

We're checking out ...	my vy-izh-*dzha*-ye-mo/ vy-se-*lya*-ye-mo-sya	Ми виїжджаємо/ виселяємося ...
today	s'o-*ho*-dni	сьогодні
tonight	s'o-*ho*-dni u-*ve*-che-ri	сьогодні увечері
tomorrow	*zaw*-tra	завтра

I'd like to pay the bill.
ya *kho*-chu za-pla-*ty*-ty
ra-*khu*-nok

Я хочу заплатити рахунок.

Can I pay with a travellers cheque?
mo-zhna za-pla-*ty*-ty
do-*rozh*-nim *che*-kom?
Можна заплатити
дорожнім чеком?

МОЖНА

Remember to use
mo-zhna (можна)
before any request
you make.

There's a mistake in the bill.
u ra-*khun*-ku
po-*myl*-ka

У рахунку помилка.

Could I have a receipt, please?
mo-zhna kvy-*tan*-tsi-yu,
bud' *la*-ska?

Можна квитанцію, будь ласка?

Can I leave my luggage here?
ya *mo*-zhu za-ly-*shy*-ty tut
sviy ba-*hazh*?

Я можу залишити тут свій багаж?

RENTING

ВИНАЙМ ЖИТЛА

Do you have any flats to rent?
u vas ye kvar-*ty*-ry
na *vy*-naym?

У вас є квартири
на винайм?

I want to rent a flat.
ya *kho*-chu *vy*-nay-nya-ty
kvar-*ty*-ru

Я хочу винайняти
квартиру.

I need a (one-roomed/two-roomed)
flat with telephone.
me-*ni* po-*trib*-na
(o-dno-kim-*nat*-na/
dvo-kim-*nat*-na) kvar-*ty*-ra
z te-le-*fo*-nom

Мені потрібна
(однокімнатна/
двокімнатна) квартира
з телефоном.

How much is it per week/month?
skil'-ky za
tyzh-den'/*mi*-syats'?

Скільки за
тиждень/місяць?

I'd like to rent it for
(one) month.
ya viz'-*mu* yi-*yi* na
(o-*dyn*) *mi*-syats

Я візьму її на
(один) місяць.

PAPERWORK

АНКЕТИ

name	i-*mya*	ім'я
surname	*pri*-zvy-shche	прізвище
patronymic	po-*bat'*-ko-vi	по-батькові
address	a-*dre*-sa	адреса
work	sluzh-*bo*-va	службова
home	do-*mash*-nya	домашня
telephone	te-le-*fon*	телефон
date of birth	*da*-ta	дата
	na-*ro*-dzhen-nya	народження
place of birth	*mi*-stse	місце
	na-*ro*-dzhen-nya	народження
nationality	nat-si-o-*nal'*-nist'	національність
age	vik	вік
sex	stat'	стать

ACCOMMODATION

ACCOMMODATION

marital status	si-*mey*-ny stan	сімейний стан
single	ne-o-*dru*-zhe-ny/	неодружений/
	ne-o-*dru*-zhe-na (m/f)	неодружена
married	o-*dru*-zhe-ny/	одружений/
	o-*dru*-zhe-na (m/f)	одружена
divorced	ro-*zlu*-che-ny/	розлучений/
	ro-*zlu*-che-na (m/f)	розлучена
widower/	wdi-*vets'*/	вдівець/
widow	wdo-*va*	вдова
religion	re-*li*-hi-ya	релігія
profession	pro-*fe*-si-ya	професія
place of employment	*mi*-stse ro-*bo*-ty	місце роботи
position held	po-*sa*-da	посада
purpose of visit	me-*ta* pry-*yi*-zdu	мета приїзду
passport number	*no*-mer *pa*-spor-ta	номер паспорта
identification	do-ku-*ment*	документ
birth certificate	svi-*dots*-tvo pro	свідоцтво про
	na-*ro*-dzhen-nya	народження
drivers licence	pra-*va* vo-di-*ya*	права водія
car registration certificate	tekh-*nich*-ny *pa*-sport	технічний паспорт
car registration number	re-ye-stra-*tsiy*-ny *no*-mer ma-*shy*-ny	реєстраційний номер машини

У МІСТІ AROUND TOWN

LOOKING FOR

ДЕ ТУТ ...?

Excuse me, where's a/an/the ...?	*vy*-ba-chte, de tut ...?	Вибачте, де тут ...?
art gallery	kar-*tyn*-na ha-le-*re*-ya; mu-*zey* my-*stets*-tva	картинна галерея; музей мистецтва
bank	bank	банк
city centre	tsentr (*mi*-sta)	центр (міста)
... consulate	*kon*-sul'-stvo ...	консульство ...
... embassy	po-*sol'*-stvo ...	посольство ...
… hotel	ho-*tel'* ...	готель ...
market	*ry*-nok	ринок
museum	mu-*zey*	музей
police station	mi-*li*-tsi-ya	міліція
post office	*po*-shta	пошта
public telephone	te-le-*fon*- aw-to-*mat*	телефон- автомат
public toilet	hro-mad-*s'ky* tu-a-*let*	громадськнй туалет
town square	tsen-*tral'*-na *plo*-shcha	центральна площа
tourist office	tu-ry-*stych*-ne byu-*ro*	туристичне бюро

AROUND TOWN

HEY YOU!

It's best to always address people you have just met with the more polite form of 'you' – vy (Ви), which sounds just like the plural 'you' (ви). Use the more familiar 'you' – ty (ти) – if you're invited to do so.

101

AT THE BANK   У БАНКУ

The Ukrainian unit of currency is the *hryvnia*, *hryw*-nya
(гривня), plural: *hryvni*, *hryw*-ni (гривні). The *hryvnia* contains
100 ko-*piy*-*ky* (копійки), singular: ko-*piy*-ka (копійка). The
Ukrainian abbreviation for *hryvnia* is грн. and is written after
the number. The currency code is *UAH*. It's against the law to
use currencies other than Ukrainian *hryvni* to pay for goods and
services, except in clearly marked establishments.

The most easily exchanged currencies are the US dollar and the
Euro. Money can be exchanged both at banks and at special
currency exchange kiosks. There are many of these in central
locations in the cities. The exchange rates of the most popular
currencies are prominently displayed, and there's little variation
from outlet to outlet.

Banknotes with writing on them are almost always rejected in
Ukraine. Don't be tempted by exchange offers from individuals
in the street. Such transactions are illegal, and you run the risk
of being ripped off.

There are no universal banking hours. Many bank branches
will close for a period in the middle of the day.

Most hotels, restaurants and supermarkets and many shops
will accept major credit cards. Automatic teller machines can be
easily found in the major cities as well as in smaller towns.

AROUND TOWN

SIGNS

БАНК	BANK
КАСИР	CASHIER
ОБМІН ВАЛЮТИ	CURRENCY EXCHANGE
КЕРІВНИК/	MANAGER
МЕНЕДЖЕР	

What time does the
bank open/close?
  o ko-*triy* ho-*dy*-ni
  vid-kry-*va*-yet'-sya/
  za-kry-*va*-yet'-sya bank?

О котрій годині
відкривається/
закривається банк?

Do you change travellers cheques?
  vy mi-*nya*-ye-te do-*rozh*-ni
  che-ky?

Ви міняєте дорожні
чеки?

Can I use my credit card
to withdraw money?
  chy *mozh*-na *znya*-ty
  hro-shi z kre-*dyt*-no-yi
  kart-ky?

Чи можна зняти
гроші з кредитної
картки?

What's the exchange rate?
  ya-*ky* kurs (*ob*-mi-nu
  va-*lyu*-ty)?

Який курс (обміну
валюти)?

How many *hryvni* per dollar?
  ya-*ky* kurs *hry*-wni
  do *do*-la-ra?

Який курс гривні
до долара?

I'd like to change ...	ya b kho-*tiw*/ kho-*ti*-la ob-mi-*nya*-ty ... (m/f)	Я б хотів/ хотіла обміняти ...
a travellers cheque	do-*ro*-zhniy chek	дорожній чек
this money into *hryvni*	tsi *hro*-shi na *hry*-wni	ці гроші на гривні
100 dollars/ pounds/ Euros	sto *do*-la-riw/ *fun*-tiw/ *yew*-ro	сто доларів/ фунтів/ євро

How many ... will that be?
  skil'-ky ... tse *bu*-de?

Скільки ... це буде?

Could you write that down?
  vy *mo*-zhe-te tse
  za-py-*sa*-ty?

Ви можете це
записати?

Can I have some money
transferred to here?
  chy *mo*-zhna
  pe-re-ve-*sty* mo-*yi*
  hro-shi syu-*dy*?

Чи можна
перевести мої
гроші сюди?

How long will it take?
  skil'-ky *cha*-su
  tse zay-*me*?

Скільки часу
це займе?

Could I speak to the manager?
  chy *mo*-zhna po-ho-vo-*ry*-ty
  z ke-riw-ny-*kom*?

Чи можна поговорити
з керівником?

The automatic teller machine
(ATM) has swallowed my card!
  ban-ko-*mat* pro-kow-*tnuw*
  mo-*yu kar*-tku!

Банкомат проковтнув
мою картку!

ATM	ban-ko-*mat*	банкомат
bank note	ban-*kno*-ta/	банкнота/
	ku-*pyu*-ra	купюра
credit card	kre-*dyt*-na *kart*-ka	кредитна картка
exchange	punkt *ob*-mi-nu	пункт обміну
	va-*lyu*-ty	валюти
identification	do-ku-*ment*	документ
personal cheques	o-so-*by*-sti *che*-ky	особисті чеки
signature	*pid*-pys	підпис
sum	*su*-ma	сума
travellers cheques	do-*ro*-zhni *che*-ky	дорожні чеки

Euro	*yew*-ro	євро
UK pounds	an-*hliys'*-ki *fun*-ty	англійські фунти
	(*ster*-lin-hiw)	(стерлінгів)
US dollars	a-me-ry-*kans'*-ki	американські
	do-la-ry	долари
yen	ya-*pons'*-ki *ye*-ny	японські єни

AT THE POST OFFICE НА ПОШТІ

The services you'll find in a branch of the Ukrainian Post Office include some that are not offered in most Western countries. In addition to the usual transactions – stamp and envelope sales, dispatch of letters, parcels, telegrams and faxes – post office staff pack parcels (very efficiently, using thick paper and strong string) and accept subscriptions for periodicals. Many post offices have telephone booths for long-distance calls. The Ukrainian Post Office is quite well-organised, and overseas airmail posted in Ukraine usually reaches its destination within two weeks.

Where's the post office?
de *po*-shta? Де пошта?

What time does the
post office open?
ko-*ly* pra-*tsyu*-ye Коли працює
po-shta? пошта?

```
                           SIGNS

      ОБЕРЕЖНО!              BE CAREFUL!
      ЗАЧИНЕНО               CLOSED
      НЕ ДОТОРКАТИСЯ!        DON'T TOUCH!
      ВХІД                  ENTRY
      ВИХІД                 EXIT
      ДОВІДКА;              INFORMATION
         ДОВІДКОВЕ
         БЮРО
      НЕМАЄ ВХОДУ           NO ENTRY
      НЕМАЄ ВИХОДУ          NO EXIT
      НЕ ПАЛИТИ             NO SMOKING
      ВІДЧИНЕНО             OPEN
      ПЕРЕХІД               PEDESTRIAN
                              CROSSING
      МІЛІЦІЯ               POLICE
      ЗАБОРОНЕНО            PROHIBITED
      ТУАЛЕТ                TOILET
```

Where's the nearest letterbox?
de nay-*blyzh*-cha
po-*shto*-va *skryn'*-ka?

Де найближча
поштова скринька?

I'd like to send this letter
to (Australia).
me-*ni* po-*trib*-no
na-di-*sla*-ty ly-*sta* do
(aw-*stra*-li-yi)

Мені потрібно
надіслати листа до
(Австралії).

How much is a stamp
(within Ukraine/abroad)?
skil'-ky *ko*-shtu-ye *mar*-ka
(w *me*-zhakh u-kra-*yi*-ny;
za kor-*don*)?

Скільки коштує марка
(в межах України;
за кордон)?

How much does it cost
to send this to ...?
skil'-ky *ko*-shtu-ye,
shchob *vy*-sla-ty
tse do ...?

Скільки коштує,
щоб вислати
це до ...?

I want to send a ...	ya *kho*-chu na-di-*sla*-ty ...	Я хочу надіслати ...
letter	ly-*sta*	листа
parcel	po-*syl*-ku	посилку
registered letter	re-ko-men-*do*-va-no-ho ly-*sta*	рекомен-дованого листа
by airmail	a-vi-a-*po*-shto-yu	авіапоштою
by regular mail	zvy-*chay*-no-yu *po*-shto-yu	звичайною поштою
by express mail	eks-*pres po*-shto-yu	експрес-поштою

I want to buy a/an...	ya *kho*-chu ku-*py*-ty ...	Я хочу купити ...
envelope	kon-*vert*	конверт
postcard	po-*shtiw*-ku	поштівку
stamp	*mar*-ku	марку

I want to send
a fax/telegram.
  ya *kho*-chu vid-*pra*-vy-ty
  faks/te-le-*hra*-mu

Я хочу відправити
факс/телеграму.

Where's the poste-restante office?
  de vid-*di*-len-nya
  o-*der*-zhan-nya
  ko-re-spon-*den*-tsi-yi?

Де відділення
Одержання
кореспонденції?

Do I have any mail?
  dlya *me*-ne ye *po*-shta?

Для мене є пошта?

AROUND TOWN

SIGNS

ЦЕНТРАЛЬНИЙ ПОШТАМТ	CENTRAL POST OFFICE
ЕКСПРЕС-ПОШТА	EXPRESS MAIL
ВІДПРАВЛЕННЯ ФАКСОВИХ ПОВІДОМЛЕНЬ	FAX SERVICE
МІСЦЕВА КОРЕСПОНДЕНЦІЯ	LOCAL MAIL
ГОЛОВПОШТАМТ	MAIN POST OFFICE
ПОСИЛКИ	PARCELS
ПОШТОВЕ ВІДДІЛЕННЯ	POSTAL SERVICES
ОДЕРЖАННЯ КОРЕСПОНДЕНЦІЇ	POSTE RESTANTE
ПОШТА	POST OFFICE
ЛИСТИ НА ЗАМОВЛЕННЯ	REGISTERED MAIL
ТЕЛЕГРАФ	TELEGRAPH
ТЕЛЕФОН	TELEPHONE

AROUND TOWN

address	a-*dre*-sa	адреса
aerogram	a-e-ro-*hra*-ma	аерограма
envelope	kon-*vert*	конверт
letter	lyst	лист
padded bag	pa-*ket* iz	пакет із
	pro-*klad*-ko-yu	прокладкою
pen	*ruch*-ka	ручка
pencil	o-li-*vets'*	олівець
post code	(po-*shto*-vy)	(поштовий)
	in-deks	індекс
postcard	ly-*stiw*-ka	листівка
receipt	chek;	чек;
	kvy-*tan*-tsi-ya;	квитанція;
	roz-*py*-ska pro	розписка про
	o-*der*-zhan-nya	одержання
registered letter	re-ko-men-*do*-va-ny	рекомендований
	lyst	лист
sender	vid-*praw*-nyk	відправник
stamp (postage)	*mar*-ka	марка
stamp (rubber)	shtamp/pe-*cha*-tka	штамп/печатка
telegram	te-le-*hra*-ma	телеграма
telegram form	blank	бланк
	(te-le-*hra*-my)	(телеграми)

SIGNS

ТЕЛЕФОН	**TELEPHONE**
ТЕЛЕФОНИ-АВТОМАТИ	**PUBLIC TELEPHONES**
МІЖМІСЬКИЙ ТЕЛЕФОН	**LONG-DISTANCE TELEPHONE**
МІЖМІСЬКИЙ ПЕРЕГОВОРНИЙ ПУНКТ	**LONG-DISTANCE CALLS CAN BE MADE HERE**
ТЕЛЕФОННА КАРТКА	**PHONECARD**

TELECOMMUNICATIONS ТЕЛЕЗВ'ЯЗОК

Telephone Телефон

The telephone service in Ukraine is quite good. Virtually every household in a city has a phone and the majority of people have mobile phones. Public phone booths carry the inscription tak-so-*fon* (таксофон). They can be used for both domestic and international calls. Methods of payment can differ in various locations, but usually phonecards are used. You can buy a phonecard at the post office or from a street kiosk. These, however, are valid only within cities where they are purchased and can't be used in other places. Also, long-distance and international calls can be made from main post offices and railway stations. The mobile network covers almost the whole territory of Ukraine, including most of the Carpathian Mountains from where you can easily say 'Hello!' to your friends. Note that wire phones are less frequent in rural areas and people there largely rely on mobiles.

What's your phone number?
    ya-*ky* vash/tviy *no*-mer
    te-le-*fo*-na? (pol/inf)

Який Ваш/твій номер телефона?

Where's the nearest public phone?
    de nay-*blyzh*-chy te-le-*fon*-
    aw-to-*mat*/ta-kso-*fon*

Де найближчий телефон-автомат/таксофон?

Can I look at a phone book?
    mozh-na *hlya*-nu-ty
    te-le-*fon*-nu *kny*-hu

Можна глянути телефонну книгу?

How much does it cost per minute?
    skil'-ky *ko*-shtu-ye
    khvy-*ly*-na?

Скільки коштує хвилина?

The number is ...
    no-mer ...

Номер - ...

I need to call ... urgently.
    me-*ni* ter-mi-*no*-vo *tre*-ba
    po-dzvo-*ny*-ty ...

Мені терміново треба подзвонити ...

What's the area code for ...?
    ya-*ky* kod ...?

Який код ...?

Could I have extension
(number) ...?
  bud' *la*-ska, *wnu*-tri-shniy
  (*no*-mer) ...

Будь ласка, внутрішній
(номер) ...

I've got the wrong number.
  ya po-my-*lyw*-sya/
  po-my-*ly*-la-sya
  no-me-rom (m/f)

Я помилився/
помилилася
номером.

We were cut off.
  nas roz-ye-*dna*-ly

Нас роз'єднали.

I want to ...	ya *kho*-chu ...	Я хочу ...
buy a chip phonecard	ku-*py*-ty te-le-*fon*-nu *kart*-ku	купити телефонну картку
call (Singapore)	po-dzvo-*ny*-ty do (sin-ha-*pu*-ru)	подзвонити до (Сінгапуру)
make a (local) call	po-dzvo-*ny*-ty (po *mi*-stu)	подзвонити (по місту)
reverse the charges	po-dzvo-*ny*-ty za ra *khu*-nok a-bo-*nen*-ta	подзвонити за рахунок абонента
send an email/ SMS	vi-di-*sla*-ty i-*meyl*/es-em-*es*	відіслати імейл/SMS
speak for (five) minutes	po-ho-vo-*ry*-ty (pyat') khvy-*lyn*	поговорити (п'ять) хвилин

AROUND TOWN

THEY MAY SAY ...

zay-nya-to	The number is engaged.
za-che-*kay*-te, bud' *la*-ska	Please wait.
vy na-*bra*-ly ne-is-*nu*-yu-chy *no*-mer	The number you dial does not exist.
no-mer ne vid-po-vi-*da*-ye	There's no reply.
ne-*ma*-ye hud-*kiw*	There's no dial tone.

Mobile/Cell Phone

What are the call rates?
ya-*ki* ta-*ry*-fy na dzvin-*ky*?
(70 kopiykas) per minute.
(sim-de-*syat*) ko-pi-*yok*
za khvy-*ly*-nu

Мобільний телефон

Які тарифи на дзвінки?

(Сімдесят копійок)
за хвилину.

I'd like a ...	ya b kho-*tiw/* kho-*ti*-la ... (m/f)	Я б хотів/ хотіла ...
charger for my phone	za-*ryad*-ku dlya svo-*ho* te-le-*fo*-na	зарядку для свого телефона
mobile/cell phone for hire	*vy*-nay-nya-ty mo-*bil'*-ny te-le-*fon*	винайняти мобільний телефон
prepaid mobile/ cell phone	mo-*bil'*-ny te-le-*fon* z pe-red-*pla*-to-yu	мобільний телефон з передплатою
SIM card for your network	sim-*kar*-tu dlya *va*-sho-yi me-*re*-zhi	SIM-карту для Вашої мережі

Making a Call

Hello!
al-*lo*!; *do*-bry den'!
I'd like to speak to ...
po-pro-*sit'*, bud' *la*-ska,
do te-le-*fo*-nu ...
This is ... speaking.
tse ho-*vo*-ryt'/*dzvo*-nyt' ...
Does anyone there speak English?
chy khtos' ho-*vo*-ryt'
an-*hliys'*-ko-yu (*mo*-vo-yu)?

Телефонний дзвінок

Алло!; Добрий день!

Попросіть, будь ласка,
до телефону ...

Це говорить/дзвонить ...

Чи хтось говорить
англійською (мовою)?

Can I leave a message?
pe-re-*day*-te, bud' *la*-ska,
shcho ...

Передайте, будь ласка,
що ...

Please tell ... I called.
pe-re-*day*-te, bud' *la*-ska,
..., shcho ya dzvo-*nyw*/
dzvo-*ny*-la (m/f)

Передайте, будь ласка,
..., що я дзвонив/
дзвонила.

The Internet

Інтернет

I'd like to ...
ya b kho-*tiw*/
kho-*ti*-la ... (m/f)

Я б хотів/
хотіла ...

    check my email
pe-re-*vi*-ry-ty
i-*meyl*

перевірити
імейл

    burn a CD
za-py-*sa*-ty
kom-pakt-*dysk*

записати
компакт-диск

    download my
    photos
za-van-*ta*-zhy-ty
svo-*yi fo*-to

завантажити
свої фото

    get Internet access
zay-*ty* w
in-ter-*net*

зайти в
Інтернет

    use a printer/
    scanner
sko-ry-*sta*-ty-sya
pryn-te-rom/
ska-ne-rom

скористатися
принтером/
сканером

Can I connect
my ... to this
computer?
chy *mozh*-na
pry-ye-*dna*-ty sviy/
svo-*yu* ... do ts'o-*ho*
kom-*pyu*-te-ra?

Чи можна
приєднати свій/
свою ... до цього
комп'ютера?

    camera
fo-to-a-pa-*rat*
фотоапарат

    media player
me-di-a-*ple*-yer
медіа-плеєр

    portable hard
    drive
pe-re-nos-*ny*/
por-ta-*tyw*-ny
vin-*che*-ster

переносний/
портативний
вінчестер

    USB drive
flesh-ku
флешку

How much per ...?
skil'-ky
ko-shtu-ye ...?

Скільки
коштує ...?

    hour
ho-*dy*-na
година

    (five) minutes
(pyat') khvy-*lyn*
(п'ять) хвилин

    page
sto-*rin*-ka
сторінка

How do I log on?
yak za-lo-hu-*va*-ty-sya/
zay-*ty*?

Як залогуватися/
зайти?

I've finished.
ya za-*kin*-chyw/
za-*kin*-chy-la (m/f)

Я закінчив/
закінчила.

It's crashed.
za-*vy*-slo

Зависло.

SIGHTSEEING   ЕКСКУРСІЇ

Ukrainian cities are rich with museums. In Kyiv most museums have English-speaking guides. Kyiv is well-known for its historical sites, but Lviv, with its baroque churches, is also waiting for you. The world has yet to discover the Carpathian Mountains, kar-*pa*-ty (**Карпати**), in the west, and the marshlands of Polissia, po-*lis*-sya (**Полісся**), in the north-west. Visit places with evocative names like Kamianets-Podilsky, the health spas Truskavets and Morshyn, salt mines in Solotvyno, the Crimean Tatar town of Bakhchysaray and its fountain of love, or the ancient Greek city of Chersonesos (**Херсонес**) on the Black Sea shore.

Where's the tourist office?
de tu-ry-*stych*-ne byu-*ro*?

Де туристичне бюро?

Do you have a city/local map?
u vas ye *kar*-ta [*mi*-sta;
tsi-*ye*-yi mi-*stse*-vo-sti]?

У вас є карта [міста;
цієї місцевості]?

I want to go on an excursion.
ya *kho*-chu pi-*ty*/
po-*yi*-kha-ty na
ek-*skur*-si-yu

Я хочу піти/
поїхати на
екскурсію.

What are the opening hours?
ko-*ly* tut vid-*chy*-ne-no?

Коли тут відчинено?

How much is the entry fee?
  ya-*ka pla*-ta za wkhid?

Яка плата за вхід?

Do you have student/
seniors'/children's discounts?
  vy da-*ye*-te *znyzh*-ky
  stu-*den*-tam/
  pen-si-o-*ne*-ram/*di*-tyam?

Ви даєте знижки
студентам/
пенсіонерам/дітям?

Is there an English-
speaking guide?
  u vas ye an-hlo-*mo*-wny
  ek-skur-so-*vod*/hid?

У вас є англомовний
екскурсовод/гід?

May I take photographs?
  tut *mo*-zhna
  fo-to-hra-fu-*va*-ty?

Тут можна
фотографувати?

It's ...	tse ...	Це ...
beautiful	*har*-no	гарно
impressive	wra-*zha*-ye	вражає
interesting	tsi-*ka*-vo	цікаво
strange	*dyw*-no	дивно

AROUND TOWN

FOLK FEATURES

Ukrainian folk oral literature includes a wealth of fairy tales kaz-*ky* (казки), animal tales bay-*ky* (байки), proverbs pry-*sli*-vya (прислів'я), and riddles za-*had*-ky (загадки). It's still possible at funerals in country areas to hear highly elaborate lamentations, ho-lo-*sin*-nya (голосіння). An important branch of folklore is the demonological tale figuring such spirits as the water nymph ru-*sal*-ka (русалка), the wood nymph *maw*-ka (мавка), the vampire u-*pyr* (упир), the house-spirit do-mo-*vyk* (домовик), and, of course, the devil chort (чорт) and the witch vid'-ma (відьма).

antiquity	*pa*-mya-tka	пам'ятка
	sta-ro-vy-*ny*	старовини
art gallery	kar-*tyn*-na	картинна
	ha-le-*re*-ya	галерея
building	bu-*dy*-nok	будинок
cathedral	so-*bor*	собор
castle	*za*-mok	замок
church	*tser*-kva	церква
icon	i-*ko*-na	ікона
iconostasis	i-ko-no-*stas*	іконостас
monastery	mo-na-*styr*	монастир
monument	*pa*-mya-tnyk	пам'ятник
museum	mu-*zey*	музей
park	park	парк
statue	*sta*-tu-ya	статуя

AROUND TOWN

DANCE, MUSIC & FOLKLORE

Ukraine has a wealth of fascinating folk rituals, oral literature, folk music and dance, as well as traditional costumes, crafts and building methods. These have been carefully documented and studied from the 19th century onward. Despite urbanisation and modernisation, many expressions of traditional culture have survived, especially in country areas, and there are superb ethnographic museums and collections in many cities.

Folk Songs

Many Ukrainian folksongs na-*ro*-dni pi-*sni* (народні пісні) accompany seasonal festivals and rituals. At Christmas, carols, ko-*lyad*-ky (колядки), are sung in the family circle and by groups of singers who go from house to house. New Year's carols are called shche-*driw*-ky (щедрівки). Spring songs, ve-*snyan*-ky (веснянки), sung by young women and accompanied by ritual movements and games, welcome the return of warmth and growth. In Western Ukraine these ve-*snyan*-ky are called ha-*hil*-ky (гагілки) and are incorporated into the celebration of Easter. At high summer, on St. John's Eve, special songs – ku-*pal's'*-ki pi-*sni* (купальські пісні) – were sung by girls as they floated wreaths downstream to foretell whether they were soon to be married.

Whereas the seasonal folksongs are mostly of pre-Christian origin, *du*-my (думи) – historical narrative songs about the Cossacks – date from the 16th and 17th centuries. Traditionally, a *du*-ma (дума) would be performed in recitative, rather than sung, by a blind minstrel kob-*zar* (кобзар), who accompanied himself on a many-stringed instrument called a *kob*-za (кобза). Nowadays, *du*-my are performed almost exclusively by professional musicians. The authorship of many of the best-known songs from the Cossack period is popularly attributed to a legendary songstress, Marusya Churay. A special repertoire is connected to the chu-ma-*ky* (чумаки), traders who carried salt by bullock wagon from the Black Sea coast to the Ukrainian heartland.

A great many folksongs are concerned with love, and celebrate an image of feminine beauty that includes dark eyes, *ka*-ri o-chi (карі очі), and black eyebrows, *chor*-ni *bro*-vy (чорні брови).

There are songs for the harvest season, for weddings and funerals, cradle songs, ko-ly-*sko*-vi pi-*sni* (колискові пісні), and humorous songs, including the epigrammatic and sometimes ribald ko-lo-*my*-ky (коломийки), whose name suggests the city of Kolymyia in the Carpathian Mountains.

Folk Dance

Folk dance, too, had its origin in pre-Christian ritual and in agricultural dance games, the kho-ro-*vo*-dy (хороводи); these were usually circular dances, and were originally accompanied by song. Musical instruments were introduced later to maintain rhythm. Some dances were originally the domain of women only, like the me-te-ly-*tsia* (метелиця); this word also means 'snowstorm', others of men only, like the ho-*pak* (гопак); the chu-*mak* (чумак), named for the already mentioned salt-traders; the ar-*kan* (аркан), whose name means 'lasso'; and the za-po-ro-*zhets* (запорожець), the dance of the Cossacks 'below the Dnipro rapids' – see page 197). More recently, most of these dances have come to be danced by groups of men and women, pairs, and solo dancers. The ho-*pak*, the most spectacular of Ukrainian dances and the one most likely to form the climax of any concert of folk dance, requires great physical strength and agility on the part of the male dancers, and some people are convinced that it derives from a form of martial arts.

Folk Music

The best-known Ukrainian folk musical instrument is the ban-*du*-ra (бандура), an instrument with up to 60 strings descended from the earlier kobza. Modified in the twentieth century, it is now often heard as a concert instrument on which vocalists accompany themselves. Other folk instruments include the clavichord-like tsym-*ba*-ly (цимбали), the hurdy-gurdy, *li*-ra (ліра), and the Jew's harp, *drym*-ba (дримба). Among wind instruments, pipes of various kinds of wood have the generic name so-*pil*-ka (сопілка). In the Carpathian Mountains, the trem-*bi*-ta (трембіта) is a tapered wooden tube up to 2.5 metres in length, traditionally played solo on the high pastures. Folk ensembles that accompanied dances usually included the violin, *skryp*-ka (скрипка), bass viol, pid-*ba*-sok (підбасок) or ba-*so*-lya (басоля), and drum, *bu*-bon (бубон).

ENTERTAINMENT

РОЗВАГИ

The main Ukrainian cities have rich cultural offerings, and if you enjoy classical music, opera and operetta, music for choir, theatre or ballet, you'll have a feast. Some prestige venues charge a lot for their very best seats, but you can see almost anything at prices that are very low by Western standards. Special cultural events abound, including folkloric festivals that feature Ukrainian traditional song and dance. There are theatres especially for children. Note, however, that very little happens in summer. 'The Season' starts in mid-September.

Ukrainians are great patrons of high culture and are likely to invite you to join them for a concert or at the theatre.

Opportunities for more popular kinds of entertainment are much the same as in other European cities. There are abundant nightclubs, bars, casinos and restaurants with performers appealing to all musical tastes.

What's there to do in
the evenings?
　shcho tut *ro*-blyat'
　ve-cho-*ra*-my?

Що тут роблять
вечорами?

What's on tonight?
　shcho yde s'o-*ho*-dni
　wve-che-ri?

Що йде сьогодні
ввечері?

Is there (live) music?
　tut *hra*-ye (zhy-*va*)
　mu-zy-ka?

Тут грає (жива)
музика?

Is the movie in English?
　tsey fil'm an-*hliy*-s'ko-yu
　mo-vo-yu?

Цей фільм англійською
мовою?

Do you have a table free?
　u vas ye *vil'*-ny *sto*-lyk?

У вас є вільний столик?

Where's the theatre
ticket office?
　de tut te-a-*tral'*-ni *ka*-sy?

Де тут театральні каси?

Are there any tickets for ...?
  chy ye kvyt-*ky* na ...?   Чи є квитки на ...?
Could I have two tickets?
  mo-zhna dva kvy-*tky*?   Можна два квитки?
When does the
performance begin?
  ko-*ly* po-*cha*-tok vy-*sta*-vy? Коли початок вистави?
Where are our seats?
  de *na*-shi mi-*stsya*?   Де наші місця?
Could I have a
program, please?
  mo-zhna ku-*py*-ty   Можна купити
  pro-*hram*-ku?   програмку?
Where can I get refreshments?
  de tut bu-*fet*?   Де тут буфет?

I'd like to go   ya *kho*-chu pi-*ty* ...   Я хочу піти ...
to a/the ...
   bar   do *ba*-ru   до бару
   cafe   w ka-*fe*   в кафе
   casino   w ka-zy-*no*   в казино
   circus   do *tsyr*-ku   до цирку
   concert   na kon-*tsert*   на концерт
   disco   na   на
                    dy-sko-*te*-ky   дискотеку
   football match   na   на
                    fut-*bol*'-ny   футбольний
                    match   матч
   movie   do/w ki-*no*   до/в кіно
   nightclub   u nich-*ny*   у нічний
                    klub   клуб
   opera   na *o*-pe-ru   на оперу
   restaurant   do   до
                    re-sto-*ra*-nu   ресторану
   theatre   do te-*a*-tru   до театру

AROUND TOWN

Invitations

		Запрошення
What are you doing this ...?	shcho [ty *ro*-bysh; vy *ro*-by-te] ...? (inf; pol or pl)	Що [ти робиш; ви робите] ...?
evening	s'o-*ho*-dni *wve*-che-ri	сьогодні ввечері
weekend	pid chas vy-khi-*dnykh*	під час вихідних

Would you like to go out somewhere?
[ty *kho*-chesh; vy *kho*-che-te] ku-*dys'* pi-*ty* s'o-*ho*-dni? (inf; pol or pl)
[Ти хочеш; Ви хочете] кудись піти сьогодні?

Do you know a good restaurant (that's cheap)?
vy *zna*-ye-te *do*-bry (de-*she*-vy) re-sto-*ran*?
Ви знаєте добрий (дешевий) ресторан?

Would you like to go for a meal?
vy-de-mo po-*yi*-sty?
Вийдемо поїсти?

My shout!
ya pla-*chu*!
Я плачу!

Do join us!
pry-*e*-dnuy-tes' do nas!
Приєднуйтесь до нас!

We're having a party.
my zby-*ra*-ye-mos'
Ми збираємось.

Responding to Invitations

Як відповідати на запрошення

Sure!
zvy-*chay*-no!
Звичайно!

Yes, I'd love to!
tak, [iz za-do-*vo*-len-nyam; *du*-zhe ra-*do*]!
Так, [із задоволенням; дуже радо]!

Yes. Where shall we go?
tak, ku-*dy* my pi-*de*-mo?
Так, куди ми підемо?

No, I'm afraid I can't.
ni, na zhal', ya ne *mo*-zhu.
Ні, на жаль, я не можу.

What about tomorrow?
a *za*-wtra?
А завтра?

Arranging to Meet

[What time; Where]
shall we meet?
   ko-*ly*/de nam
   zu-*stri*-ty-sya?
Let's meet in the foyer 20
minutes before the beginning.
   zu-*stri*-ne-mos' u fo-*ye*
   za *dva*-tsyat'
   khvy-*lyn* do po-*cha*-tku
Sorry I'm late.
   vy-bach-te, ya
   spi-z*nyw*-sya/
   spi-z*ny*-la-sya (m/f)

Домовляємося про зустріч

Коли/Де нам
зустрітися?

Зустрінемось у фойє
за двадцять
хвилин до початку.

Вибачте, я
спізнився/
спізнилася.

Nightclubs & Bars

Are there any good nightclubs?
   chy ye ya-*kis' do*-bri
   nich-*ni klu*-by?
How do you get to this club?
   yak do-*yi*-kha-ty do
   ts'o-ho *klu*-bu?
Do you have to pay to enter?
   chy *tre*-ba pla-*ty*-ty
   za wkhid?
How much is it to get
into this disco?
   skil'-ky *ko*-shtu-ye wkhid
   na dy-sko-*te*-ku?

Нічні клуби і бари

Чи є якісь добрі
нічні клуби?

Як доїхати до
цього клубу?

Чи треба платити
за вхід?

Скільки коштує вхід
на дискотеку?

The music here is great.
    tut *do*-bra *mu*-zy-ka

Тут добра музика.

I don't like the music here.
    me-*ni* tut *mu*-zy-ka ne
    po-*do*-ba-yet'-sya

Мені тут музика не подобається.

It's very smoky here.
    tut *du*-zhe na-*ku*-re-no

Тут дуже накурено.

AROUND TOWN

СІМ'Я

FAMILY

QUESTIONS & ANSWERS

Are you married?
    vy o-*dru*-zhe-ni;
    vy za-mu-zhem/
    za-*mi*-zhnya? (only to a woman)

Ви одружені;
Ви замужем/
заміжня?

I'm (not) married.
    ya (ne-)o-*dru*-zhe-ny/a (m/f);
    ya (ne) za-mu-zhem/
    za-*mi*-zhnya (f)

Я (не)одружений/а;
Я (не) замужем/
заміжня.

I'm divorced/separated.
    ya ro-*zlu*-che-ny/
    ro-*zlu*-che-na (m/f)

Я розлучений/
розлучена.

I'm a widower/widow.
    ya wdi-*vets'*/wdo-*va*

Я вдівець/вдова.

Do you have any children?
    u vas ye *di*-ty?

У вас є діти?

I have [one child/two children].
    u *me*-ne [od-*na* dy-*ty*-na;
    dvo-ye di-*tey*]

У мене [одна дитина;
двоє дітей].

I don't have any children.
    u *me*-ne ne-*ma*-ye di-*tey*

У мене немає дітей.

FAMILY MEMBERS

ЧЛЕНИ СІМ'Ї

aunt	*ti*-tka	тітка
boy	*khlo*-pets'	хлопець
brother	brat	брат
child	dy-*ty*-na	дитина
children	*di*-ty	діти
dad	*ta*-to	тато
daughter	do-*chka*/ don'-ka	дочка/донька
elder (adj)	*star*-shy	старший
father	*bat'*-ko	батько
father-in-law		
husband's side	*sve*-kor	свекор
wife's side	test'	тесть

girl	*diw*-chy-na	дівчина
granddaughter	o-*nu*-chka	онучка
grandfather	di-*dus'*	дідусь
grandmother	ba-*bu*-sya	бабуся
grandson	o-*nuk*	онук
husband	cho-lo-*vik*	чоловік
little boy	*khlop*-chyk	хлопчик
little girl	*diw*-chyn-ka	дівчинка
mother	*ma*-ty	мати
mother-in-law		
husband' side	sve-*kru*-kha	свекруха
wife's side	*te*-shcha	теща
mum	*ma*-ma	мама
old	sta-*ry*	старий
sister	se-*stra*	сестра
son	syn	син
uncle	*dyad'*-ko	дядько
wife	dru-*zhy*-na	дружина
young (adj)	mo-lo-*dy*	молодий
younger	mo-*lod*-shy	молодший

SWEET JANE

Ukrainian has a large number of diminutive suffixes. These suffixes generally also suggest that the speaker expresses affection toward the thing or person named. A single word or name can give rise to many diminutives, each carrying a slightly different emotional nuance. For example, the name ma-*ri*-ya (Марія), 'Mary', has the common diminutives ma-*riy*-ka (Марійка), ma-*ru*-sya (Маруся), and ma-*ru*-sen'-ka (Марусенька), in increasing order of tenderness.

On the other hand, there are also suffixes that express a negative attitude toward the thing named, suggesting that it's coarse or excessively large.

TALKING WITH PARENTS

When are you expecting the baby?
ko-*ly* che-*ka*-ye-te
dy-*ty*-nu?

Коли чекаєте
дитину?

Is this your first child?
tse *va*-sha *per*-sha
dy-*ty*-na?

Це ваша перша
дитина?

How many children do you have?
skil'-ky u vas di-*tey*?

Скільки у вас дітей?

Do you have a son/daughter?
vy *ma*-ye-te *sy*-na/*don'*-ku?

Ви маєте сина/доньку?

How old are your children?
skil'-ky ro-kiw
va-shym *di*-tyam?

Скільки років
вашим дітям?

Does he/she attend school?
vin/vo-*na* wzhe
kho-dyt' do *shko*-ly?

Він/Вона вже
ходить до школи?

What grade is he/she in?
u ko-*tro*-mu vin/
vo-*na kla*-si?

У котрому він/
вона класі?

Do you have grandchildren?
u vas ye o-*nu*-ky?

У вас є онуки?

What a well-behaved child!
ya-*ka chem*-na dy-*ty*-na!

Яка чемна дитина!

He/She looks very much like you!
vin/vo-*na du*-zhe
skho-zhy/*skho*-zha (m/f)
na vas!

Він/Вона дуже
схожий/схожа
на вас!

TALKING WITH CHILDREN

РОЗМОВА З ДІТЬМИ

What's your name?
 yak [te-*be zva*-ty; ty
 na-zy-*va*-yesh-sya]?

Як [тебе звати;
ти називаєшся]?

How old are you?
 skil'-ky to-*bi* ro-kiw?

Скільки тобі років?

When's your birthday?
 ko-*ly* tviy den'
 na-*ro*-dzhen-nya?

Коли твій день
народження?

Do you have brothers and sisters?
 u *te*-be ye bra-*ty*
 i *se*-stry?

У тебе є брати
і сестри?

Do you go to kindergarten/school?
 ty *kho*-dysh
 [u sa-*do*-chok;
 do *shko*-ly]?

Ти ходиш
[у садочок;
до школи]?

Do you like the teachers?
 to-*bi* po-*do*-ba-yut'sya
 wchy-te-*li*?

Тобі подобаються
вчителі?

What grade are you in?
 u ya-*ko*-mu ty *kla*-si?

У якому ти класі?

Are you learning English?
 ty wchysh/vyw-*cha*-yesh
 an-*hliy*-s'ku *mo*-vu?

Ти вчиш/вивчаєш
англійську мову?

Do you play sport?
 ty zay-*ma*-yesh-sya
 spor-tom?

Ти займаєшся
спортом?

Do you have a cat or dog?
 u *te*-be ye kit chy
 so-*ba*-ka?

У тебе є кіт чи
собака?

A DANE IN UKRAINE

Dogs are extremely popular in the cities, even though conditions for them are less than ideal. Do not be surprised if you encounter a Great Dane in your hosts' two-bedroom 16th-floor apartment.

FAMILY

PETS

ДОМАШНІ ТВАРИНИ

I have a ...	u *me*-ne ye ...	У мене є ...
bird	*pta*-shka	пташка
cat	kit/*ki*-shka	кіт/кішка
dog	so-*ba*-ka	собака
fish	*ryb*-ka	рибка
guinea pig	mor-*s'ka svyn*-ka	морська свинка
kitten	ko-she-*nya*	кошеня
parrot	pa-*pu*-ha	папуга
puppy	tsu-tse-*nya*	цуценя
rabbit	*kro*-lyk	кролик
tortoise	che-re-*pa*-kha	черепаха

FAMILY

ЗАЦІКАВЛЕННЯ

INTERESTS

COMMON INTERESTS & HOBBIES

ПОПУЛЯРНІ ЗАЦІКАВЛЕННЯ

What do you do in your spare time?
chym vy zay-*ma*-ye-tes' u *vil'*-ny chas?

Чим Ви займаєтесь у вільний час?

I (don't) like ... ya (ne) lyu-*blyu* ... Я (не) люблю ...
Do you like ...? vy *lyu*-by-te ...? Ви любите ...?

art	my-*stets*-tvo	мистецтво
cooking	ho-tu-*va*-ty	готувати
dancing	tan-tsyu-*va*-ty	танцювати
film	ki-*no*	кіно
fishing	lo-*vy*-ty ry-bu	ловити рибу
going out	hu-*lya*-ty	гуляти
hiking	pi-sho-*khid*-ny	пішохідний
	tu-*ryzm*	туризм
music	*mu*-zy-ku	музику
reading	chy-*ta*-ty	читати
painting	ma-lyu-*va*-ty	малювати
photography	fo-to-hra-fu-*va*-ty	фотографувати
playing chess	*hra*-ty w *sha*-khy	грати в шахи
playing soccer	*hra*-ty u fut-*bol*	грати у футбол
playing sport	zay-*ma*-ty-sya *spor*-tom	займатися спортом
shopping	kho-*dy*-ty po ma-ha-*zy*-nakh	ходити по магазинах
skating/skiing	ka-*ta*-ty-sya na *ly*-zhakh/ kow-za-*nakh*	кататися на лижах/ ковзанах
the theatre	te-*atr*	театр
travelling	po-do-ro-zhu-*va*-ty	подорожувати
watching TV	dy-*vy*-ty-sya te-le-*vi*-zor	дивитися телевізор

129

INTERESTS

wood carving	riz'-*by*-ty	різьбити
writing (poetry)	py-*sa*-ty (po-*e*-zi-yu/ *vir*-shi)	писати (поезію/ вірші)
writing letters to friends	ly-stu-*va*-ty-sya z *dru*-zya-my	листуватися з друзями

I collect ...	ya zby-*ra*-yu ...	Я збираю ...
books	knyzh-*ky*	книжки
coins	mo-*ne*-ty	монети
insects	ko-*makh*	комах
postcards	ly-*stiw*-ky	листівки
stamps	*mar*-ky	марки

SPORT   СПОРТ

For a country with few resources to spare for elite level sport, Ukraine does well in international competition, especially in athletics, gymnastics, boxing, wrestling, sailing and swimming. Prior to independence, Ukrainian athletes collected a large percentage of the Soviet Union's medals at the Olympic Games. Competitors representing independent Ukraine also performed well in the Games held since independence. Ukraine's best-known athlete of recent times is Serhy Bubka, who broke the world pole vault record 35 times. Nevertheless, Ukrainians as a rule are not passionate about sport (with the exception of soccer). Despite this, many children and young people participate in a very wide range of sports. This activity is organised mainly through clubs. Among unstructured sports, soccer, hockey and winter sports are popular among the young. There are numerous specialised schools that teach and train promising sportspeople. Participation in sport among adults is less widespread.

INTERESTS

Do you like sport?
vy *lyu*-by-te sport?   Ви любите спорт?
I like playing sport.
ya lyu-*blyu* zay-*ma*-ty-sya   Я люблю займатися
spor-tom   спортом.
I prefer to watch rather than
play sport.
me-*ni* bil'-she   Мені більше
po-*do*-ba-yet'-sya   подобається
dy-*vy*-ty-sya na sport, nizh   дивитися на спорт, ніж
zay-*ma*-ty-sya nym   займатися ним.
Do you play ...?
vy *hra*-ye-te w ...?   Ви граєте в ...?
Would you like to play ...?
[vy *kho*-che-te; ty *kho*-chesh]   [Ви хочете; Ти хочеш]
zi-*hra*-ty w ...? (pol/inf)   зіграти в ...?

baseball	beys-*bol*	бейсбол
basketball	ba-sket-*bol*	баскетбол
boxing	boks	бокс
cricket	kry-*ket*	крикет
diving	stryb-*ky* u *vo*-du	стрибки у воду
fishing	ry-*bal*'-stvo	рибальство
football	fut-*bol*	футбол
gymnastics	him-*na*-sty-ka	гімнастика
hockey	kho-*key*	хокей
keeping fit	*bu*-ty u *for*-mi	бути у формі
martial arts	vo-*yen*-ne	воєнне
	my-*stets*-tvo	мистецтво
rugby	*reg*-bi	реґбі
soccer	fut-*bol*	футбол
swimming	*pla*-van-nya	плавання
tennis	*te*-nis	теніс
skiing	*ly*-zhny sport	лижний спорт

INTERESTS

BOXING

бокс (boks)

BROTHERS IN THE RING

Ukraine's best-known professional boxers are heavyweights Vitaliy and Volodymyr Klychko (Klitschko), who between them hold many international titles. The Klychko brothers used to live and train in Germany where they have a large and enthusiastic following. They are active in public and political life of modern Ukraine. Both hold higher degrees.

INTERESTS

FOOTBALL   ФУТБОЛ

In Ukraine, the most popular spectator sport is, without any doubt, soccer, which is referred to, of course, as fut-*bol* (футбол), 'football'. Men of all social profiles are likely to be quite erudite about the game and the current local, national and international competitions. Three Ukrainian clubs (Shakhtar from Donetsk, Dynamo from Kyiv, and Dnipro from Dnipropetrovsk) are ranked among top 100 European teams. Clubs enjoy cult status in their cities. Ukrainian soccer crowds are generally well behaved and football violence is practically unknown.

Do you follow soccer?
  vy tsi-*ka*-vy-te-sya   Ви цікавитеся
  fut-*bo*-lom?   футболом?
What team do you support?
  za ya-*ku* ko-*man*-du   За яку команду
  vy wbo-li-*va*-ye-te?   Ви вболіваєте?
Who's playing (at the
Central Stadium) today?
  khto *hra*-ye s'o-*ho*-dni   Хто грає сьогодні
  (na tsen-*tral*'-no-mu   (на Центральному
  sta-di-*o*-ni)?   стадіоні)?
(Dynamo Kyiv) is playing
(Manchester United).
  (dy-*na*-mo *ky*-iw) *hra*-ye ("Динамо" Київ) грає
  z (man-*che*-ste-rom).   з ("Манчестером").
What's the score?
  ya-*ky* ra-*khu*-nok?   Який рахунок?
The score is 1-0 in favour
of (Shakhtar).
  ra-*khu*-nok – o-*dyn* – nul' Рахунок – 1–0
  na *ko*-ryst' (shakh-ta-*rya*) на користь ("Шахтаря").

THEY MAY YELL!

hol !	Гол!	Goal!
pe-*nal*'-ti!	Пенальті!	Penalty!
of-*sayd*!	Офсайд!	Off-side!

INTERESTS

TV & VIDEO   ТЕЛЕБАЧЕННЯ ТА ВІДЕО

Ukrainian TV shows the usual mix of news and current affairs, documentaries, series and films. There's some excellent programming for children. Some imported TV series have achieved extraordinary levels of popularity. There are also many political and musical programs.

I often watch TV.
  ya *cha*-sto dy-*wlyus'*
  te-le-*vi*-zor
Я часто дивлюсь телевізор.

What's on TV tonight?
  shcho yde s'o-*ho*-dni
  po te-le-*vi*-zo-ru?
Що йде сьогодні по телевізору?

Can we change the channel?
  mo-zhna pe-re-klyu-*chy*-ty
  pro-*hra*-mu?
Можна переключити програму?

Would you mind turning
the volume up/down?
  mo-zhna ho-lo-s*ni*-she/
  ty-*khi*-she?
Можна голосніше/ тихіше?

Do you get foreign channels here?
  vy di-sta-*ye*-te za-kor-*don*-ni
  pro-*hra*-my/ka-*na*-ly?
Ви дістаєте закордонні програми/канали?

This program/ advertisement is ...	tsya pro-*hra*-ma/ re-*kla*-ma ...	Ця програма/ реклама ...
very good	*du*-zhe *do*-bra	дуже добра
interesting	tsi-*ka*-va	цікава
uninteresting	ne-tsi-*ka*-va	нецікава
(just) dreadful	(*pro*-sto) zha-*khly*-va	(просто) жахлива

THE IDIOT BOX

Though reading has traditionally been very important to Ukrainians, the role of TV has increased greatly. Reading probably reached its peak in the late 1980s, during the last years of being a part of the Soviet Union. Censorship was practically discontinued, the periodical press printed revelation upon revelation about the Soviet past, and subscriptions to journals skyrocketed. But in the early years of independent Ukraine high inflation impoverished most of the population. People had much less cash to spare for reading matter, and many had recourse to TV as their main, and often only, source of news, information and entertainment.

Ukraine has a state-owned TV company, as well as several privately owned broadcasters. In addition, many people receive foreign channels. In the early 1990s there was a great deal of incisive and critical current affairs journalism. Subsequently many have begun to feel that the domestic channels have passed into the ownership of interests close to government and no longer provide an independent commentary on public affairs.

cartoon	mul't-*fil'm*	мультфільм
current affairs program	po-li-*tych*-ny *o*-hlyad	політичний огляд
children's program	dy-*tya*-cha pro-*hra*-ma	дитяча програма
(documentary) film	(do-ku-men-*tal'*-ny) fil'm	(документальний) фільм
news	no-*vy*-ny	новини
soap opera	*myl'*-na *o*-pe-ra	мильна опера
TV series	te-le-se-ri-*al*	телесеріал
weather forecast	pro-*hnoz* po-*ho*-dy	прогноз погоди

INTERESTS

DATING

ПОБАЧЕННЯ

Would you like to go somewhere ...?	[vy b ne kho-*ti*-ly; *mo*-zhe b nam] ku-*dys'* pi-*ty* ...?	[Ви б не хотіли; Може б нам] кудись піти ...?
today	s'o-*ho*-dni	сьогодні
tomorrow	*za*-wtra	завтра
this evening	u-*ve*-che-ri	увечері

Yes, I'd love to.
tak, [iz za-do-*vo*-len-nyam; *du*-zhe ra-*do*]

Так, [із задоволенням; дуже радо].

Thanks, but I'm busy.
dya-ku-yu, a-*le ya* zay-nya-ty/*zay*-nya-ta (m/f)

Дякую, але я зайнятий/зайнята.

Where would you like to go?
ku-*dy* b nam pi-*ty*?

Куди б нам піти?

Can I ring you?
mo-zhna vam/to-*bi* pe-re-dzvo-*ny*-ty? (pol/inf)

Можна Вам /тобі передзвонити?

I'll phone you tomorrow.
ya po-dzvo-*nyu* vam/to-*bi za*-wtra (pol/inf)

Я подзвоню Вам /тобі завтра.

I like you (very much).
ty me-*ni* (*du*-zhe) po-*do*-ba-yesh-sya

Ти мені (дуже) подобаєшся.

I love you.
ya te-*be* ko-*kha*-yu/lyu-*blyu*

Я тебе кохаю/люблю.

boyfriend	*khlo*-pets/druh	хлопець/друг
girlfriend	*diw*-chy-na/*po*-dru-ha	дівчина/подруга
to go out with ...	zu-stri-*cha*-ty-sya z ...	зустрічатися з ...

Note that the words *khlo*-pets and *diw*-chy-na stand for 'boyfriend' and 'girlfriend' only if preceded by a possessive word ('my', 'your' etc). In other instances they are just words for 'boy' and 'girl' in the general sense.

Do you mind if I join you?
mo-zhna do vas pry-e-*dna*-ty-sya?

Можна до вас приєднатися?

I'm with friends.
 ya z *dru*-zya-my   Я з друзями.
Would you like to dance?
 mo-zhna vas za-pro-*sy*-ty   Можна Вас запросити
 na *ta*-nets'?   на танець?
Can I see you home?
 mo-zhna vas/te-*be* pro-ves-*ty*   Можна Вас/тебе провести
 do-*do*-mu? (pol/inf)   додому?

WRITING LETTERS   ЛИСТИ

Once you get back home, you may want to drop a line to people you met.

In all correspondence use initial capitals for the pronouns ty (Ти) and vy (Ви) and remember to use the polite form when writing to people whom you don't know very well or who are older than you.

POLITE FORM	INFORMAL FORM
Dear ... Шановний/Шановна ... (m/f)	Dear ... Дорогий/Дорога ... (m/f)
I'm sorry it's taken me so long to write. Вибачте, що я так довго не писав/писала. (m/f)	I'm sorry it's taken me so long to write. Вибач, що я так довго не писав/писала. (m/f)
It was great to meet you. Було приємно з Вами познайомитися.	It was great to meet you. Було приємно з Тобою познайомитися.
Thank you so much for your hospitality. Дуже дякую за Вашу гостинність.	Thank you so much for your hospitality. Дуже дякую за Твою гостинність.
I miss you. (sg) Я скучаю за Вами.	I miss you. (sg) Я скучаю за Тобою.
Say 'hi' to ... and ... for me. Передавайте ... і ... вітання від мене.	Say 'hi' to ... and ... for me. Передавай ... і ... вітання від мене.

INTERESTS

INTERESTS

GENERAL PHRASES

I miss (all of) you. (pl)
Я скучаю за всіма вами.

I had a fantastic time in ...
Я прекрасно провів/провела час у ... (m/f)

My favourite place was ....
Мені найбільше сподобався ...

I hope to visit ... again.
Я [хотів би; хотіла б] знову відвідати ... (m/f)

I'd love to see you again.
Дуже хотілось би зустрітися знову.

Write soon!	Пишіть!
With love,	Ваш/Ваша, (pol, m/f)
With love,	Твій/Твоя, (inf, m/f)
Regards,	Всього найкращого,

CYRILLIC IF YOU CAN

The Ukrainian Post Office recommends that the front of the envelope should be used for all addresses. The addressee should appear in the bottom right-hand quarter of the envelope, the sender in the top left-hand corner. The preferred format for both addresses is as follows:

Микола Тарасович Степаненко
вул. Січових Стрільців, 8, кв. 26
м. Київ
04050
УКРАЇНА

Use Cyrillic if you can, but your letter will still reach its destination if you address it in Roman letters, thus:

Mykola Tarasovych Stepanenko
vul. Sichovykh Stril'tsiv, 8, kv. 26
m. Kyiv
04050
UKRAINE

The five-digit postcode comes as the last line of domestic addresses. Patronymics are optional.

Also see Addresses in Getting Around, Page 70.

POLITICS

INTERESTS

ПОЛІТИКА

Ukrainians elect a president and a unicameral parliament, ver-*khow*-na *ra*-da (Верховна Рада). The parliamentary coalition is responsible for the appointment of the Cabinet of Ministers, headed by the Prime Minister. Most people believe that a lot of power resides with a small number of so-called 'oligarchs' who combine political office with great personal wealth.

Since Ukraine became independent in 1991 the main issue of domestic politics has been the mostly painful transition from a planned to a market economy. Another major issue has been how much the state should promote Ukrainian language and culture. Internationally Ukraine has tried to cooperate closely with the European Union and the USA while maintaining cordial relations with the Russian Federation.

Because of the failure of successive governments to improve the lot of ordinary people, many Ukrainians are sceptical about politicians, and there's less discussion of politics than might be expected.

Did you know that ...?
   vy *zna*-ye-te, shcho …?   Ви знаєте, що …?
I heard on the TV news that ...
   po te-le-*ba*-chen-ni   По телебаченні
   pe-re-da-*va*-ly, shcho ...   передавали, що ...
I read in the paper that ...
   ya chy-*taw*/chy-*ta*-la   Я читав/читала
   w ha-*ze*-ti, shcho ... (m/f)   в газеті, що ...
I'm [in favour of; against] ...
   ya za/*pro*-ty ...   Я за/проти ...

INTERESTS

When are the elections?
ko-*ly vy*-bo-ry?   Коли вибори?

What's the position of the ... on this issue?	yak *sta*-wlyat'-sya do *ts'o*-ho ...?	Як ставляться до цього ...?
centrists	tsen-*try*-sty	центристи
communists	ko-mu-*ni*-sty	комуністи
national democrats	na-tsi-o-*nal* de-mo-*kra*-ty	націонал-демократи
regionals	re-hi-o-*na*-ly	регіонали
socialists	so-tsi-a-*lis*-ty	соціалісти

BLUE SKIES

The Ukrainian flag is divided into two equal horizontal bars, the top one light blue, bla-*ky*-tny (блакитний), the lower one yellow, zhow-ty (жовтий). The colours derive from the coat of arms of the medieval princes of Halych, which showed a golden lion rampant on a field of azure. Many people think of the flag as representing the blue skies and golden wheat fields of Ukraine.

The state emblem is the trident, try-*zub* (тризуб), in a design derived from one used in the coinage of the medieval princes of Kyiv, especially Volodymyr the Great (who ruled from 980 to 1015). The try-*zub* is much older, however: archaeological finds showing tridents are dated as early as the 1st century AD. The original meaning of the trident is unknown, though it's assumed to have been a mystical symbol and a sign of authority.

(blue and yellow) flag	(zho-wto-bla-*kyt*-ny) *pra*-por	(жовто-блакитний) прапор
emblem	herb	герб
national insignia	na-tsi-o-*nal'*-na sym-vo-li-ka	національна символіка

INTERESTS

That's a ... policy.	tse ... po-*li*-ty-ka	Це ... політика.
bad	po-*ha*-na	погана
dangerous	ne-bez-*pech*-na	небезпечна
practical	prak-*tych*-na	практична
wise	*mu*-dra	мудра
armed forces	*zbroy*-ni *sy*-ly	збройні сили
constitution	kon-sty-*tu*-tsi-ya	конституція
corruption	ko-*rup*-tsi-ya	корупція
defence	o-bo-*ro*-na	оборона
democracy	de-mo-*kra*-ti-ya	демократія
economics/economy	e-ko-*no*-mi-ka	економіка
elections	*vy*-bo-ry	вибори
local (municipal and regional)	mi-*stse*-vi	місцеві
general/national	za-*hal'*-ni	загальні

Europe	yew-*ro*-pa	Європа
European Union	yew-ro-*peys*'-ky so-*yuz*	Європейський Союз
(foreign) investment	(za-kor-*don*-ni) in-ve-*sty*-tsi-yi	(закордонні) інвестиції
foreign policy	za-kor-*don*-na po-*li*-ty-ka	закордонна політика
former Soviet Union	ko-*ly*-shniy ra-*dyans*'-ky so-*yuz*	колишній Радянський Союз
government	*u*-ryad	уряд
human rights	pra-*va* lyu-*dy*-ny	права людини
International Monetary Fund	mizh-na-*ro*-dny va-*lyu*-tny fond	Міжнародний Валютний Фонд

INTERESTS

law	za-*kon*	закон
majority	*bil'*-shist'	більшість
minister	mi-*nistr*	міністр
minority	*men*-shist'	меншість
NATO	*na*-to	НАТО
oligarch	o-li-*harkh*	олігарх
opposition	o-po-*zy*-tsi-ya	опозиція
ownership	*wlas*-nist'	власність
state	der-*zhaw*-na	державна
private	pry-*vat*-na	приватна
party	*par*-ti-ya	партія
policy/politics	po-*li*-ty-ka	політика
privatisation	pry-va-ty-*za*-tsi-ya	приватизація
president	pre-zy-*dent*	президент
prime minister	prem-*yer*-mi-*nistr*	прем'єр-міністр
parliament	par-*la*-ment	парламент
state language	der-*zhaw*-na *mo*-va	державна мова
Supreme Council	ver-*khow*-na *ra*-da	Верховна Рада
tax(es)	po-*da*-tok/po-*dat*-ky	податок/податки
transition economy	pe-re-khi-*dna* e-ko-*no*-mi-ka	перехідна економіка
unemployment	bez-ro-*bit*-tya	безробіття
United States	spo-*lu*-che-ni *shta*-ty (a-*me*-ry-ky)	Сполучені Штати (Америки)

KNOW YOUR NEIGHBOURS

Ukraine's neighbours listed clockwise from the Black Sea, *chor*-ne *mo*-re (Чорне Море), are:

Romania	ru-*mu*-ni-ya	Румунія
Moldova	mol-*do*-va	Молдова
Hungary	u-*hor*-shchy-na	Угорщина
Slovakia	slo-*vach*-chy-na	Словаччина
Poland	*pol'*-shcha	Польща
Belarus	bi-lo-*rus'*	Білорусь
Russia	ro-*si*-ya	Росія

ENVIRONMENT

НАВКОЛИШНЄ
СЕРЕДОВИЩЕ

INTERESTS

Ukraine has diverse natural resources. Most of its territory are flat-lands with fertile soil, while mountains are found in the west (the Carpathians) and in the southern part of the Crimean Peninsula. The country's rivers, lakes and forests are great places for spending time outdoors. Like in other heavily industrialised countries, air, water and soil pollution are important issues in Ukraine. In order to preserve the unique environment, six biosphere reserves have been established: Chornomorsky, Askania-Nova, Carpathian, Danube Delta, East Carpathians and Shatsky.

Can your country do
without nuclear power?
    va-sha kra-*yi*-na *mo*-zhe
    o-biy-*ty*-sya bez
    a-to-mno-yi e-ner-*he*-ty-ky?

Ваша країна може
обійтися без
атомної енергетики?

What alternative energy sources
are used in your country?
    ya-ki al'-ter-na-tyw-ni
    dze-re-la e-ner-hi-yi
    vy-ko-ry-sto-vu-yut u
    va-shiy kra-yi-ni?

Які альтернативні
джерела енергії
використовують у
вашій країні?

What animals/plants are found
in this reserve?
    ya-*ki* tva-*ry*-ny/ro-*sly*-ny ye
    w *ts'o*-mu za-po-*vid*-ny-ku?

Які тварини/рослини є
в цьому заповіднику?

What fish lives in this river/lake?
    ya-*ka ry*-ba *vo*-dyt'-sya w
    [tsiy *rich*-tsi; *ts'o*-mu *o*-ze-ri]?

Яка риба водиться в
[цій річці; цьому озері]?

The water in this spring is clean.

vo-*da* w *ts'o*-mu
dzhe-re-*li chy*-sta

Вода в цьому
джерелі чиста.

Don't drink tap water.

ne *py*-te vo-*dy* z *kra*-na

Не пийте води з крана.

Can mushrooms/berries be
picked up here?

tut *mo*-zhna zby-*ra*-ty
hry-*by*/ya-ho-*dy*?

Тут можна збирати
гриби/ягоди?

carbon dioxide	vu-hle-*ky*-sly haz	вуглекислий газ
(chemical) fertilisers	(khi-*mich*-ni)	(хімічні)
	do-*bry*-va	добрива
emissions	*vy*-pa-ry	випари
endangered species	vyd, shcho	вид, що
	zna-*kho*-dyt'-sya	знаходиться
	pid za-*hro*-zo-yu	під загрозою
greenhouse effect	par-ny-*ko*-vy	парниковий
	e-*fekt*	ефект
hydroelectric	hi-dro-e-lek-tro-	гідроелектро-
power station	*stan*-tsi-ya (hes)	станція (ГЕС)
pesticide	pe-sty-*tsyd*	пестицид
pollution	za-*bru*-dnen-nya	забруднення
power station	e-lek-tro-*stan*-tsi-ya	електростанція
atomic	*a*-to-mna	атомна
thermal	te-plo-*va*	теплова
radioactivity	ra-di-o-ak-*tyw*-nist'	радіоактивність
reserve	za-po-*vid*-nyk	заповідник
sarcophagus	sar-ko-*fah*	саркофаг

(stone coffin; in Chornobyl the concrete shield around the
stricken reactor)

SOCIAL ISSUES

What do people
here feel about ...?
   yak *lyu*-dy
   staw-lyat'-sya do ...?

СОЦІАЛЬНІ ПИТАННЯ

Як люди
ставляться до ...?

abortion	a-*bort*	аборт
AIDS	snid	СНІД
alcoholism	al-ko-ho-*lizm*	алкоголізм
compulsory military	o-bo-vyaz-*ko*-va	обов'язкова
service	viys'-*ko*-va	військова
	sluzh-ba	служба
crime	zlo-*chyn*-nist'	злочинність
divorce	roz-*lu*-chen-nya	розлучення
drug addiction	nar-ko-*ma*-ni-ya	наркоманія
... education	... o-s*vi*-ta	... освіта
public	der-*zha*-wna	державна
private	pry-*va*-tna	приватна
higher	*vy*-shcha	вища
emigration	e-mi-*hra*-tsi-ya	еміграція
(high) mortality	(vy-*so*-ka)	(висока)
	smert-nist'	смертність
inequality	ne-*riw*-nist'	нерівність
minority rights	pra-*va*	права
	men-sho-stey	меншостей
poverty	*bi*-dnist'	бідність
prostitution	pro-sty-*tu*-tsi-ya	поституція
refugee(s)	*bi*-zhe-nets'/	біженець/
	bi-zhen-tsi	біженці
trade union(s)	prof-*spil*-ka/	профспілка/
	prof-*spil*-ky	профспілки
unemployment	bez-ro-*bit*-tya	безробіття
veteran(s)	ve-te-*ran*/	ветеран/
	ve-te-*ra*-ny	ветерани

INTERESTS

THEY MAY SAY ...

(po-wni-styu) po-*ho*-dzhu-yu-sya
    I (absolutely) agree.
tse *pra*-wda
    That's true.
vy *ma*-ye-te *ra*-tsi-yu
    You're right.
na mo-*yu dum*-ku ...
    In my opinion ...
mozh-*ly*-vo, a-*le* ...
    Maybe, but ...
nu, khay *bu*-de po-va-sho-mu
    OK, you win.
ne wsi tak *du*-ma-yut'
    Not everyone would agree with you.
tut ya-*kes'* ne-po-ro-zu-*min*-nya
    There's a misunderstanding here.
pro tse i *mo*-vy ne *mo*-zhe *bu*-ty
    That's out of the question.
vy me-*ne* ne zro-zu-*mi*-ly
    You haven't understood me.
ya zo-wsim ne te ho-vo-*ryw*/ho-vo-*ry*-la (m/f)
    That's not what I said.
pro shcho zh vy ho-vo-ry-te?
    What are you talking about?

МАГАЗИНИ   SHOPPING

There are several different kinds of outlet for goods – shops, kiosks (small shops in prefabricated huts set up in public places), supermarkets and markets. Some shops may close for an hour during the day.

shop	ma-ha-*zyn*/ kram-*ny*-tsya	магазин/ крамниця
kiosk	ki-*osk*	кіоск
supermarket	su-per-*mar*-ket	супермаркет
market	ry-*nok*/ba-*zar*	ринок/базар

LOOKING FOR ...   У ПОШУКАХ ...

Where can I buy ...?	de [*mozh*-na; ya *mo*-zhu] ku-*py*-ty ...?	Де [можна; я можу] купити ...?
Where's the nearest ...?	de nay-*blyzh*-chy/ a/e/i ...? (m/f/neut/pl)	Де найближчий/ a/e/i ...?
bank	bank	банк
bookshop	kny-*har*-nya	книгарня
camera shop	fo-to-to-*va*-ry	фототовари
chemist/pharmacy	a-*pte*-ka	аптека
clothing store	ma-ha-*zyn* o-dya-hu	магазин одягу
department store	u-ni-ver-*mah*	універмаг
hairdresser	pe-ru-*kar*-nya	перукарня
laundry	*pral*'-nya	пральня
market	ry-*nok*	ринок
music shop	mu-*zych*-ni to-*va*-ry	музичні товари
newsagency	ha-*zet*-ny ki-*osk*	газетний кіоск
shoe shop	wzut-*tye*-vy ma-ha-*zyn*	взуттєвий магазин
souvenir shop	su-ve-*nir*-ny ma-ha-*zyn*	сувенірний магазин
supermarket	su-per-*mar*-ket	супермаркет

SHOPPING

MAKING A PURCHASE   КУПУЄМО

I'd like to buy ...
  ya b kho-*tiw*/kho-*ti*-la
  ku-*py*-ty ... (m/f)

Я б хотів/хотіла
купити ...

Where can I buy ...?
  de ya *mo*-zhu ku-*py*-ty ...?

Де я можу купити ...?

Do you have/sell ...?
  u vas ye/pro-da-*yet'*-sya ...?

У вас є/продається ...?

Please show me ...
  po-ka-*zhit'* (me-*ni*),
  bud' *la*-ska ...

Покажіть (мені),
будь ласка ...

How much does it cost?
  skil'-ky tse (vin/vo-*na*)
  ko-shtu-ye? (m/f)

Скільки це (він/вона)
коштує?

Please write down the price.

na-py-*shit*', bud' *la*-ska, tsi-*nu*

Напишіть, будь ласка, ціну.

OK, I'll take it.

ha-*razd*, ya viz'-*mu*

Гаразд, я візьму.

I (don't) like it.

me-*ni* (ne) po-*do*-ba-yet'-sya

Мені (не) подобається.

I'm just looking.

ya ly-*she* dy-*wlyu*-sya

Я лише дивлюся.

Thanks for your help/advice.

dya-ku-yu za do-po-*mo*-hu/ po-*ra*-du

Дякую за допомогу/ пораду.

Please pack it.

u-pa-*kuy*-te, bud' *la*-ska

Упакуйте, будь ласка.

How much all together?

skil'-ky *ko*-shtu-ye wse *ra*-zom?

Скільки коштує все разом?

Could I have a receipt, please?

mo-zhna kvy-*tan*-tsi-yu, bud' *la*-ska?

Можна квитанцію, будь ласка?

Do you take ...?	vy pry-*ma*-ye-te ...?	Ви приймаєте ...?
credit cards	kre-*dy*-tni	кредитні
	kar-*tky*	картки
foreign currency	i-no-*ze*-mnu	іноземну
	va-*lyu*-tu	валюту

SIGNS

On doors you'll see:

ДО СЕБЕ	**PULL**
ВІД СЕБЕ	**PUSH**

That's all, thanks.

tse wse, *dya*-ku-yu

Це все, дякую.

SHOPPING

BARGAINING   ТОРГУЄМОСЬ

Prices are fixed in shops. It might be worth trying to bargain at the market, as well as in small privately owned shops at the market.

That's too expensive.
  tse *nad*-to *do*-ro-ho   Це надто дорого.
What's your best price?
  ya-*ka va*-sha   Яка ваша
  o-sta-*toch*-na tsi-*na*?   остаточна ціна?

Can you make me
a better price?
  a de-*shew*-she ne *bu*-de?   А дешевше не буде?
I can give you ...
  ya *mo*-zhu *da*-ty ...   Я можу дати ...
I have no/little money.
  u *me*-ne ne-*ma*-ye/*ma*-lo   У мене немає/мало
  hro-*shey*   грошей.

YOU'RE KIDDING!

Really?	*praw*-da?	Правда?
Indeed?	ne-*wzhe*?	Невже?
You're kidding!	vy zhar-*tu*-ye-te!	Ви жартуєте!
I'm not a millionaire!	ya ne mil'-*yo*-ner!	Я не мільйонер!

ESSENTIAL GROCERIES

ОСНОВНІ ТОВАРИ

Where can I find ...?

de pro-da-*yet'*-sya/
pro-da-*yut'*-sya ...? (sg/pl)

Де продається/
продаються ...?

I'd like ...

ya [kho-*tiw* by;
kho-*ti*-la b]
ku-*py*-ty... (m/f) ;
day-te, bud' *la*-ska ...

Я [хотів би;
хотіла б]
купити ...;
Дайте, будь ласка ...

batteries	ba-ta-*rey*-ky	батарейки
bread	khlib	хліб
butter	*ma*-slo	масло
candles	svich-*ky*	свічки
cheese	syr	сир
chocolate bar	sho-ko-*lad*-ku	шоколадку
chocolates	sho-ko-*lad*-ni	шоколадні
	tsu-*ker*-ky	цукерки
eggs	*yay*-tsya	яйця
flour	*bo*-ro-shno	борошно
gas cylinder	*ha*-zo-vy ba-*lon*	газовий балон
ham	*shyn*-ku	шинку
honey	med	мед
margarine	mar-ha-*ryn*	маргарин
matches	sir-ny-*ky*	сірники
milk	mo-lo-*ko*	молоко
pepper	*pe*-rets'	перець
salt	sil'	сіль
shampoo	sham-*pun'*	шампунь
soap	*my*-lo	мило
sugar	*tsu*-kor	цукор
toilet paper	tu-a-*let*-ny pa-*pir*	туалетний папір
toothpaste	zub-*nu pas*-tu	зубну пасту
washing powder	*pral'*-ny po-ro-*shok*	пральний порошок
yogurt	*yo*-hurt	йогурт

SHOPPING

SOUVENIRS   СУВЕНІРИ

You'll find painted Easter eggs, py-san-*ky* (писанки), everywhere.
Every region has hundreds of distinct patterns, each one with a
particular meaning. Embroidery, especially embroidered shirts
and blouses, as well as ceramics and carvings are also popular
souvenirs. Don't be tempted by the matryoshki dolls (wooden
dolls that fit inside each other) if you're looking for genuine local crafts. There's nothing Ukrainian about them. Antique icons
should be avoided, firstly because there's a chance that they have
been stolen from abandoned churches during the Soviet period,
and secondly because you'll need to obtain an export licence to
get them out of the country legally. This is also the case for any
items that may have cultural heritage value, including works of
art and books.

amber	bur-*shtyn*	бурштин
ceramics	ke-*ra*-mi-ka	кераміка
crockery	*po*-sud	посуд
earrings	se-*rezh*-ky	сережки
embroidered ...	*vy*-shy-ti ...	вишиті ...
embroidered shirt	vy-*shy*-van-ka	вишиванка
items of wood	*vy*-ro-by z	вироби з
	de-re-va	дерева
jewellery (single item)	pry-*kra*-sa	прикраса
necklace	na-*my*-sto	намисто
necklace (of coral)	ko-*ra*-li	коралі
painting	kar-*ty*-na	картина
serviettes	ser-*vet*-ky	серветки
tablecloth	ska-ter-*ty*-na	скатертина
towels	ru-shny-*ky*	рушники

Note that embroidered ru-shny-*ky* (рушники) are not used as
towels, but for decoration.

CLOTHING | | ОДЯГ

baby's suit	kom-bi-ne-*zon*	комбінезон
bra	byust-*hal'*-ter	бюстгальтер
cardigan (women's)	*ko*-fta	кофта
dress	*su*-knya/*plat*-tya	сукня/плаття
dressing gown	kha-*lat*	халат
hat	ka-pe-*lyukh*	капелюх
jacket	zha-*ket*/*kur*-tka	жакет/куртка
jeans	*dzhyn*-sy	джинси
jumper	*dzhem*-per	джемпер
overalls	kom-bi-ne-*zon*	комбінезон
overcoat	pal'-*to*	пальто
panties (women's and children's)	*tru*-sy-ky	трусики
pants/undershorts	tru-*sy*	труси
panty hose	kol-*ho*-ty	колготи
pyjamas	pi-*zha*-ma	піжама
raincoat	plashch	плащ
shirt	so-*ro*-chka	сорочка
shorts	*shor*-ty	шорти
skirt	spi-*dny*-tsya	спідниця
socks	shkar-*pet*-ky	шкарпетки
stockings	pan-*cho*-khy	панчохи
suit	ko-*styum*	костюм
sweater	svetr	светр
swimming trunks (men's)	*plaw*-ky	плавки
swimsuit (women's)	ku-*pal'*-nyk	купальник
trousers	shta-*ny*	штани
underclothes	*ny*-zhnya bi-*lyz*-na	нижня білизна

SHOPPING

Can I try them/it on?
  mo-zhna po-*mi*-rya-ty?   Можна поміряти?
My size is ...
  u *me*-ne *roz*-mir ...   У мене розмір ...
It doesn't fit; They don't fit.
  tse ne miy *roz*-mir   Це не мій розмір.

It's too ...	tse ...	Це ...
big	za-ve-*ly*-ke	завелике
long	za-*dow*-he	задовге
short	za-ko-*ro*-tke	закоротке
small	za-ma-*le*	замале

Can I try another size?
mo-zhna po-*mi*-rya-ty
in-shy *roz*-mir?

Можна поміряти
інший розмір?

It doesn't suit me.
me-*ni* tse ne pa-*su*-ye

Мені це не пасує.

Do you have a mirror?
u vas ye *dzer*-ka-lo?

У вас є дзеркало?

HOPAK HIDE

The regions of Ukraine have a great variety of folk costumes, and it's worth visiting an ethnographic museum to get an idea of their wealth and beauty.

In modern times it has become customary to focus on one or two regional styles as representing the national costume. The best known of these is the garb that dancers wear when performing the most spectacular of Ukrainian dances, the ho-*pak* (гопак). This outfit follows the folk costume of the Poltava region. Over a long (calf-length) embroidered shirt, so-*roch*-ka (сорочка), a woman wears a woven wrap, *pla*-khta (плахта), an embroidered apron, far-*tukh* (фартух), and a tight-fitting sleeveless jacket, ker-*se*-tka (керсетка). Her floral headdress with long multicoloured ribbons, known as stri-*chky* (стрічки), is called a vi-*nok* (вінок).

Men also wear an embroidered shirt, wide trousers, sha-ro-*va*-ry (шаровари), in red or another bright colour, and a contrasting wide cloth belt, po-*yas* (пояс). Both men and women wear leather boots called *cho*-bo-ty (чоботи).

Also well known is the costume of the inhabitants of the Carpathian Mountains, the Hutsuly, hu-*tsu*-ly (гуцули), with its picturesque sheepskin waistcoat, the ke-*ptar* (кептар).

Accessories

Аксесуари

belt	*po*-yas	пояс
button	*gu*-dzyk	ґудзик
earrings	se-*rezh*-ky	сережки
glasses/spectacles	o-ku-*lya*-ry	окуляри
gloves	ru-ka-*vy*-chky	рукавички
handkerchief	no-so-*va*	носова
	khu-sto-chka;	хусточка;
	no-so-vy-*chok*	носовичок
headscarf	*khus*-tka	хустка
(shoe)lace	shnu-*riw*-ka	шнурівка
necklace	na-*my*-sto	намисто
ring	*pers*-ten'	перстень
scarf	sharf	шарф
tie	kra-*vat*-ka	краватка
umbrella	pa-ra-*so*-lya	парасоля
zipper	*bly*-skaw-ka/za-*mok*	блискавка/замок

SHOPPING

THIS & THAT

It's easy to remember the word tse (це). It means 'This/That is ...' or 'These/Those are ...'.

Footwear

Взуття

boots	*cho*-bo-ty	чоботи
lace-up shoes/boots	che-re-*vy*-ky	черевики
mules	*shl'o*-pan-tsi	шльопанці
sandals	san-*da*-li/	сандалі/
	bo-so-*nizh*-ky	босоніжки
shoes	*tuf*-li/*me*-shty	туфлі/мешти
slippers	do-*mash*-ni *kap*-tsi	домашні капці
trainers/runners	kro-*siw*-ky	кросівки

MATERIALS

cardboard	kar-*ton*	картон
cotton	ba-*vow*-na	бавовна
crystal	krysh-*tal'*	кришталь
fur	*khu*-tro	хутро
artificial	*shtuch*-ne	штучне
natural	na-tu-*ral'*-ne	натуральне
glass	sklo	скло
gold	*zo*-lo-to	золото
leather	*shki*-ra	шкіра
linen	l'on	льон
paper	pa-*pir*	папір
plastic	plas-*ma*-sa	пластмаса
porcelain	por-tse-*lya*-na/	порцеляна/
	far-for	фарфор
satin	at-*las*	атлас
silk	showk	шовк
silver	*sri*-blo	срібло
suede	*zam*-sha	замша
synthetics	syn-*te*-ty-ka	синтетика
velour	ve-*lyur*	велюр
velvet	o-ksa-*myt*	оксамит
velveteen	vel'-*vet*	вельвет
viscose	vi-*sko*-za	віскоза
wood	*de*-re-vo	дерево
wool	sherst'/*vow*-na	шерсть/вовна

SHOPPING

HOW DO YOU GO?

Remember that Ukrainian has two verbs meaning 'to go'. One refers to going somewhere by a means of transport: *yi*-kha-ty (їхати). The other refers to going on foot: *i*-ty (іти). They're not interchangeable.

COLOURS

		КОЛІР
black	*chor*-ny	чорний
light blue	bla-*ky*-tny	блакитний
dark blue; navy	*sy*-niy	синій
brown	ko-*rych*-ne-vy	коричневий
gold(en)	zo-lo-*ty*/	золотий/
	zo-lo-*ty*-sty	золотистий
green	ze-*le*-ny	зелений
grey	*si*-ry	сірий
orange	o-*ran*-zhe-vy/	оранжевий/
	po-ma-*ran*-che-vy	помаранчевий
pink	ro-*zhe*-vy	рожевий
purple	fi-o-*le*-to-vy	фіолетовий
red	cher-*vo*-ny	червоний
silver	*srib*-ny/	срібний/
	srib-*lya*-sty	сріблястий
white	*bi*-ly	білий
yellow	*zhow*-ty	жовтий

SHOPPING

STATIONERY & PUBLICATIONS

КАНЦТОВАРИ Й ПРЕСА

Major Western newspapers can usually be found in the large hotels.

Is there a newsagent nearby?
  chy ye tut ne-da-*le*-ko
  ha-*zet*-ny ki-*osk*?

Чи є тут недалеко
газетний кіоск?

Is there an English-language
bookshop nearby?
  chy ye po-*bly*-zu
  kny-*har*-nya z
  knyzh-*ka*-my
  an-*hliys*'-ko-yu *mo*-vo-yu?

Чи є поблизу
книгарня з
книжками
англійською мовою?

Is there an English-
language section?
  chy ye *vid*-dil z
  knyzh-*ka*-my
  an-*hliys*'-ko-yu *mo*-vo-yu?

Чи є відділ з
книжками
англійською мовою?

SHOPPING

Do you have/ sell (a)...?	u vas pro-da-*yet*'-sya ...?/pro-da-*yut*'-sya ...? (sg/pl)	У вас продається.../про-даються ...?
books	knyzh-*ky*	книжки
book on art	*kny*-ha z my-*stets*-tva	книга з мистецтва
big/pocket dictionary	ve-*ly*-ky/ ky-shen'*ko*-vy slow-*nyk*	великий/ кишеньковий словник
guidebook of the town	pu-tiw-*nyk* po *mi*-sti	путівник по місті
magazines	zhur-*na*-ly	журнали
newspapers	ha-*ze*-ty	газети
novels in English	ro-*ma*-ny an-*hliys*'-ko-yu *mo*-vo-yu	романи англійською мовою
town map	*kar*-ta *mi*-sta	карта міста
Ukrainian– English dictionary	u-kra-*yins*'-ko an-*hliys*'-ky slow-*nyk*	українсько– англійський словник

I need (a/an) ...	me-*ni* po-*tri*-ben/ po-*trib*-na ... (m/f)	Мені потрібен/ потрібна ...
CD	kom-*pakt*-dysk	компакт-диск
envelope	kon-*vert*	конверт
eraser	*gum*-ka	ґумка
notebook	blo-*knot*	блокнот
pen	*ru*-chka	ручка
pencil	o-li-*vets*'	олівець
ruler	li-*niy*-ka	лінійка
writing paper	pa-*pir*	папір

TOILETRIES   ПРЕДМЕТИ ТУАЛЕТУ

You're more likely to find the items listed below in one of the kiosks that line the streets of the big cities than in a pharmacy.

Can I have (a) ...?	*mo*-zhna ...?;	Можна ...?;
	day-te,	Дайте,
	bud'*la*-ska, ...	будь ласка, ...
comb	hre-bi-*nets'*	гребінець
condoms	pre-zer-va-*ty*-vy	презервативи
deodorant	de-zo-do-*rant*	дезодорант
eye shadow	*ti*-ni	тіні
hair spray	lak dlya	лак для
	vo-*lo*-sya	волосся
hand cream	krem dlya ruk	крем для рук
insect repellent	ri-dy-*nu* vid	рідину від
	ko-*makh*	комах
lipstick	po-*ma*-du	помаду
mascara	tush	туш
mirror	*dzer*-ka-lo	дзеркало
moisturiser	zvo-*lo*-zhu-val'-ny	зволожувальний
	krem	крем
nail polish	lak dlya *nikh*-tiw	лак для нігтів
packet of tissues	*pach*-ku ser-*ve*-tok	пачку серветок
razor	*bryt*-vu	бритву
razor blade(s)	*le*-zo/*le*-za	лезо/леза
sanitary napkins	pro-*klad*-ky	прокладки
shampoo	sham-*pun'*	шампунь
shaving cream	krem dlya	крем для
	ho-*lin*-nya	гоління
soap	*my*-lo	мило
sunblock	za-khy-*sny* krem;	захисний крем;
	krem vid *son*-tsya	крем від сонця
tampons	tam-*po*-ny	тампони
toilet paper	tu-a-*let*-ny	туалетний
	pa-*pir*	папір
toothbrush	zub-*nu shchit*-ku	зубну щітку
tube of toothpaste	*tyu*-byk zub-*no*-yi	тюбик зубної
	pa-sty	пасти

SHOPPING

SHOPPING

FOR THE BABY

Can I have (a/some) ...?	mo-zhna ...?; day-te, bud'la-ska, ...	**ДЛЯ НЕМОВЛЯТ** Можна ...?; Дайте, будь ласка, ...
baby powder	pry-syp-ku	присипку
bib	sly-nya-wchyk	слинявчик
disposable nappies	o-dno-ra-zo-vi pid-huz-ny-ky; pam-per-sy	одноразові підгузники; памперси
dummy/pacifier	sos-ku	соску
feeding bottle	plya-shech-ku	пляшечку
nappy	pe-len-ku	пеленку
nappy rash cream	krem vid vy-syp-ky	крем від висипки
powdered milk	su-khe mo-lo-ko	сухе молоко
tinned baby food	dy-tya-chu yi-zhu w ba-no-chkakh	дитячу їжу в баночках

MUSIC

МУЗИКА

I'm looking for a ... CD.
ya shu-ka-yu
kom-pakt-dysk ...

Я шукаю
компакт-диск ...

I heard a band/singer called ...
ya chuw/chu-la (m/f)
hru-pu/vy-ko-naw-tsya ...

Я чув/чула
групу/виконавця ...

What's his/her best recording?
ya-ka na-zva yo-ho/yi-yi
nay-kra-shcho-ho za-py-su?

Яка назва його/її
найкращого запису?

Can I listen to the CD here?
chy mo-zhna tut
pro-slu-kha-ty tsey
kom-pakt-dysk?

Чи можна тут
прослухати цей
компакт-дикс?

I need a blank tape.
me-ni po-trib-na
chy-sta ka-se-ta.

Мені потрібна
чиста касета.

VIDEO & PHOTOGRAPHY

ВІДЕО Й ФОТО

I'd like a ...	ya b kho-*tiw*/ kho-*ti*-la ... (m/f)	Я б хотів/ хотіла ...
blank tape	*chy*-stu ka-*se*-tu	чисту касету
CD	kom-pakt (-*dysk*)/si-*di*	компакт (-диск)/CD
DVD	di-vi-*di*(-dysk)	DVD(-диск)
video tape	*vi*-de-o-ka-*se*-tu	відеокасету

Can I listen to this?

mo-zhna tse pro-*slu*-kha-ty?

Можна це прослухати?

Will this work on any DVD player?

chy tse *bu*-de *hra*-ty na *bud'*-ya-ko-mu di-vi-di-*ple*-ye-ri?

Чи це буде грати на будь-якому DVD-плеєрі?

Is this for a (PAL/SECAM/NTSC) system?

tse pid-*kho*-dyt' dlya sy-*ste*-my (pal/se-*kam*/ en-ti-es-*si*)?

Це підходить для системи (PAL/SECAM/ NTSC)?

video camera	*vi*-de-o-ka-*ka*-me-ra	відеокамера

SHOPPING

IT'S IN THE BAG!

bag	*sum*-ka	сумка
box	ko-*rob*-ka	коробка
briefcase	port-*fel'*	портфель
pack	*pach*-ka	пачка
packet	pa-*ket*	пакет
plastic bag	ku-*l'ok*	кульок
purse	ha-ma-*nets'*	гаманець
suitcase	va-*li*-za/va-*liz*-ka/ che-mo-*dan*	валіза/валізка/ чемодан

... camera	... fo-to-a-pa-*rat*	... фотоапарат
digital	tsy-fro-*vy*	цифровий
disposable	od-no-*ra*-zo-vy	одноразовий
underwater	pid-*vod*-ny	підводний

Can you ...?	vy mo-zhe-te ...?	Ви можете ...?
develop this film	pro-ya-*vy*-ty tsyu *pliw*-ku	проявити цю плівку
enlarge this photo	*zbil'*-shy-ty [tse *fo*-to; tsyu fo-to-*bra*-fi-yu]	збільшити [це фото; цю фотографію]
load my film	za-rya-*dy*-ty *pliw*-ku	зарядити плівку
print digital photos	na-dru-ku-*va*-ty tsy-fro-*vi* *fo*-to(-*bra*-fi-yi)	надрукувати цифрові фото(графії)
recharge the battery for my digital camera	za-rya-*dy*-ty ba-ta-*re*-yu dlya mo-*ho* fo-to-a-pa-*ra*-ta	зарядити батарею для мого фото-апарата
transfer photos from my camera to CD	pe-re-py-*sa*-ty *fo*-to(-*bra*-fi-yi) z mo-*ho* fo-to-a-pa-*ra*-ta na kom-pakt-*dysk*/si-*di*	переписати фото(графії) з мого фотоапарата на компакт-диск/CD

Do you have ... for this camera?	u vas ye ... dlya *tsyo*-ho fo-to-a-pa-*ra*-ta?	У вас є ... для цього фотоапарата?
batteries	ba-ta-*re*-yi/ a-ku-mu-*lya*-to-ry	батареї/ акумулятори
flashbulbs	*spa*-lakh	спалах
(zoom) lenses	(*zbil'*-shu-val'-ni) *lin*-zy	(збільшувальні) лінзи
light meters	eks-po-*no*-metr	експонометр
memory cards	*kar*-ty *pa*-mya-ti	карти пам'яті

I need ... film for this camera.	me-*ni* po-*tri*-bna ... *pliw*-ka dlya fo-to-a-pa-*ra*-ta	Мені потрібна ... плівка для фотоапарата.
APS	a-pe-*es*/dva-tsya-*ty*-cho-*ty*-ry-mi-li-me-*tro*-va	APS/24-міліметрова
B&W	chor-no-*bi*-la	чорно-біла
colour	ko-*l'o*-*ro*-va	кольорова
slide	*slay*-do-va	слайдова
(200) ASA	chu-*tly*-vi-styu (*dvi*-sti)	чутливістю (200)

I need a cable to connect my camera to a computer.

me-*ni* po-*tri*-ben *ka*-bel', *shcho*-by pid-ye-*dna*-ty fo-to-a-pa-*rat* do kom-*pyu*-te-ra

Мені потрібен кабель, щоби під'єднати фотоапарат до комп'ютера.

I need a cable to recharge this battery.

me-*ni* po-*tri*-ben *ka*-bel' dlya za-*ryad*-ky ba-ta-*re*-yi

Мені потрібен кабель для зарядки батареї.

I need a video cassette for this camera.

me-*ni* po-*tri*-bna vi-de-o-ka-*se*-ta dlya ta-*ko*-yi *ka*-me-ry

Мені потрібна відео-касета для такої камери.

When will it be ready?

ko-*ly* tse *bu*-de ho-*to*-ve?

Коли це буде готове?

I need a passport photo taken.

me-*ni* *tre*-ba zro-*by*-ty *fo*-to na *pas*-port

Мені треба зробити фото на паспорт.

I'm not happy with these photos.

me-*ni* ne *du*-zhe po-*do*-ba-yut'-sya tsi *fo*-to

Мені не дуже подобаються ці фото.

I don't want to pay the full price.

ya ne *kho*-chu pla-*ty*-ty *pow*-nu tsi-*nu*

Я не хочу платити повну ціну.

SIZES & COMPARISONS   РОЗМІРИ

I want something ...   ya *kho*-chu shchos' ...   Я хочу щось ...

a bit cheaper	*tro*-khy de-*shew*-she	трохи дешевше
a bit smaller	*tro*-khy *men*-she	трохи менше
a bit larger	*tro*-khy *bil*'-she	трохи більше
of a different colour/size	*in*-sho-ho *ko*-l'o-ru/*roz*-mi-ru	іншого кольору/розміру

a couple	*pa*-ru	пару
a little/few	*ma*-lo	мало
a lot/much/many	ba-*ha*-to	багато
bad	po-*ha*-ny	поганий
best	nay-*kra*-shchy	найкращий
better	*kra*-shchy	кращий
big	ve-*ly*-ky	великий
bigger/larger	*bil*'-shy	більший
dark	*tem*-ny	темний
good/fine	*har*-ny/*do*-bry	гарний/добрий
heavy/difficult	vazh-*ky*	важкий
less/fewer	*men*-she	менше
light/bright	*svit*-ly	світлий
light/easy	leh-*ky*	легкий
long	*do*-why	довгий
more	*bil*'-she	більше
narrow/tight	vuz'-*ky*	вузький
short	ko-*ro*-tky	короткий
small	ma-*ly*/ma-*len*'-ky	малий/маленький
some/several	de-*kil*'-ka	декілька
thin	ton-*ky*	тонкий
too little/few	za-*ma*-lo	замало
too much/many	za-ba-*ha*-to	забагато
wide/broad	shy-*ro*-ky	широкий
worse	*hir*-shy	гірший
worst	nay-*hir*-shy	найгірший

ЇЖА

FOOD

Ukrainian cuisine is very varied, and Ukrainians are famed for their hospitality. The food reflects not only the range of national dishes, but also the contact that Ukrainians have had over the centuries with neighbouring peoples. In recent years, international cuisine has begun to make its presence felt and fast-food outlets have made an appearance.

THROUGH THE DAY   ПРОТЯГОМ ДНЯ

The maxim that a hearty breakfast is an essential foundation for a successful day enjoys wide currency in Ukraine. If you're staying with relatives or friends you may be offered a morning meal that includes meat and potatoes. But people will understand that Westerners may prefer a lighter breakfast. Below are the Ukrainian names of some of the more 'Western' breakfast foods.

cereal	*ka*-sha	каша
coffee	*ka*-va	кава
corn flakes	ku-ku-*ru*-dzya-ni	кукурудзяні
	pla-stiw-*tsi*	пластівці
eggs	*yay*-tsya	яйця
boiled	*va*-re-ni	варені
scrambled	*sma*-zhe-ni	смажені
muesli	*myu*-sli	мюслі
omelette	om-*let*	омлет
orange juice	a-pel'-*sy*-no-vy sik	апельсиновий сік
tea	chay	чай
toast	*hrin*-ka/tost	грінка/тост

breakfast	sni-*da*-nok	сніданок
lunch	o-*bid*	обід
dinner	ve-*che*-rya	вечеря

Lunch is usually the main meal of the day and can be served at any time in the afternoon. It's a serious affair of more than one course, even if you have it at the workplace cafeteria. Of course, many people take a cut lunch to work. In that case their evening meal may be more substantial.

VEGETARIAN & SPECIAL MEALS ВЕГЕТАРІАНСЬКА ТА СПЕЦІАЛЬНА ЇЖА

Some Ukrainians are vegetarian by choice, but vegetarianism is not widespread, and the idea of well-being and prosperity is associated in the minds of many with the frequent consumption of meat. On the other hand, there are many delicious foods in Ukraine that do not involve meat, so it's easy to have a vegetarian meal at a restaurant without a special menu. However, if you're vegetarian and are invited for a meal at someone's home, make sure you mention this in advance, otherwise you'll be sure to be confronted with meat.

I'm vegetarian.
ya ve-he-ta-ri-*a*-nets'/
ve-he-ta-ri-*an*-ka (m/f)

Я вегетаріанець/
вегетаріанка.

Do you serve vegetarian food?
u vas ye ve-he-ta-ri-*an*-s'ki
stra-vy?

У вас є вегетаріанські
страви?

Does this dish have meat?
chy w tsiy *stra*-vi
ye *mya*-so?

Чи в цій страві є
є м'ясо?

Can I get this without meat?
mo-zhna tse za-*mo*-vy-ty
bez *mya*-sa?

Можна це замовити
без м'яса?

I don't eat dairy products.
ya ne yim mo-*loch*-nykh
pro-*duk*-tiw

Я не їм молочних
продуктів.

I don't eat meat/pork/fish.
ya ne yim *mya*-sa/
svy-*ny*-ny/*ry*-by

Я не їм м'яса/
свинини/риби.

FOOD

I'm allergic to (peanuts).
> u *me*-ne a-ler-*hi*-ya na
> (a-*ra*-khis).

У мене алергія на
(арахіс).

Is this kosher?
> tse ko-*sher*-ne?

Це кошерне?

Is this organic?
> tse bez khi-mi-*ka*-tiw?

Це без хімікатів?

EATING OUT   У РЕСТОРАНІ

In recent years a number of restaurants, bars and cafes have
opened, offering excellent food at reasonable prices with standards
of service to match. On menus in Ukraine the adjective describ-
ing how an item is cooked follows the name of the item itself,
for example, kar-*to*-plya *sma*-zhe-na (картопля смажена) is
literally 'potato fried', ba-*lyk* o-se-*tro*-vy (балик осетровий)
is literally 'fillet sturgeon cured'. The amount of each item that
you can expect for your money is still given on some menus, eg
100 г (100 grams) or 1 шт (one piece).

THE PLATE IS NEVER EMPTY

If you're lucky enough to be invited into a Ukrainian
home, you can be sure of a treat. Ukrainians gladly
spend a lot of time and energy in the kitchen prepar-
ing food for guests. Virtually everything has to be
prepared at home as pre-prepared and frozen foods
are not widely available. A traditional festive meal in
domestic surroundings begins with a huge number
of cold dishes, followed by hot dishes. Come hungry,
as the aim is to ensure that a guest's plate is never
empty. The meal is punctuated by frequent toasts
and the guests are also expected to take part, so be
prepared! *bud'*-mo! (Будьмо!), 'Cheers!'.

See page 179 for some toasts in Ukrainian.

FOOD

FOOD

Do you have a table for (two)?
    u vas ye *sto*-lyk
    na (dvokh)?

У вас є столик
на (двох)?

Do you have any free tables?
    u vas ye *vil'*-ni
    sto-ly-ky?

У вас є вільні
столики?

I want to book a table for
tomorrow at (six).
    ya *kho*-chu za-*mo*-vy-ty
    sto-lyk na *zaw*-tra na
    (*sho*-stu ho-*dy*-nu)

Я хочу замовити
столик на завтра на
(шосту годину).

Can I/we see the menu?
    mo-zhna po-dy-*vy*-ty-sya
    me-*nyu*?

Можна подивитися
меню?

Do you have a menu in
English?
    u vas ye me-*nyu*
    an-*hliys'*-ko-yu *mo*-vo-yu?

У вас є меню
англійською мовою?

What do you recommend?
    shcho vy po-*ra*-dy-te?

Що ви порадите?

What special dishes do you have?
    ya-*ki* u vas ye
    fir-*mo*-vi *stra*-vy?

Які у вас є
фірмові страви?

What's this/that?
    shcho tse?

Що це?

SIGNS

БАР	**BAR**
БУФЕТ	**BUFFET**
КАФЕ (КАВ'ЯРНЯ)	**CAFE**
ЇДАЛЬНЯ	**CAFE; EATING HOUSE**
РЕСТОРАН	**RESTAURANT**
МІСЦЬ НЕМАЄ	**RESTAURANT FULL**
САМООБСЛУГОВУВАННЯ	**SELF SERVICE**

I'd like ...
  ya viz'-*mu* ...;
  ya b kho-*tiw*/
  kho-*ti*-la ... (m/f)

Я візьму ...;
Я б хотів/
хотіла ...

Can I try that?
  mo-zhna po-ku-shtu-*va*-ty
  ts'o-ho?

Можна покуштувати
цього?

Could you bring us a good
local wine?
  vy *mo*-zhe-te pry-ne-*sty*
  do-bro-ho mi-*stse*-vo-ho
  vy-*na*?
  Ви можете принести
  доброго місцевого
  вина?

THANKS

Remember the word
for 'Thank you' is
dya-ku-yu (дякую).

I love this dish!
  tse pre-*kra*-sna *stra*-va!

Це прекрасна страва!

The meal was delicious.
  bu-*lo du*-zhe *smach*-no.

Було дуже смачно.

Compliments to the chef!
  pe-re-*day*-te po-*dya*-ku
  ku-kha-re-vi!

Передайте подяку
кухареві!

Could we have the bill?
  mo-zhna ra-*khu*-nok?

Можна рахунок?

Is service included in the bill?
  chy w ra-*khu*-nok
  wklyu-che-no
  ob-slu-*ho*-vu-van-nya?

Чи в рахунок
включено
обслуговування?

I've been waiting for a long time.
  ya daw-*no* che-*ka*-yu

Я давно чекаю.

Please change this glass.
  po-mi-*nyay*-te, bud' *la*-ska,
  sklyan-ku.

Поміняйте, будь ласка,
склянку.

Another place setting, please.
  day-te, bud' *la*-ska,
  shche o-*dyn* pry-*bor*

Дайте, будь ласка,
ще один прибор.

FOOD

Please bring a/an/the ...	pry-ne-*sit'*, bud' *la*-ska, ...	Принесіть, будь ласка, ...
ashtray	po-*pil'*-*nych*-ku	попільничку
bill	ra-*khu*-nok	рахунок
fork	vy-*del*-ku	виделку
glass of water (with/ without ice)	*sklyan*-ku vo-*dy* (z *l'o*-dom; bez *l'o*-du)	склянку води (з льодом; без льоду)
knife	nizh	ніж
plate	ta-*ril*-ku	тарілку
spoon	*lozh*-ku	ложку
teaspoon	chay-*nu lozh*-ku	чайну ложку

DINING, DANCING & DOSH

Except for the very rich, people still don't go to restaurants often unless there is a special occasion. If they do go, they will normally spend a long time and order a larger number of dishes than Westerners might. All in all, the event is likely to be rather festive, and at a traditional restaurant people expect to dance.

The days of arrogant and sloppy service are well and truly over. Waiters and waitresses are usually polite and friendly, and can be tipped with good conscience. Tipping is more or less universal, but there are no guidelines as to the amount. One might just round up to the next five *hryvni*, or make a grand gesture with an extravagant tip.

While dining at a restaurant is now, on the whole, a pleasant experience, the relationship between what's printed on the menu and what's actually available may still be sketchy. It's always useful to ask the waiter to recommend something.

FOOD

bitter	hir-ky	гіркий
boiled	va-re-ny	варений
bottle	plya-shka	пляшка
bottle opener	shto-por/	штопор/
	kor-ko-tyah	коркотяг
broiled (stewed)	tu-shko-va-ny	тушкований
cork	ko-rok	корок
... course	stra-va ...	страва ...
first	per-sha	перша
second	dru-ha	друга
sweet	so-lod-ka	солодка
cup	hor-nyat-ko/	горнятко/
	chash-ka	чашка
fork	vy-del-ka	виделка
fried	sma-zhe-ny	смажений
glass (long drinks)	sklyan-ka	склянка
glass (shots)	char-ka	чарка
glass (wine)	fu-zher/ke-lykh	фужер/келих
hot (spicy)	ho-stry	гострий
ice	lid	лід
jellied	za-lyw-ny	заливний
knife	nizh	ніж
manager (restaurant)	ad-mi-ni-stra-tor	адміністратор
marinated	ma-ry-no-va-ny	маринований
napkin	ser-vet-ka	серветка
plate	ta-ril-ka	тарілка
reservation/order	za-mow-len-nya	замовлення
roast/baked	pe-che-ny	печений
salty/salted	so-lo-ny	солоний
saucer	blyud-tse	блюдце
service	ob-slu-ho-vu-van-nya	обслуговування
sour	ky-sly	кислий
spoon	lozh-ka	ложка
sweet	so-lod-ky	солодкий
tablecloth	ska-ter-ty-na	скатертина
waiter	o-fi-tsi-ant	офіціант

FOOD

UKRAINIAN SPECIALTIES

УКРАЇНСЬКІ СТРАВИ

The following Ukrainian specialties are definitely worth a try:

borshch   борщ
soup based on beetroot with other vegetables and meat; served with sour cream. There are many regional varieties.

va-*re*-ny-ky   вареники
ravioli-like pasta stuffed with potato, cabbage, mushrooms, meat or cheese, or with cherries as a sweet dish

ho-lub-*tsi*   голубці
cabbage rolls stuffed with rice and vegetables, or possibly with spiced minced meat, and stewed slowly in the oven

de-ru-*ny*   деруни
pancakes made from grated potato and flour and fried; served with sour cream

FOOD

kho-lo-*dets'* холодець
brawn made by boiling pigs' trotters. The meat is picked off the
bone and the gravy sets around it into a jelly as it cools; served
with horseradish or mustard.

sa-lo сало
pork fat; no description of Ukrainian cuisine would be complete
without it. Ukrainians like their pigs to be fat for their *sa*-lo
(сало). Spices are rubbed into the skin and the fat is then allowed
to stand. It's eaten in thin slices on black bread with garlic and
salt and washed down with ice-cold vodka. Especially delicious
is the smoked version, kop-*che*-ne *sa*-lo (копчене сало).

do-*ma*-shnya kow-ba-*sa* домашня ковбаса
domestic sausage; it's an injustice to call it salami. The only way
to sample true home-prepared sausage is by experiencing it for
yourself with the sights and smells of the markets of Ukraine.

mlyn-*tsi* млинці
pancakes, often made with soured milk for a lighter batter. Thin-
ner pancakes are called na-*ly*-sny-ky (налисники), which are
rolled and served with a stuffing, usually fruit or jam.

ENOUGH IS ENOUGH!

FOOD

Thanks, I'm full.	
dya-ku-yu, ya na-*yiw*-sya/ na-*yi*-la-sya (m/f)	Дякую, я наївся/ наїлася.
[I don't want to; I can't] eat any more.	
ya *bil'*-she ne *kho*-chu (mo-zhu)	Я більше не хочу (можу).
I don't drink. (alcohol)	
ya ne pyu	Я не п'ю.
I'm on a diet.	
ya na di-ye-ti	Я на дієті.
The doctor doesn't allow me to eat/drink that.	
me-*ni* ne do-zvo-*lya*-ye li-kar	Мені не дозволяє лікар.
Enough!	
do-*syt'*!	Досить!

TYPICAL DISHES
ТИПОВІ СТРАВИ

Appetisers

assorted cold platter with ...	... a-sor-*ti*	... асорті
fish	*ryb*-ne (adj)	рибне
meat	mya-*sne* (adj)	м'ясне
fish/meat in aspic	za-*lyw*-ne	заливне
hors d'oeuvres	za-*ku*-sky	закуски
meat in jelly	kho-lo-*dets'*	холодець
pate	pa-*shtet*	паштет
salad	sa-*lat*	салат

Soups

Soups form a very important part of the Ukrainian diet. They are often thick enough to be a meal in themselves. Some are served with special buns or breads. You might see z pam-pu-*shka*-my (з пампушками) written next to a soup on the menu; if you go for this one, your soup will be served 'with small garlicky buns'.

first course	*per*-sha *stra*-va	перша страва
beetroot soup	borshch	борщ
bouillon	bul'-*yon*	бульйон
soup	sup	суп
bean	kva-so-*lya*-ny	квасоляний
buckwheat	hre-*cha*-ny	гречаний
mushroom	hryb-*ny*	грибний
pea	ho-ro-kho-vy	гороховий
potato	kar-to-*plya*-ny	картопляний
vegetable	o-vo-*che*-vy	овочевий

FOOD

Main Courses

beef (cold)	*rost*-bif	ростбіф
beef stroganoff	bef-*stro*-ha-now	беф-строганов
beefsteak	bif-*shteks*	біфштекс
chop	vid-byw-*na*	відбивна
cutlet	ko-*tle*-ta	котлета
meatballs	tyuf-*tel*'-ky	тюфтельки
meatloaf	ru-*let*	рулет
omelette	o-*mlet*	омлет
sausage (frankfurter)	so-*sy*-ska	сосиска
saveloy	sar-*del*'-ka	сарделька
schnitzel	*shni*-tsel'	шніцель
second course	*dru*-ha *stra*-va	друга страва
shashlik/kebab	sha-*shlyk*	шашлик

Desserts

In a restaurant, you can order cakes or ice cream for dessert, usually accompanied by a cup of coffee or tea. A meal in domestic surroundings is quite another matter. Baking cakes and pies for a festive meal is common in every household. You may also be offered ky-*sil*' (кисіль), something resembling drinkable fruit jelly.

cake (large)	tort	торт
cake (small)	*ti*-stech-ko	тістечко
confectionery	tsu-*ker*-ky	цукерки
fruit jelly (drinkable)	ky-*sil*'	кисіль
honey	med	мед
ice cream	mo-ro-zy-vo	морозиво
jelly	zhe-*le*	желе
marmalade	va-*ren*-nya	варення
pie	py-*rih*	пиріг

Jams aren't usually thought of as breakfast foods in Ukraine, but are rather eaten as dessert. There are different types of jam – va-*ren*-nya (варення) has fruit and is usually too runny to spread on bread, but can be eaten with little spoons when having tea; po-*vy*-dlo (повидло) is most often made from plums or apples and is also runny; like dzhem (джем), which is thicker, it can be spread on bread.

FOOD

Staples

Bread's the staple that is present at every meal. The tasty black bread, made from rye flour, comes in several varieties; the ones to look out for are u-kra-*yins'*-ky (Український) and dar-*nyts'*-ky (Дарницький). A popular form of white bread is ba-*ton* (батон).

Other staple foods are the various kinds of *ka-sha* (каша) made from grain. Translating *ka-sha* as 'porridge' is misleading, because of the association that the word has with the lumpy grey mass that forms part of the English breakfast cuisine. Buckwheat *ka-sha* is generally drier and much more textured than porridge. It's an excellent accompaniment to many meat dishes, and can be a vegetarian dish on its own.

bread	khlib	хліб
black	*chor*-ny	чорний
white	*bi*-ly	білий
breadroll	*bul*-ka	булка
buckwheat	*hrech*-ka	гречка
egg	yay-*tse*	яйце
fried egg	ya-*yech*-nya	яєчня
kasha	*ka*-sha	каша
millet	pshe-*nych*-na kru-*pa*	пшенична крупа
pasta	ma-ka-ro-*ny*/ ver-mi-*shel*'/ *lok*-shy-na	макарони/ вермішель/ локшина
rice	rys	рис
semolina	*man*-na kru-*pa*	манна крупа

Condiments

horseradish	khrin	хрін
mayonnaise	ma-yo-*nez*	майонез
mustard (spicy)	hir-*chy*-tsya	гірчиця
oil	o-*li*-ya	олія
pepper	pe-*rets*'	перець
salt	sil'	сіль
sauce	*so*-us	соус
spices	spe-tsi-*yi*	спеції
sugar	*tsu*-kor	цукор
vinegar	o-*tset*	оцет

FOOD

DRINKS НАПОЇ
Nonalcoholic Drinks Безалкогольні напої

Black coffee is always served in small cups, white coffee in larger ones. Tea is almost always drunk black and can be sweetened with sugar and even honey. If you want milk, you should ask for it. Tea and coffee are often served with biscuits, cakes and pastries. You may be served a glass containing a fruit liquid with pieces of fruit floating in it; this is kom-*pot* (компот).

One very refreshing nonalcoholic drink that you may not find on restaurant menus (but will be able to buy on the street) is kvas (квас), made from fermented black bread.

cocoa	ka-*ka*-o	какао
coffee	*ka*-va	кава
instant	roz-*chyn*-na	розчинна
with milk	z mo-lo-*kom*	з молоком
Turkish	po-tu-*rets*'-ky	по-турецьки
cappuccino	ka-pu-*chi*-no	капучіно
espresso	*ka*-va e-*spre*-so	кава-еспресо
iced coffee	*ka*-va hlya-*se*	кава-глясе
juice	sik	сік
apple	*ya*-bluch-ny	яблучний
birch	be-*re*-zo-vy	березовий
grape	vy-no-*hra*-dny	виноградний
orange	a-pel'-*sy*-no-vy	апельсиновий
tomato	to-*ma*-tny	томатний
mineral water	mi-ne-*ral*'-na vo-*da*	мінеральна вода
soft drink	so-*lod*-ka vo-*da*;	солодка вода;
	ly-mo-*nad*	лимонад
tea	chay	чай
with lemon	z ly-*mo*-nom	з лимоном
with milk	z mo-lo-*kom*	з молоком
water	vo-*da*	вода

FOOD

GOING DUTCH IN UKRAINE

Nowadays in Ukraine, a man and a woman who have dined together usually share the bill – still, on some occasions the man can be expected to pay.

Alcoholic Drinks   Алкогольні напої

The institution of pre-dinner drinks has no equivalent in Ukraine. It's also not usual to have a progression from white wine to red wine and then to liqueur or brandy in the course of a meal. People usually stay with one kind of drink throughout a meal.

Men often drink vodka or brandy, the latter known in Ukraine as kon'-*yak* (коньяк). Vodka, ho-*ril*-ka (горілка), should be drunk 'neat'. There are also vodkas with flavouring. Perhaps the most striking is the one with chilli peppers – pepper-flavoured vodka! Fruit and alcohol combine to produce an infusion, na-*lyw*-ka (наливка), that may seem innocuously sweet until you try to stand up; one particularly tasty variety is based on cherries – vy-*shniw*-ka (вишнівка).

Women are more likely to drink wine or the excellent sparkling wine, always known as sham-*pan*-s'ke (шампанське). The wines of Crimea have long enjoyed a worldwide reputation.

beer	*py*-vo	пиво
brandy/cognac	kon'-*yak*	коньяк
liqueur	li-*ker*	лікер
moonshine	sa-mo-*hon*	самогон
port	port-*veyn*	портвейн
rum	rom	ром
sherry	*khe*-res	херес
sparkling wine	sham-*pan*-s'ke	шампанське
vodka	ho-*ril*-ka	горілка
Ukrainian	u-kra-*yin*-s'ka	українська
pepper-flavoured	z *per*-tsem	з перцем
wine	vy-*no*	вино
dessert (sweet)	de-*ser*-tne	десертне
dry	su-*khe*	сухе
red	cher-*vo*-ne	червоне
table	sto-*lo*-ve	столове
white	*bi*-le	біле

Making a Toast   Тости

Toasts are made throughout special meals. Everyone around the table will be expected to propose at least one toast during the meal.

A word of warning: the small glasses of vodka are supposed to be downed in one gulp when a toast has been proposed. To sip would be regarded as an insult. If you do not think that you'll be able to last, it's better to say at the outset that you do not drink alcohol at all. And if you do drink, be especially wary of any home-produced spirits, sa-mo-*hon* (самогон). Needless to say, domestic distilling is illegal, but some people do it and the results – although sometimes better than commercially produced vodka in terms of taste – can be overpowering.

За вас!

FOOD

Bon appetit!	
smach-*no*-ho!	Смачного!
Cheers!	
bud'-mo!	Будьмо!
Here's to you!	
za vas!	За вас!
Here's to your health!	
za (*va*-she) zdo-*ro*-wya!	За (ваше) здоров'я!
Here's to our hosts!	
za ho-*spo*-da-riw!	За господарів!
Here's to the guests!	
za ho-*stey*!	За гостей!
Here's to our friends!	
za *dru*-ziw!	За друзів!

At a birthday party the first toast is always to the person whose birthday is being celebrated: za i-me-*nyn*-ny-ka/i-me-*nyn*-ny-tsyu! (m/f) (За іменинника/іменинницю!), 'Here's to the person whose birthday it is!'. The second toast can be to the parents: za bat'-*kiw*! (За батьків!), 'Here's to the parents!'. The third toast is usually to love: za lyu-*bow*! (За любов!), or to women: za zhi-*nok*! (За жінок!) and men can drink it standing up.

AT THE MARKET
Meat

НА РИНКУ
М'ясо

beef	*ya*-lo-vy-chy-na	яловичина
chicken	ku-*rya*-ty-na/*kur*-ka	курятина/курка
duck	*kach*-ka	качка
goose	*hu*-ska	гуска
ham	*shyn*-ka	шинка
lamb	ba-*ra*-ny-na	баранина
pork	svy-*ny*-na	свинина
turkey	in-*dyk*	індик
veal	te-*lya*-ty-na	телятина

SIGNS

КАСА	**CASHIER**
ВІДДІЛ	**DEPARTMENT/SECTION**
ПРОДТОВАРИ	**FOOD**
ГАСТРОНОМ	**FOOD STORE**
ОВОЧІ ФРУКТИ	**GREENGROCER**
БАКАЛІЯ	**GROCER**
БАЗАР/РИНОК	**MARKET**
КУЛІНАРІЯ	**PREPARED FOOD**
КОНДИТЕРСЬКА	**PATISSERIE**
УНІВЕРСАМ	**SELF-SERVICE STORE**
СУПЕРМАРКЕТ	**SUPERMARKET**

Seafood

		Рибні страви
carp	*ko-rop*	короп
caviar	i-*kra*	ікра
black	*chor*-na	чорна
red	che-*rvo*-na	червона
cod liver	pe-*chin*-ka tri-*sky*	печінка тріски
cod	tri-*ska*	тріска
crabs	*kra*-by	краби
fish	*ry*-ba	риба
fresh	*svi*-zha	свіжа
smoked	kop-*che*-na	копчена
herring	o-se-*le*-dets'	оселедець
mackerel	*skum*-bri-ya	скумбрія
octopus	kal'-*ma*-ry	кальмари
pike	*shchu*-ka	щука
plaice	*kam*-ba-la	камбала
prawns	kre-*ve*-tky	креветки
salmon	lo-*sos'*	лосось
sardine	sar-*dy*-na	сардина
sprats	*shpro*-ty	шпроти
sturgeon	o-se-*try*-na	осетрина

FOOD

Vegetables

Овочі

English	Pronunciation	Ukrainian
aubergine	ba-kla-*zhan*	баклажан
beetroot	bu-*ryak*	буряк
cabbage	ka-*pu*-sta	капуста
capsicum	*pe*-rets'	перець
carrot	*mor*-kva	морква
celery	se-*le*-ra	селера
chilli pepper(s)	*ho*-stry *pe*-rets	гострий перець
cucumber	o-hi-*rok*	огірок
dill	krip	кріп
garlic	cha-*snyk*	часник
lettuce	sa-*lat*	салат
marrow	ka-ba-*chok*	кабачок
mushroom	hryb	гриб
onion	tsy-*bu*-lya	цибуля
parsley	pe-*tru*-shka	петрушка
potato	kar-*to*-plya	картопля
radish	re-*dys*	редис
sweetcorn	ku-ku-*ru*-dza	кукурудза
tomato	po-mi-*dor*	помідор

FOOD

MIND THE MUSHROOMS

Think twice before you buy any mushrooms. Due to the fall-out of the Chornobyl nuclear accident, mushrooms appear to harbour high concentrations of radioactive elements. If you want to play it safe, don't pick them unless you have experience and don't buy them at open markets.

Dairy Produce   Молочні продукти

Ukrainians are very fond of milk and dairy products. Sour milk – not milk that has gone off, but milk with a particular bacterial culture – is especially valued for its beneficial effects upon the digestion. Two products have no counterpart in English: ke-*fir* (кефір) – somewhat like drinking yogurt, only tastier – and *rya*-zhan-ka (ряжанка) – try it, if you can find it! Butter in Ukraine is always unsalted.

butter	*ma*-slo	масло
cheese	syr	сир
cream	ver-*shky*	вершки
margarine	mar-ha-*ryn*	маргарин
milk	mo-lo-*ko*	молоко
sour cream	sme-*ta*-na	сметана

Fruit   Фрукти

alpine strawberry	su-*ny*-tsya	суниця
apple	*ya*-blu-ko	яблуко
apricot	a-bry-*kos*	абрикос
banana	ba-*nan*	банан
blackcurrant	*chor*-na	чорна
	smo-*ro*-dy-na	смородина
cherry	*vy*-shnya	вишня
(dark, juicy, sweet-sour taste)		
cherry	che-*re*-shnya	черешня
(pale, sweet, firm)		
gooseberry	*a*-grus	аґрус
grapes	vy-no-*hrad*	виноград
lemon	ly-*mon*	лимон
mandarin	man-da-*ryn*	мандарин
melon	*dy*-nya	диня
orange	a-pel'-*syn*/	апельсин/
	po-ma-*ran*-cha	помаранча
peach	*per*-syk	персик
pear	*hru*-sha	груша

FOOD

pineapple	a-na-*nas*	ананас
plum	*sly*-va	слива
pomegranate	hra-*nat*	гранат
raspberry	ma-*ly*-na	малина
redcurrant	po-*rich*-ka	порічка
strawberry	po-lu-*ny*-tsya	полуниця
watermelon	ka-*vun*	кавун

FALSE FRIENDS

Some Ukrainian words sound very much like English ones, but have unexpected meanings. Be careful with the following:

To translate 'preservatives', say kon-ser-*van*-ty (консерванти). The word pre-zer-va-*ty*-vy (презервативи) exists, but means 'condoms'.

To translate 'panel' (such as might occur at a conference), you should use the term *kru*-hly stil, 'round table' (круглий стіл), because na pa-*ne*-li (на панелі) is a phrase applied to prostitutes on the lookout for clients.

FOOD

ЗА МІСТОМ
IN THE COUNTRY

CAMPING ПІД НАМЕТАМИ

Camping as a leisure activity for families is only becoming popular. For schoolchildren, however, the most common way of spending part of the summer holidays is at a summer camp. Camp sites are usually located on the edge of major cities and can be difficult to get to by public transport. It is also possible to organise camping during walking tours in the wilderness, especially in the mountains, where there are many free camp sites.

Where's the camping ground?
de *kem*-pinh? Де кемпінг?

May I camp here?
mo-zhna tut ro-*zby*-ty Можна тут розбити
ta-bir? табір?

How much is it per ...?	*skil'*-ky za ...?	Скільки за ...?
night	o-*dnu* nich	одну ніч
person	o-*so*-bu	особу
tent	na-*met*	намет
vehicle	ma-*shy*-nu	машину

Where's the office?
de kon-*to*-ra/ Де контора/
a-dmi-ni-*stra*-tsi-ya/ адміністрація/
dy-*rek*-tsi-ya? дирекція?

Where are the toilets?
de tu-a-*le*-ty? Де туалети?

Can we light a fire?
chy *mo*-zhna roz-*kla*-sty Чи можна розкласти
ba-*hat*-tya/vo-*hon*? багаття/вогонь?

Where can I get water?
de *mo*-zhna na-*bra*-ty Де можна набрати
vo-*dy*? води?

backpack	ryug-*zak*/na-*plech*-nyk	рюкзак/наплечник
campfire	*vo*-hny-shche	вогнище
camping	ta-bo-ru-*van*-nya	табрування
camp site	*ta*-bir	табір
can opener	vid-kry-*vach*-ka	відкривачка
compass	*kom*-pas	компас
hammer	mo-lo-*tok*	молоток
hut	kha-*tyn*-ka/	хатинка/
	bu-*dy*-no-chok	будиночок
map	*kar*-ta	карта
mattress	ma-*trats*	матрац
rope	shnur/ka-*nat*/tros	шнур/канат/трос
rucksack	ryug-*zak*	рюкзак
sleeping bag	*spal'*-ny mi-*shok*	спальний мішок
tent pegs	kil-*ky*	кілки
tent	na-*met*	намет
torch	li-*khta*-ryk	ліхтарик
trail	*stezh*-ka	стежка
water bottle	*plya*-shka na *vo*-du	пляшка на воду
well (n)	kry-*ny*-tsya	криниця

MUSHROOMS & BERRIES

The Ukrainian forests are home to a great variety of mushrooms, berries and hazelnuts. That is why mushrooming and picking berries and nuts are favourite pastimes. If you are experienced, you can try participating in this activity and you'll get a lot of enjoyment from it. However, if you want to play it safe, don't pick them in industrial regions, but rather choose some remote areas. Among Ukrainians, it's quite popular to buy mushrooms and berries at the market because they are fresh and cheaper than in the shops.

berries	*ya*-ho-dy	ягоди
(hazel)nuts	(li-so-*vi*) ho-*ri*-khy	(лісові) горіхи
mushroom(s)	hryb/hry-*by*	гриб/гриби
to gather mushrooms	zby-*ra*-ty	збирати
	hry-*by*	гриби

HIKING

ПІШОХІДНИЙ ТУРИЗМ

Hiking – as well as mountaineering and caving – at all levels of difficulty is quite popular and well organised. However, Ukraine has yet to develop hiking as a tourist activity for foreign visitors.

Where can I find out
about hiking trails?

de *mo*-zhna di-*zna*-tys' pro
tu-ry-*stych*-ni mar-*shru*-ty?

Де можна дізнатись про
туристичні маршрути?

I'd like to talk to someone
who knows this area.

ya [kho-*tiw* by/kho-*ti*-la b]
po-ho-vo-*ry*-ty z *ky*-mos',
khto *zna*-ye tsyu
mi-*stse*-vist' (m/f)

Я [хотів би/хотіла б]
поговорити з кимось,
хто знає цю
місцевість.

Is this path safe?

tsya *stezh*-ka bez-*pech*-na?

Ця стежка безпечна?

Do we need a guide?

nam po-*trib*-ny
pro-vi-*dnyk*?

Нам потрібний
провідник?

How long is the trail?

ya-*ka* dow-zhy-*na* ts'o-ho
mar-*shru*-tu?

Яка довжина цього
маршруту?

Is the track well marked?

stezh-ka *do*-bre
po-*zna*-che-na?

Стежка добре
позначена?

How high is the climb?

yak *vy*-so-ko yde
tsey pid-*yom*?

Як високо йде
цей підйом?

Which is the shortest/
easiest route?

ko-*try* mar-*shrut*
nay-ko-*rot*-shy/
nay-*leh*-shy?

Котрий маршрут
найкоротший/
найлегший?

Is the path open?
    tsya *stezh*-ka vid-*kry*-ta?   Ця стежка відкрита?
When does it get dark?
    o ko-*triy* ho-*dy*-ni te-*mni*-ye?   О котрій годині темніє?
Where can I buy supplies?
    de *mo*-zhna di-*sta*-ty   Де можна дістати
    za-*pa*-sy?   запаси?

THE VILLAGE

If you're invited to visit a village, you should take the opportunity. You'll be the centre of attention and the object of sincere and generous hospitality. Ukrainian villages differ from region to region, but they're picturesque and neat, notwithstanding the economic hardship of recent years. The black soil, chor-no-*zem* (чорнозем), is a revelation. You will discover what tomatoes really taste like (and corn, and cucumbers, and strawberries, and all the other wonders that people have in their back gardens). You'll see apple, pear and walnut trees growing to their natural size, share the muddy streets with ducks and geese, and visit houses that inside can be like museums of folk art, especially in the Carpathian region.

You may warm yourself at the traditional wood stove, drink water drawn from a well, and sleep under incredibly soft and sweet-smelling goose-down quilts. You may stroll to a nearby lake, stream or forest, and in Western Ukraine you'll certainly inspect the local church.

'Green' tourism is becoming more and more popular. Note, however, that in the villages the facilities can be found outdoors.

On the Path

На стежці

Please tell me the way to ...
  po-ka-*zhit'*, bud' *la*-ska,
  do-*ro*-hu do ...

Покажіть, будь ласка,
дорогу до ...

Does this path go to ...?
  chy tsya *stezh*-ka
  ve-*de* do ...?

Чи ця стежка
веде до ...?

Is it far to the ...?	chy da-*le*-ko do ...?	Чи далеко до ...?
ancient temple	sta-ro-*vyn*-no-ho *khra*-mu	старовинного храму
beach	*plya*-zhu	пляжу
castle	*zam*-ku	замку
cave	pe-*che*-ry	печери
cemetery	*tsvyn*-ta-rya/ kla-do-*vy*-shcha	цвинтаря/ кладовища
forest	*li*-su	лісу
gorge	u-*shche*-ly-ny	ущелини
lake	*o*-ze-ra	озера
mountain(s)	ho-*ry*/hir	гори/гір
national park	za-po-*vi*-dny-ka	заповідника
river	ri-*ky*	ріки
sanatorium	sa-na-*to*-ri-yu	санаторію
sea shore	be-re-ha *mo*-rya	берега моря
spring	dzhe-re-*la*	джерела
summer house	*da*-chi	дачі
top/foot of the mountain	ver-*shy*-ny/ pi-*dnizh*-zhya ho-*ry*	вершини/ підніжжя гори
town	*mi*-sta	міста
village	se-*la*	села
waterfall	vo-do-*spa*-du	водоспаду

How many hours will it take?
    skil'-ky ho-*dyn* tse zay-*me*?   Скільки годин це займе?

Are there signs?
    chy tam ye wka-zi-wny-*ky*/   Чи там є вказівники/
    zna-ky?   знаки?

How many kilometres?
    skil'-ky ki-lo-*me*-triw?   Скільки кілометрів?

I'm lost.
    ya za-hu-*by*-wsya/   Я загубився/
    za-hu-*by*-la-sya (m/f)   загубилася.

Is the water safe to drink?
    tsyu *vo*-du *mo*-zhna *py*-ty?   Цю воду можна пити?

I DO!

Ukrainian folk culture is best preserved in the villages. The folk wedding was associated with elaborate rituals, some of which are still widely observed. A wedding bread, ko-ro-*vay* (коровай), is baked and the bride and groom each invite their guests in person, usually some hundreds of them, by going house to house.

The bride and groom sometimes wear ornate traditional costume at the wedding ceremony, although Western bridal dress is much more common today. In church, the bridal couple stands on an embroidered ritual cloth called ru-shnyk (рушник).

The reception is lavish and may continue over several days. Guests queue up to present the bride and groom with gifts of money. It's usual for the young men present to 'kidnap' the bride and for the groom to pay a 'ransom', *vy*-kup (викуп).

The resources required for a full-scale wedding are enormous and not easily marshalled except in a village community. Nonetheless, some folk customs are often incorporated into urban weddings.

Directions

		Вказівки
Which way?	ku-*dy*?	Куди?
By which road?	ya-*ko*-yu do-*ro*-ho-yu?	Якою дорогою?
Left.	li-*vo*-ruch	Ліворуч.
Right.	pra-*vo*-ruch	Праворуч.
Straight ahead.	*prya*-mo	Прямо.
Back.	na-*zad*	Назад.
Past the village.	powz se-*lo*	Повз село.
Before the village.	*pe*-red se-*lom*	Перед селом.
To the east.	na skhid	На схід.
To the west.	na *za*-khid	На захід.
To the north.	na *piw*-nich	На північ.
To the south.	na *piw*-den'	На південь.

AT THE BEACH   НА ПЛЯЖІ

The shores of the Black Sea, and especially the south coast of Crimea, are a favourite summer holiday destination. The Crimean peninsula is a unique place, with mountains, picturesque sea views and healthy air, and offering all sorts of recreational activities. The best-known Crimean resorts include Yalta, Alupka, Hurzuf and Alushta. The coast there is dotted with guesthouses and sanatoriums – as with many Eastern Europeans, Ukrainians like to think of their holidays as opportunities for a health cure. Many holiday-makers also rent private rooms, apartments or houses.

Can we swim here?	
tut *mo*-zhna *pla*-va-ty?	Тут можна плавати?
Is it safe to swim here?	
tut bez-*pech*-no *pla*-va-ty?	Тут безпечно плавати?
What time is high/low tide?	
ko-*ly* pry-*plyw*/vid-*plyw*?	Коли приплив/відплив?
Where can we change?	
de *mo*-zhna pe-re-wdya-*hnu*-ty-sya?	Де можна перевдягнутися?

coast	*be*-reh	берег
fishing	ry-*bal'*-stvo	рибальство
reef	ryf	риф
rock	ska-*la*	скала
sand	pi-*sok*	пісок
sea	*mo*-re	море
snorkelling	*pla*-van-nya z *ma*-sko-yu	плавання з маскою
sunblock	krem vid *son*-tsya	крем від сонця
sunglasses	*te*-mni o-ku-*lya*-ry	темні окуляри
surf	pry-*biy*	прибій
swimming	*pla*-van-nya	плавання
towel	ru-*shnyk*	рушник
waterskiing	*vo*-dni *ly*-zhi	водні лижі
wave(s)	*khvy*-lya/*khvy*-li	хвиля/хвилі
windsurfing	vind-*ser*-finh	вінд-серфінг

TAKING A DIP

The Crimean beaches are mostly pebbly and need to be negotiated in footwear. During the holiday season there's a great deal to do at the coast in addition to swimming, snorkelling, sunbathing and boating: the resorts have extensive entertainment and cultural programs, and holiday-makers can enjoy a hectic social life if they so choose. The mountainous hinterland is picturesque, and sightseeing excursions are plentiful.

WEATHER   ПОГОДА

In summer the temperature can climb to 35°C. If you prefer the cold, go in winter when the temperature can range from -2°C right down to -30°C. The thermometer manages to climb to just above zero in March and November – bring an umbrella. Spring is in the air in April but there can be sharp changes in temperature. The best months for a visit are undoubtedly May and September. It's warm, but not too hot, and it doesn't rain very often. Moreover, the lilac and the chestnut trees, for which Kyiv is famous, are in bloom. pry-izh-*dzhay*-te do *ky*-e-va w *traw*-ni (Приїжджайте до Києва в травні), 'Come to Kyiv in May'.

It's ...

bright	*svi*-tlo	Світло.
cold	*kho*-lo-dno	Холодно.
cool	pro-kho-*lo*-dno	Прохолодно.
damp	vo-*lo*-ho	Волого.
dark	*te*-mno	Темно.
hot	*zhar*-ko	Жарко.
humid	*sy*-ro	Сиро.
raining	i-*de* doshch	Іде дощ.
snowing	i-*de* snih	Іде сніг.
sunny	s'o-*ho*-dni	Сьогодні
	so-nyach-ny den'	сонячний день.
windy outside	na *vu*-ly-tsi *vi*-ter	На вулиці вітер.

What will the weather be like today?
ya-*ka* s'o-*ho*-dni *bu*-de po-*ho*-da?

Яка сьогодні буде погода?

What's the forecast for tomorrow?
ya-*ky* pro-*hnoz* po-*ho*-dy na *za*-wtra?

Який прогноз погоди на завтра?

What's the temperature?
ya-*ka* tem-pe-ra-*tu*-ra?;
skil'-ky s'o-*ho*-dni *hra*-du-siw?

Яка температура?;
Скільки сьогодні градусів?

It's plus/minus 10 outside today.

	s'o-*ho*-dni na *vu*-ly-tsi plyus/*mi*-nus *de*-syat'	Сьогодні на вулиці плюс/мінус десять.

I'm...	me-*ni* ...	Мені ...
cold	*kho*-lo-dno	холодно
hot	*zhar*-ko	жарко
warm	*te*-plo	тепло

black ice	o-zhe-*le*-dy-tsya	ожеледиця
cold (n)	*kho*-lod	холод
dawn	svi-*ta*-nok	світанок
degree	*hra*-dus	градус
downpour	*zly*-va	злива
dusk	*pry*-smerk	присмерк
fog	tu-*man*	туман
hail	hrad	град
hoarfrost	*i*-niy	іній
hot weather	*spe*-ka	спека
ice	lid	лід
lightning	*bly*-skaw-ka	блискавка
rain	doshch	дощ
snow	snih	сніг
storm	*bu*-rya	буря
sunrise	skhid *son*-tsya	схід сонця
sunset	*za*-khid *son*-tsya	захід сонця
thunder	hrim	грім
thunderstorm	hro-*za*	гроза

FAUNA ФАУНА

animal	tva-*ry*-na	тварина
wild animal	zvir	звір
bear	ve-*dmid'*	ведмідь
beaver	bo-*ber*	бобер
bison	zubr	зубр
cat	kit	кіт
deer	*o*-len'	олень
dog	so-*ba*-ka/pes	собака/пес

elk	los'	лось
fox	ly-*sy*-tsya	лисиця
hare	*za*-yets'	заєць
squirrel	*bil*-ka	білка
wolf	vowk	вовк

BIRDS · ПТАХИ

bird	ptakh	птах
crane	zhu-ra-*vel'*	журавель
crow	vo-*ro*-na	ворона
cuckoo	zo-*zu*-lya	зозуля
duck	*kach*-ka	качка
finch	sni-*hur*	снігур
goose	*hus*-ka	гуска
owl	so-*va*	сова
pigeon	*ho*-lub	голуб
seagull	*chay*-ka	чайка
sparrow	ho-ro-*bets'*	горобець
stork	le-*le*-ka	лелека
swan	*le*-bid'	лебідь
tit	sy-*ny*-tsya	синиця
woodpecker	*dya*-tel	дятел

INSECTS & OTHER CREATURES · КОМАХИ ТА ІНШЕ

ant	mu-*ra*-shka	мурашка
bee	bdzho-*la*	бджола
fly	*mu*-kha	муха
insect	ko-*ma*-kha	комаха
jellyfish	me-*du*-za	медуза
lizard	*ya*-shchir-ka	ящірка
mosquito	ko-*mar*	комар
snake	zmi-*ya*	змія
spider	pa-*vuk*	павук
wasp	o-*sa*	оса

FLORA

ФЛОРА

birch	be-*re*-za	береза
bush	kushch	кущ
bramble	o-*zhy*-na	ожина
camomile	ro-*ma*-shka	ромашка
carnation	hvo-*zdy*-ka	гвоздика
chestnut	ka-*shtan*	каштан
cornflower	vo-*lo*-shka	волошка
cranberry bush	zhu-raw-*ly*-na	журавлина
fir	ya-*ly*-na	ялина

GREEN SUMMER CIRCLES

Most larger cities are encircled by a recreational belt where people have summer houses. A summer house, da-cha (дача), can be anything from a humble shack to a large and ostentatious villa. Many city-dwellers use the land around their summer houses for growing fruit and vegetables to reduce their living costs and ensure a supply of fresh greens.

flower	*kvi*-tka	квітка
gladiolus	hla-di-*o*-lus	гладіолус
grass	tra-*va*	трава
guelder-rose	ka-*ly*-na	калина
lilac	bu-*zok*	бузок
lily	*li*-li-ya	лілія
lily of the valley	kon-*va*-li-ya	конвалія
linden	*ly*-pa	липа
narcissus	nar-*tsys*	нарцис
oak	dub	дуб
pine	so-*sna*	сосна
poplar	to-*po*-lya	тополя
poppy	mak	мак
rose	tro-*yan*-da	троянда
tree	*de*-re-vo	дерево
walnut tree	vo-*los*'-ky ho-*rikh*	волоський горіх
willow	ver-*ba*	верба

THE WET & THE WILD

Most of Ukraine consists of flat lowlands and uplands, except for the Carpathian Mountains in the west and the Crimean Mountains along the southern coast of the peninsula. The mountains are not very high – the highest peak in Ukraine, Hoverla (Говерла) in the Carpathians, is 2061 metres above sea level.

Three great bands of natural vegetation stretch from east to west. In the north you'll find forest, both deciduous and coniferous, in the middle a mixture of steppe and forest – Ukrainian has a special word for this: li-so-*step* (лісостеп) – and in the south the steppe. The steppe, of course, is the landscape of tall grasses most closely associated with the activities of the Ukrainian Cossacks (from the 16th to the 18th century).

Two large rivers, the Dnipro (often written 'Dnieper' in English) and the Dnister, as well as several smaller ones flow into the Black Sea. The long inlets into which these rivers flow are called ly-*ta*-ny (лимани). The Dnipro, on which Kyiv is situated, is rich in historical associations. Its lower course used to be interrupted by a series of great cascades, the Porohy, po-*ro*-hy (Пороги). The Cossacks had their headquarters, the Sich, sich (Січ), downstream from the cascades, za po-*ro*-ha-my (за порогами), and were thus also called the Zaporozhtsi.

Today one of the large industrial cities along the Dnipro bears the name Zaporizhzhya, za-po-*rizh*-zhya (Запоріжжя), but the Porohy have disappeared beneath huge artificial lakes – Ukrainians refer to them as seas – created by damming the Dnipro.

GEO GROUPS

cascade	po-*ro*-hy	пороги
estuary	ly-*man*	лиман
Dnipro estuary	dni-*prow*-s'ky	Дніпровський
	ly-*man*	лиман
lake	o-ze-ro	озеро
mountain(s)	ho-*ra*/ho-ry	гора/гори
Carpathian Mountains	kar-*pa*-ty	Карпати
Crimean Mountains	*kryms'*-ki *ho*-ry	Кримські гори
Hoverla	ho-*ver*-la	Говерла
reservoir	vo-do-*skho*-vy-shche	водосховище
river	ri-chka/ri-*ka*	річка/ріка
Dnipro/Dnieper	dni-*pro*	Дніпро
Dnister	dni-*ster*	Дністер
sea	*mo*-re	море
Black Sea	*chor*-ne *mo*-re	Чорне море
Sea of Azov	a-zow-s'ke *mo*-re	Азовське море
vegetation	ro-s*lyn*-nist'	рослинність
forest	lis	ліс
forest-steppe	li-so-*step*	лісостеп
steppe	step	степ

ЗДОРОВ'Я   HEALTH

Health-insurance requirements are subject to change, so be sure to clarify the issue with your travel agent or the embassy. Generally, all foreigners arriving in Ukraine have to take out compulsory emergency health cover. The premium depends on the intended length of the visit. Under this insurance, emergency care, including ambulance, is provided efficiently and to Western standards. Travellers should, however, have general health insurance to cover other health needs.

In addition to the state health-care system, which is free but short of resources, there are many private health professionals and centres, which charge fees comparable to those in Western countries.

If you require regular medication, take sufficient supplies with you, together with a note for the customs officials. You should also take any proprietary medicines, eg cough mixtures or headache tablets, because local pharmaceuticals have different names from the ones that you'll be familiar with.

Where's the nearest
chemist/hospital?
    de nay-*blyzh*-cha ap-*te*-ka/   Де найближча аптека/
    li-*kar*-nya?   лікарня?
Please call a doctor.
    vy-klych-te, bud' *la*-ska,   Викличте, будь ласка,
    li-ka-rya   лікаря.
Is there a doctor here?
    tut ye *li*-kar?   Тут є лікар?

OH WHAT A TRILL!

Remember that the r, represented in Cyrillic script by the character p, is always pronounced as a trilled 'r'.

HEALTH

AT THE DOCTOR У ЛІКАРЯ

I feel ill.
me-*ni* po-*ha*-no — Мені погано.

My friend has fallen ill.
miy druh za-khvo-*riw* (m); — Мій друг захворів;
mo-*ya* *po*-dru-ha — Моя подруга
za-khvo-*ri*-la (f) — захворіла.

I feel sick. (nauseous)
me-*ne nu*-dyt' — Мене нудить.

It hurts here.
u *me*-ne bo-*lyt'* tut — У мене болить тут.

I have a pain in the ...u *me*-ne bo-*lyt'* ... У мене болить ...

ear	*vu*-kho	вухо
head	ho-lo-*va*	голова
liver	pe-*chin*-ka	печінка
stomach/belly	zhy-*vit*	живіт
throat	*hor*-lo	горло
tooth	zub	зуб

(See also Parts of the Body, page 208.)

SIGNS

АПТЕКА	CHEMIST/PHARMACY
ТРАВМПУНКТ	EMERGENCY
МЕДПУНКТ	FIRST-AID POINT
ПОЛІКЛІНІКА	HEALTH CENTRE
ЛІКАРНЯ	HOSPITAL
ПРИЙМАЛЬНІ ГОДИНИ	OPENING HOURS
АПТЕЧНИЙ КІОСК	PHARMACY KIOSK
РЕЦЕПТУРНИЙ	PRESCRIPTIONS
РЕЄСТРАТУРА	REGISTRATION

HEALTH

I've caught a cold.
 ya za-stu-*dyw*-sya/
 za-stu-*dy*-la-sya (m/f)

Я застудився/
застудилася.

I have a temperature.
 u *me*-ne tem-pe-ra-*tu*-ra

У мене температура.

I have a sharp/dull pain
in my chest.
 ya vid-chu-*va*-yu *ho*-stry/
 tu-*py* bil' u *hru*-dyakh

Я відчуваю гострий/
тупий біль у грудях.

I've burned myself.
 ya ob-*pik*-sya/
 ob-pe-*kla*-sya (m/f)

Я обпікся/
обпеклася.

I have food poisoning.
 u *me*-ne khar-cho-*ve*
 o-*tru*-yen-nya

У мене харчове
отруєння.

He/She has been   u *nyo*-ho/*ne*-yi   У нього/неї
poisoned by ...   o-*tru*-yen-nya ...   отруєння ...
  medicine   *li*-ka-my   ліками
  mushrooms   hry-*ba*-my   грибами
  tinned food   kon-*ser*-va-my   консервами

It's difficult for   me-*ni vazh*-ko ...   Мені важко ...
me to ...
  breathe   *dy*-kha-ty   дихати
  swallow   kow-*ta*-ty   ковтати
  walk   kho-*dy*-ty   ходити

I can't sleep/walk.
 ya ne *mo*-zhu *spa*-ty/
 kho-*dy*-ty

Я не можу спати/
ходити.

I've been stung by ...
 me-*ne* u-*zha*-lyw/
 u-*zha*-ly-la ... (m/f)

Мене ужалив/
ужалила ...

I've been bitten by ...
 me-*ne* wku-*syw*/
 wku-*sy*-la ... (m/f)

Мене вкусив/
вкусила ...

HEALTH

THE DOCTOR MAY ASK ...

shcho z *va*-my?
  What's the matter?

Що з Вами?

vy vid-chu-*va*-ye-te bil'?
  Do you feel any pain?

Ви відчуваєте біль?

de bo-*lyt*'?
  Where does it hurt?

Де болить?

u vas men-stru-*a*-tsi-ya?
  Are you menstruating?

У Вас менструація?

u vas tem-pe-ra-*tu*-ra?
  Do you have a
  temperature?

У Вас температура?

yak *dow*-ho tse u vas?
  How long have you
  been like this?

Як довго це у Вас?

u vas tse wzhe bu-*lo*?
  Have you had this
  before?

У Вас це вже було?

vy pry-*ma*-ye-te *li*-ky?
  Are you on
  medication?

Ви приймаєте ліки?

vy *pa*-ly-te?
  Do you smoke?

Ви палите?

vy wzhy-*va*-ye-te
al-ko-*hol*'?
  Do you drink?

Ви вживаєте
алкоголь?

vy wzhy-*va*-ye-te
nar-*ko*-ty-ky?
  Do you take drugs?

Ви вживаєте
наркотики?

u vas a-ler-*hi*-ya na
bud' shcho?
  Are you allergic to
  anything?

У Вас алергія на
будь-що?

vy va-*hit*-ni?
  Are you pregnant?

Ви вагітні?

You need ...	vam ne-ob-*khid*-no ...	Вам необхідно ...
an examination	zro-*by*-ty ob-*ste*-zhen-nya	зробити обстеження
an injection	zro-*by*-ty i-*nyek*-tsi-yu	зробити ін'єкцію
an operation	zro-*by*-ty o-pe-*ra*-tsi-yu	зробити операцію
to submit samples	*zda*-ty a-*na*-li-zy	здати аналізи
to have your blood pressure taken	po-*mi*-rya-ty tysk (*kro*-vi)	поміряти тиск (крові)

Take this ...	*vy*-py-te ...	Випийте ...
tablet	tsyu ta-*ble*-tku	цю таблетку
mixture	tsyu miks-*tu*-ru	цю мікстуру
powder	tsey po-ro-*shok*	цей порошок

I'll write you a prescription.

   ya *vy*-py-shu vam re-*tsept* — Я випишу Вам рецепт.

You must take it with water.

   tre-ba za-*py*-ty vo-*do*-yu — Треба запити водою.

You must take the medicine three times a day.

   vam *tre*-ba pry-*ma*-ty *li*-ky *try*-chi na den' — Вам треба приймати ліки тричі на день.

Order this medicine at the chemist.

   za-*mow*-te tsi *li*-ky v ap-*te*-tsi. — Замовте ці ліки в аптеці.

HEALTH

HEALTH

AILMENTS ХВОРОБИ

English	Pronunciation	Ukrainian
I have (a/an) ...	u *me*-ne ...	У мене ...
I've had (a/an) ...	u *me*-ne buw/bu-*la*/ bu-*lo* ... (m/f/neut)	У мене був/була/ було ...
accident	ne-*shcha*-sny *vy*-pa-dok	нещасний випадок
AIDS	snid	СНІД
appendicitis	a-pen-dy-*tsyt*	апендицит
asthma	*a*-stma	астма
burn	*o*-pik	опік
cold	za-*stu*-da	застуда
constipation	za-*por*	запор
cough	*ka*-shel'	кашель
diarrhoea	pro-*nos*	пронос
drug addiction	nar-ko-*ma*-ni-ya	наркоманія
fracture	pe-re-*lom*	перелом
heart attack	in-*farkt*	інфаркт
haemorrhage	kro-vo-*te*-cha	кровотеча
high blood pressure	hi-per-to-*ni*-ya; vy-*so*-ky tysk (*kro*-vi)	гіпертонія; високий тиск (крові)
illness	khvo-*ro*-ba	хвороба
indigestion	ne-*traw*-len-nya *shlun*-ku	нетравлення шлунку
infection	za-*ra*-zhen-nya/ in-*fek*-tsi-ya	зараження/ інфекція
inflammation	za-*pa*-len-nya	запалення
influenza	hryp	грип
injury	*traw*-ma	травма
low blood pressure	hi-po-to-*ni*-ya	гіпотонія
nausea	nu-*do*-ta	нудота
scratch	po-*drya*-py-na	подряпина
sprain	roz-*tya*-hnen-nya	розтягнення

stomach upset	*ro*-zlad	розлад
	shlun-ku	шлунку
stroke	in-*sul't*	інсульт
swelling	*na*-bryak	набряк
temperature	tem-pe-ra-*tu*-ra	температура
high	vy-*so*-ka	висока
low	nyz'-*ka*	низька
tonsillitis	an-*hi*-na	ангіна
ulcer	*vy*-raz-ka	виразка
sexually	ve-ne-*rych*-ne	венеричне
transmitted	za-*khvo*-ryu-van-nya	захворювання
disease		
worms	hly-*sty*	глисти
wound	*ra*-na	рана

healthy	zdo-*ro*-vy	здоровий
paralysis	pa-*ra*-lich	параліч
poisoning	o-*tru*-yen-nya	отруєння
pregnancy	va-*hi*-tnist'	вагітність
pus	hniy	гній
vomit (n)	blyu-*vo*-ta	блювота

WOMEN'S HEALTH

ЖІНКА ТА ЗДОРОВ'Я

I'd like to see a female doctor.

ya kho-*ti*-la b	Я хотіла
za-py-*sa*-tys-sya	б записатися
do li-*ka*-rya *zhin*-ky	до лікаря-жінки.

I'm pregnant.

ya va-*hi*-tna	Я вагітна.

I think I'm pregnant.

me-*ni* zda-*yet'*-sya, shcho	Мені здається, що
ya va-*hi*-tna	я вагітна.

I'm on the Pill.
  ya pry-*ma*-yu
  pro-ty-za-*plid*-ni
  ta-*ble*-tky

Я приймаю
протизаплідні
таблетки.

I haven't had my period
for ... weeks.
  u *me*-ne za-*trym*-ka
  (men-stru-*a*-tsi-yi)
  na ... *ty*-zhniw

У мене затримка
(менструації)
на ... тижнів.

I'd like to use contraception.
  ya kho-*ti*-la b u-zhy-*va*-ty
  pro-ty-za-*plid*-ni
  za-so-by

Я хотіла б уживати
протизаплідні
засоби.

I'd like to have a pregnancy test.
  zro-*bit'* me-ni,
  bud' *la*-ska,
  a-*na*-liz na va-*hi*-tnist'

Зробіть мені,
будь ласка,
аналіз на вагітність.

abortion	a-*bort*	аборт
diaphragm	di-a-*frah*-ma	діафрагма
mammogram	ma-mo-*hra*-ma	мамограма
menstruation	men-stru-*a*-tsi-ya	менструація
miscarriage	*vy*-ky-den'	викидень
pap smear	ma-*zok shy*-ky	мазок шийки
	ma-tky	матки
period pain	men-stru-*al'*-ni	менструальні
	bo-li	болі
the Pill	pro-ty-za-*plid*-ni	протизаплідні
	ta-*ble*-tky	таблетки
ultrasound	ul'-tra-zvu-ko-*ve*	ультразвукове
	ob-*ste*-zhen-nya	обстеження

IUD
  vnu-trish-n'o-*ma*-tko-va spi-*ral'*
  внутрішньоматкова спіраль
premenstrual tension
  pe-red-men-stru-*al'*-ny syn-*drom*
  передменструальний синдром

ALTERNATIVE TREATMENTS
НЕТРАДИЦІЙНА МЕДИЦИНА

HEALTH

Many Ukrainians use folk remedies in the treatment of common complaints, so if you catch a cold, your friends are likely to make suggestions involving garlic, onion, honey or raspberry tea. People will often try these before turning to pharmaceuticals. Antibiotics are much less frequently prescribed than in Western countries. In addition, many alternative therapies exotic to Ukraine enjoy considerable popularity. Some mainstream medical practitioners also recommend alternative healing methods.

acupuncture	a-ku-punk-*tu*-ra	акупунктура
homeopathy	ho-me-o-*pa*-ti-ya	гомеопатія
massage	ma-*sazh*	масаж
meditation	me-dy-*ta*-tsi-ya	медитація
reflexology	re-fle-kso-*lo*-hi-ya	рефлексологія
yoga	*yo*-ha	йога

IT'S A MIRACLE!

One of the remarkable social phenomena of the late 1980s was the popularity of people claiming to possess abnormal psychic powers, including those of faith healing. Some faith healers purported to heal huge crowds assembled in football stadiums, or even TV audiences watching at home. The word coined for such psychics is eks-tra-*sens* (екстрасенс), derived from 'extrasensory'.

HEALTH

PARTS OF THE BODY   ЧАСТИНИ ТІЛА

English	Pronunciation	Ukrainian
belly	zhy-*vit*	живіт
blood	krow	кров
bone	*kist*-ka	кістка
brain	*mo*-zok	мозок
bronchial tubes	*bron*-khy	бронхи
chest/breast	*hru*-dy (pl)	груди
elbow	*li*-kot'	лікоть
face	o-*blych*-chya	обличчя
finger	*pa*-lets'	палець
gland	*za*-lo-za	залоза
gums	*ya*-sna	ясна
hand	ru-*ka*	рука
heart	*ser*-tse	серце
hip	ste-*hno*	стегно
joint	su-*hlob*	суглоб
kidney	*nyr*-ka	нирка
knee	ko-*li*-no	коліно
leg	no-*ha*	нога
lip	hu-*ba*	губа
liver	pe-*chin*-ka	печінка
lungs	le-*he*-ni (pl)	легені
mouth	rot	рот
muscle	myaz	м'яз
neck	*shy*-a	шия
nose	nis	ніс
pancreas	pid-shlun-*ko*-va *za*-lo-za	підшлункова залоза
rib	re-*bro*	ребро
shoulder	ple-*che*	плече
side	bik	бік
skin	*shki*-ra	шкіра
spine	khre-*bet*	хребет
stomach	*shlu*-nok	шлунок
throat	*hor*-lo	горло
toe	*pa*-lets' na no-*zi*	палець на нозі
tongue	ya-*zyk*	язик
tooth	zub	зуб

HEALTH

SPECIAL HEALTH NEEDS

СПЕЦІАЛЬНІ ПОТРЕБИ

I have ... — u *me*-ne ... — У мене ...
- diabetes — di-a-*bet* — діабет
- epilepsy — e-pi-*le*-psiya — епілепсія
- high blood pressure — hi-per-to-*ni*-ya — гіпертонія
- rheumatism — rew-ma-*tyzm* — ревматизм

I have an allergy to antibiotics.
u *me*-ne a-ler-*hi*-ya na an-ty-bi-*o*-ty-ky

У мене алергія на антибіотики.

I have my own syringe.
u *me*-ne ye *wla*-sny shpryts

У мене є власний шприц.

My insulin has run out.
u *me*-ne za-kin-*chyw*-sya in-su-*lin*

У мене закінчився інсулін.

I'm taking ... — ya pry-*ma*-yu ... — Я приймаю ...
- hormone pills — hor-mo-*nal'*-ni ta-*ble*-tky — гормональні таблетки
- contraceptive pills — pro-ty-za-*plid*-ni ta-*ble*-tky — протизаплідні таблетки
- painkillers — zne-*bo*-lyu-val'-ni ta-*ble*-tky — знеболювальні таблетки

HEALTH

AT THE CHEMIST   В АПТЕЦІ

Tampons and condoms are obtainable in the kiosks that line the
streets, but it's best to check the wrapping and the use-by date
before buying.

I need something for ...
   me-*ni* po-*trib*-ne   Мені потрібне
   shchos' vid ...   щось від ...
Do I need a prescription for ...?
   chy me-*ni* po-*tri*-ben   Чи мені потрібен
   re-*tsept* dlya ...?   рецепт для ...?
How many times a day?
   skil'-ky ra-*ziw* na den'?   Скільки разів на день?
When will my medicine be ready?
   ko-*ly bu*-dut'   Коли будуть
   ho-*to*-vi mo-*yi li*-ky?   готові мої ліки?

antibiotic	an-ty-bi-*o*-tyk	антибіотик
antiseptic	an-ty-*se*-ptyk	антисептик
bandage	bynt	бинт
condom	pre-ze-rva-*tyw*	презерватив
contraceptives	pro-ty-za-*plid*-ni	протизаплідні
	za-so-by	засоби
cotton wool	*va*-ta	вата
cough mixture	mik-*stu*-ra vid	мікстура від
	ka-shlyu	кашлю
... cream	krem ...	крем ...
face	dlya o-*blych*-chya	для обличчя
hand	dlya ruk	для рук
shaving	dlya ho-*lin*-nya	для гоління
nappies/diapers	*pam*-per-sy	памперси
painkillers	zne-*bo*-lyu-val'-ni	знеболювальні
plaster (sticking)	*pla*-styr	пластир
razor blades	*le*-za	леза
shampoo	sham-*pun'*	шампунь
soap	*my*-lo	мило
tampons	tam-*po*-ny	тампони
toothbrush	zub-*na shchi*-tka	зубна щітка
toothpaste	zub-*na pa*-sta	зубна паста
vitamins	vi-ta-*mi*-ny	вітаміни

HEALTH

AT THE DENTIST

I have a toothache.
   u *me*-ne bo-*lyt'* zub
A filling has fallen out.
   u *me*-ne *vy*-pa-la
   plom-ba
Please give me an anaesthetic.
   zro-*bit'*, bud' *la*-ska,
   zne-*bo*-lyu-van-nya
This tooth has to be taken out.
   tsey zub *tre*-ba
   vy-da-ly-ty
I don't want it extracted.
   ya ne *kho*-chu yo-*ho*
   vy-ry-*va*-ty/vy-da-*lya*-ty

У СТОМАТОЛОГА

У мене болить зуб.

У мене випала
пломба.

Зробіть, будь ласка,
знеболювання.

Цей зуб треба
видалити.

Я не хочу його
виривати/видаляти.

BETTER SAFE THAN SORRY

Many people in Ukraine do not drink tap water without boiling it first, or use bottled or spring water. In Kyiv, artesian wells have been sunk in many parts of the city, and attractive gazebos built over them. People queue up here to get their supply of free spring water. Many apartments have water filters installed. Travellers should take no more risks with water than the local people.

Many residents of Ukraine are concerned about the long-term effects on their health of the Chornobyl nuclear disaster, and of the polluted state of the environment more generally. The statistical incidence of cancers has increased since Chornobyl. But there are no preventive measures that can easily be taken (except for respite periods in environmentally clean locations). A degraded environment is generally recognised as one of the causes of the alarmingly low life expectancy in Ukraine (62 years for men, 74 years for women).

AT THE OPTOMETRIST   В ОКУЛІСТА

HEALTH

I need to get my [glasses;
contact lenses] fixed.

   me-*ni* po-*trib*-no   Мені потрібно
   po-*la*-ho-dy-ty [o-ku-*lya*-ry;   полагодити [окуляри;
   kon-*takt*-ni *lin*-zy]   контакті лінзи].

I need to order some
[glasses; contact lenses].

   me-*ni* po-*trib*-no   Мені потрібно
   za-*mo*-vy-ty [o-ku-*lya*-ry;   замовити [окуляри;
   kon-*takt*-ni *lin*-zy]   контакті лінзи].

When will my [glasses;
contact lenses] be ready?

   ko-*ly bu*-dut' ho-*to*-vi   Коли будуть готові
   mo-*yi* [o-ku-*lya*-ry;   мої [окуляри;
   kon-*takt*-ni *lin*-zy]?   контакті лінзи]?

СПЕЦІАЛЬНІ ПОТРЕБИ
SPECIFIC NEEDS

DISABLED TRAVELLERS

ПОДОРОЖУВАННЯ ДЛЯ ІНВАЛІДІВ

Nowadays Ukrainians are more aware of the presence of disabled people in the community, and of their needs. The government has found resources to support the Paralympic movement. Nevertheless, it's still not easy for unaccompanied disabled people to travel in Ukraine. There are few access ramps, urban public transport is not well adapted to wheelchair use, metro stations have escalators rather than lifts, and there are almost no specialised taxis.

I'm disabled.
  ya [in-va-*lid;*
  ne-pow-no-*spraw*-ni/a] (m/f)

Я [інвалід; неповносправний/а].

I need assistance.
  me-*ni* po-*trib*-na
  do-po-*mo*-ha

Мені потрібна допомога.

What services do you have for disabled people?
  ya-*ki* u vas *po*-slu-hy
  dlya in-va-*li*-diw/
  ne-pow-no-*spraw*-nykh?

Які у вас послуги для інвалідів/ неповносправних?

Is there wheelchair access?
  chy ye *do*-stup dlya
  [in-va-*lid*-no-ho viz-*ka;*
  in-va-*lid*-no-yi ko-*lya*-sky]?

Чи є доступ для [інвалідного візка; інвалідної коляски]?

I'm deaf.
  ya hlu-*khy*

Я глухий.

I have a hearing aid.
  u *me*-ne slu-kho-*vy* a-pa-*rat*

У мене слуховий апарат.

Speak more loudly, please.
  pro-shu ho-vo-*ry*-ty
  ho-lo-*sni*-she

Прошу говорити голосніше.

Are guide dogs permitted?
  chy do-pu-*ska*-yut'-sya
  so-*ba*-ky po-vo-dy-*ri*?

Чи допускаються собаки-поводирі?

braille library	bi-bli-o-*te*-ka ma-te-ri-*a*-liw *bray*-liws'-kym *shryf*-tom	бібліотека матеріалів брайлівським шрифтом
disabled person	in-va-*lid;* ne-pow-no-*spraw*-ni/a (m/f)	інвалід; неповно-справний/а
guide dog	so-*ba*-ka po-vo-*dyr*	собака-поводир
wheelchair	in-va-*lid*-ny vi-*zok;* in-va-*li*-dna ko-*lya*-ska	інвалідний візок; інвалідна коляска

GAY TRAVELLERS
ПОДОРОЖУВАННЯ ДЛЯ ГОМОСЕКСУАЛІСТІВ

Ukrainian society has some familiarity with gay culture, but it is rather considered part of the 'bohemian' lifestyle. So, gay travellers should use their discretion and be prepared for conservative attitudes in most situations, and the following inquiries should be made only if you're confident that the person you're speaking to is understanding of gay people.

Is there a place where gay/lesbian people meet?

chy ye *mi*-stse, de zby-*ra*-yut'-sya [*he*-yi; ho-mo-sek-su-a-*li*-sty]/ les-bi-*yan*-ky?

Чи є місце, де збираються [геї; гомосексуалісти]/ лесбіянки?

Is there an organisation for gay/lesbian people?

chy ye or-ha-ni-*za*-tsi-ya dlya ho-mo-sek-su-a-*li*-stiw/ les-bi-*ya*-nok?

Чи є організація для гомосексуалістів/ лесбіянок?

Where I can buy some gay/lesbian publications?

de *mo*-zhna di-*sta*-ty vy-*dan*-nya dlya ho-mo-sek-su-a-*li*-stiw/ les-bi-*ya*-nok?

Де можна дістати видання для гомосексуалістів/ лесбіанок?

TRAVELLING WITH THE FAMILY
ПОДОРОЖУВАННЯ З ДІТЬМИ

Travelling with infants can be difficult. Locals normally rely on networks of family and friends. Special facilities for travellers with babies are not widely available in public places. If you're thinking about travelling by car, consider bringing your own child seat as these may not be widely available.

SPECIFIC NEEDS

Are there facilities for babies?

chy ye u-*mo*-vy dlya pe-re-pe-le-*nan*-nya i ho-du-*van*-nya ne-mo-*wlyat*?	Чи є умови для перепеленання і годування немовлят?

Do you have a child-minding service?

chy ye *sluzh*-ba *do*-hlya-du za *dit'*-my?	Чи є служба догляду за дітьми?

Where can I find a (English-speaking) babysitter?

de *mo*-zhna znay-*ty* (an-hlo-*mo*-wnu) *nyan'*-ku?	Де можна знайти (англомовну) няньку?

Are children allowed?

mo-zhna *bra*-ty zi so-*bo*-yu di-*tey*?	Можна брати зі собою дітей?

GET A HAIRCUT!

The chronicles of the medieval state of Kyiv Rus contain records of elaborate ceremonies at which a bishop would cut the hair of the prince's sons for the first time at the age of five or seven. In more modern times the Church stopped participating in the ritual, but it continued to be carried out, mainly by the child's father.

The age of the child at the first haircut ceremony, po-*stry*-zhy-ny (**постри́жини**), the procedure followed and the meaning attributed to the ritual varied from region to region. By WWI the custom was largely extinct.

Can you put an (extra)
bed/cot in the room?
    chy *mo*-zhna po-*sta*-vy-ty
    (do-*dat*-*ko*-ve) [*lizh*-ko;
    dy-*tya*-che *li*-zhe-chko]
    w *no*-me-ri?

Чи можна поставити
(додаткове) [ліжко;
дитяче ліжечко]
в номері?

I need a car with a child seat.
    me-*ni* po-*trib*-na ma-*shy*-na
    z dy-*tya*-chym sy-*din*-nyam.

Мені потрібна машина
з дитячим сидінням.

Is it suitable for children?
    tse pid-*kho*-dyt' *di*-tyam?

Це підходить дітям?

Do you have a children's menu?
    vy *ma*-ye-te me-*nyu*
    dlya di-*tey*?

Ви маєте меню
для дітей?

Are there any activities for children?
    u vas ye bud'-*ya*-*ki*
    za-*nyat*-tya dlya di-*tey*?

У вас є будь-які
заняття для дітей?

Is there a playground nearby?
    po-*bly*-zu ye dy-*tya*-chy
    may-*dan*-chyk?

Поблизу є дитячий
майданчик?

LOOKING FOR A JOB   ПОШУКИ РОБОТИ

Many Westerners live and work in Ukraine, especially in Kyiv.
The majority have been sent to Ukraine by foreign employers. It
can be difficult (though not impossible) for Westerners living in
Ukraine for extended periods to find jobs there. However, jobs
can be easier to find in areas where native knowledge of English
is an advantage, for example in teaching, big international com-
panies, journalism, advertising or public relations.

Where can I find local
job advertisements?
    de *mo*-zhna *znay*-ty
    o-ho-*lo*-shen-nya pro
    pry-*om* na ro-*bo*-tu?

Де можна знайти
оголошення про
прийом на роботу?

Do I need a work permit?
    me-*ni* po-*tri*-ben *do*-zvil
    na *pra*-tsyu?

Мені потрібен дозвіл
на працю?

I've had experience.
u *me*-ne *do*-svid *pra*-tsi

У мене досвід праці.

I've come about the position advertised.
ya u *spra*-vi o-ho-*lo*-shen-nya pro ro-*bo*-tu

Я у справі оголошення про роботу.

I'm ringing about the position advertised.
ya dzvo-*nyu* u *spra*-vi o-ho-*lo*-shen-nya pro ro-*bo*-tu

Я дзвоню у справі оголошення про роботу.

What's the wage?
ya-*ka* zar-*pla*-ta?

Яка зарплата?

Do I have to pay tax?
ya po-*vy*-nen/po-*vyn*-na pla-*ty*-ty po-*da*-tok? (m/f)

Я повинен/повинна платити податок?

SPECIFIC NEEDS

I can start ...	ya *mo*-zhu po-*cha*-ty ro-*bo*-tu ...	Я можу почати роботу ...
today	s'o-*ho*-dni	сьогодні
tomorrow	za-*wtra*	завтра
next week	na-*stup*-no-ho *ty*-zhnya	наступного тижня
from Monday	vid po-ne-*dil*-ka	від понеділка

employer	pra-tse-*da*-vets'	працедавець
employee	pra-tsiw-*nyk*	працівник
full-time/ part-time employee	pra-tsiw-*nyk*, ya-*ky* pra-*tsyu*-ye [na *pow*-nu/ ne-*pow*-nu *staw*-ku; *pow*-ny/ne-*pow*-ny ro-*bo*-chy *tyzh*-den']	працівник, який працює [на повну/ неповну ставку; повний/неповний робочий тиждень]
job	ro-*bo*-ta	робота
occupation/trade	spe-tsi-*al*'-nist'/ pro-*fe*-si-ya	спеціальність/ професія
resume/CV	re-zyu-*me*	резюме
traineeship/work experience	*prak*-ty-ka; *do*-svid ro-*bo*-ty	практика; досвід роботи

SPECIFIC NEEDS

ON BUSINESS

У СЛУЖБОВИХ СПРАВАХ

We're attending a ...	my pry-*i*-kha-ly na ...	Ми приїхали на ...
conference	kon-fe-*ren*-tsi-yu	конференцію
meeting	zyizd	з'їзд
trade fair	tor-*ho*-vy *yar*-ma-rok	торговий ярмарок

I'm on a course.

ya *wchu*-sya na *kur*-sakh — Я вчуся на курсах.

I have an appointment with ...

ya do-*mo*-vyw-sya z ...; — Я домовився з ...;
u *me*-ne pry-*zna*-che-no — У мене призначено
zu-strich z ... — зустріч з ...

ANGLICISMS

Since the fall of the USSR and the advent of globalisation, many new loan words have entered the Ukrainian language. Some words, such as kom-*pyu*-ter (комп'ютер), have been accepted into the language without resistance. Others are felt by many speakers to be quite foreign. The fields of computer technology and business are, as one would expect, most affected. Here are a few examples:

business	*bi*-znes	бізнес
distributor	dy-stry-*byu*-tor	дистриб'ютор
image	*i*-midzh	імідж
management	*me*-ne-dzhment	менеджмент
marketing/PR	mar-*ke*-tynh/ pi-*ar*	маркетинг/піар
computer	kom-*pyu*-ter	комп'ютер
file	fayl	файл
website	sayt	сайт

The word for the computer mouse, however, is the diminutive of the Ukrainian word for the small grey rodent:

mouse	*my*-shka	мишка

Here's my business card.
os' mo-*ya* vi-*zy*-tka

Ось моя візитка.

I need an interpreter.
me-*ni* po-*tri*-ben
pe-re-kla-*dach*

Мені потрібен
перекладач.

I'd like to use a computer.
me-*ni* *tre*-ba
po-pra-tsyu-*va*-ty
na kom-*pyu*-te-ri

Мені треба
попрацювати
на комп'ютері.

I'd like to send a/an
fax/email.
me-*ni* *tre*-ba *vy*-sla-ty
[faks; i-*meyl*/
e-lek-*tron*-nu *po*-shtu]

Мені треба вислати
[факс; імейл/
електронну пошту].

client	kli-*yent*	клієнт
colleague	ko-*le*-ha	колега
customer	po-ku-*pets'*	покупець
goods	to-*va*-ry	товари
manager	me-ne-*dzher*	менеджер
mobile phone	mo-*bil'*-ny te-le-*fon*	мобільний телефон
profit	pry-*bu*-tok	прибуток
receipt	chek	чек
salesperson	pro-da-*vets'*	продавець

PILGRIMAGE & RELIGION

ПРОЩІ ТА РЕЛІГІЯ

The main religion in Ukraine is Orthodox. Sober dress is essential if you're entering a church. Women can be asked to cover their heads. Worshippers may ask you to leave if they believe that you're acting without sufficient respect.

What's your religion?
do ya-*ko*-yi re-*li*-hi-yi vy
na-*le*-zhy-te?

До якої релігії ви
належите?

In the following list, the masculine form of the word appears first.

I'm ...	ya ...	Я ...
Buddhist	bud-*dyst*/	буддист/
	bud-*dys*-tka	буддистка
Christian	khry-sty-a-*nyn*/	християнин/
	khry-sty-*an*-ka	християнка
Orthodox	pra-vo-*slaw*-ny/	православний/
	pra-vo-*slaw*-na	православна
Greek	hre-ko-ka-*to*-lyk/	греко-католик/
Catholic	hre-ko-ka-to-*lych*-ka	греко-католичка
(Roman)	(ry-mo-)ka-*to*-lyk/	(римо-)католик/
Catholic	(ry-mo-)ka-to-*lych*-ka	(римо-)католичка
Hindu	in-du-*yist*/	індуїст/
	in-du-*yis*-tka	індуїстка
Jewish	i-u-*dey*/	іудей/
	i-u-*dey*-ka	іудейка
Muslim	mu-sul'-*ma*-nyn/	мусульманин/
	mu-sul'-*man*-ka	мусульманка

I'm not religious.
  ya ne-*vi-ru*-yu-chy/
  ne-*vi*-ru-yu-cha (m/f)

Я невіруючий/
невіруюча.

I'm (Catholic),
but not practising.
  ya (ka-*to*-lyk), a-*le* ne
  kho-dzhu do *tser*-kvy

Я (католик), але не
ходжу до церкви.

I'm an atheist.
  ya a-te-*yist*

Я атеїст.

I'm agnostic.
  ya a-*hno*-styk

Я агностик.

Can I attend this service/mass?
  mo-zhna zay-*ty* na
  tsyu vid-*pra*-vu?

Можна зайти на
цю відправу?

Can I pray here?
  mo-zhna me-*ni* tut
  po-mo-*ly*-ty-sya?

Можна мені тут
помолитися?

Where can I pray/worship?
de me-*ni* *mo*-zhna
po-mo-*ly*-ty-sya?

Де мені можна
помолитися?

Where can I make confession
(in English)?
de *mo*-zhna
vy-spo-vi-da-ty-sya
(an-*hliys'*-ko-yu *mo*-vo-yu)?

Де можна
висповідатися
(англійською мовою)?

Can I receive communion here?
me-*ni* *mo*-zhna tut
pry-*nya*-ty
pry-*cha*-stya?

Мені можна тут
прийняти
причастя?

baptism/christening	*khre*-shchen-nya	хрещення
church	*tser*-kva	церква
communion	pry-*cha*-stya	причастя
confession	*spo*-vid'	сповідь
funeral	*po*-kho-ron	похорон
God	boh	Бог
god	boh	бог
monk	mo-*nakh*	монах
nun	mo-na-*khy*-nya	монахиня
prayer	mo-*ly*-tva	молитва
priest	svya-*shche*-nyk	священик
relic	*mo*-shchi (pl)	мощі
religious procession	khid	хід
saint	svya-*ty*	святий
shrine	svya-*ty*-nya	святиня
synagogue	sy-na-*ho*-ha	синагога
temple	khram	храм

(See also Cultural Differences on page 57.)

SPECIFIC NEEDS

TRACING ROOTS & HISTORY

РОДИННА ІСТОРІЯ

SPECIFIC NEEDS

(I think) My ancestors came from this area.

(ya *du*-ma-yu, shcho) mo-*yi* *pred*-ky po-*kho*-dyat' z tsykh mists'

(Я думаю, що) Мої предки походять з цих місць.

I'm looking for my relatives.

ya roz-*shu*-ku-yu svo-*yikh* ro-dy-chiw

Я розшукую своїх родичів.

I have (a) relative(s) who live(s) around here.

[miy *ro*-dych; mo-*yi* *ro*-dy-chi] des' tut zhy-*ve*/zhy-*vut'* (sg/pl)

[Мій родич; Мої родичі] десь тут живе/живуть.

Is there anyone here by the name of ...?

tut zhy-*ve* khtos' na *pri*-zvy-shche ...?

Тут живе хтось на прізвище ...?

I'd like to go to the cemetery/burial ground.

ya [kho-*tiw* by; kho-*ti*-la b] vi-*dvi*-da-ty tsvyn-tar (m/f)

Я [хотів би; хотіла б] відвідати цвинтар.

My (grandfather) fought/died here in WWI/II.

miy (did) vo-yu-*vaw*/ za-*hy*-nuw tut pid chas *per*-sho-yi/*dru*-ho-yi svi-to-*vo*-yi viy-*ny*

Мій (дід) воював/ загинув тут під час Першої/Другої світової війни.

My (grandmother) nursed here in WWI/II.

mo-*ya* (ba-*bu*-sya) bu-*la* tut med-se-*stro*-yu pid chas *per*-sho-yi/*dru*-ho-yi svi-to-*vo*-yi viy-*ny*

Моя (бабуся) була тут медсестрою під час Першої/Другої світової війни.

ЧАС, КАЛЕНДАР
I СВЯТА
TIME, DATES & FESTIVALS

TELLING THE TIME   **КОТРА ГОДИНА?**

All timetables use the 24-hour clock. In informal speech the 12-hour system may also be used.

What's the time?	ko-*tra* ho-*dy*-na?	Котра година?
... o'clock		
one	*per*-sha ho-*dy*-na	перша година
		(lit: first hour)
two	*dru*-ha ho-*dy*-na	друга година
three	*tre*-tya ho-*dy*-na	третя година
four	che-*tver*-ta ho-*dy*-na	четверта година
five	*pya*-ta ho-*dy*-na	п'ята година
six	*sho*-sta ho-*dy*-na	шоста година
seven	*s'o*-ma ho-*dy*-na	сьома година
eight	*vos'*-ma ho-*dy*-na	восьма година
nine	de-*vya*-ta ho-*dy*-na	дев'ята година
ten	de-*sya*-ta ho-*dy*-na	десята година
eleven	o-dy-*na*-tsya-ta ho-*dy*-na	одинадцята година
twelve	dva-*na*-tsya-ta ho-*dy*-na	дванадцята година

The word ho-*dy*-na (**година**), meaning 'hour', can be omitted in the list above.

223

To indicate 'half past', Ukrainian inserts the words piw or piw na (пів; пів на) before the hour. Instead of saying that it's 'half past' an hour, Ukrainians say that it's 'half into' the next hour. This construction is also used for 'quarter past', chvert' na (чверть на):

half past one	piw [na *dru*-hu; *dru*-ho-yi]	пів [на другу; другої]
half past ten	piw [na o-dy-*na*-tsya-tu; o-dy-*na*-tsya-to-yi]	пів [на одинадця-ту; одинадцятої]
quarter past two	chvert' na *tre*-tyu	чверть на третю
quarter past five	chvert' na *sho*-stu	чверть на шосту

In English it's possible to say 'one thirty' as well as 'half past one'. In Ukrainian you can use exactly the same construction:

| one thirty | *per*-sha *try*-tsyat' | перша тридцять |

The minutes of the first half-hour are constructed in a similar way to 'half past' and 'quarter past':

minute	khvy-*ly*-na	хвилина
ten past four	*de*-syat' (khvy-*lyn*) [na *pya*-tu; po chet-*ver*-tiy]	десять (хвилин) [на п'яту; по четвертій]
twenty past seven	*dva*-tsyat' (khvy-*lyn*) [na *vos'*-mu; po *s'o*-miy]	двадцять (хвилин) [на восьму; по сьомій]

Note that times from the half-hour to the next full hour have a different structure:

| quarter to four | za chvert' che-*tver*-ta | за чверть четверта |
| five to seven | za pyat' (khvy-*lyn*) *s'o*-ma | за п'ять (хвилин) сьома |

What time are you leaving?	o ko-*triy* ho-*dy*-ni vy vid-li-*ta*-ye-te?	О котрій годині ви відлітаєте?
At one pm.	o try-*na*-tsya-tiy/ *per*-shiy	О тринадцятій/ першій.
At 3.40 pm.	o p'ya-*tna*-tsya-tiy *so*-rok	О п'ятнадцятій сорок.
At 11 am.	ob o-dy-*na*-tsya-tiy	Об одинадцятій.

DAYS

What day of the week is it today?	*ya*-ky s'o-*ho*-dni den' *ty*-zhnya?	Який сьогодні день тижня?
Monday	po-ne-*di*-lok	понеділок
Tuesday	viw-*to*-rok	вівторок
Wednesday	se-re-*da*	середа
Thursday	che-*tver*	четвер
Friday	*pya*-tny-tsya	п'ятниця
Saturday	su-*bo*-ta	субота
Sunday	ne-*di*-lya	неділя
week	*ty*-zhden'	тиждень
On what day will you be in Kyiv?	u ya-*ky* den' vy *bu*-de-te w *ky*-e-vi?	У який день ви будете в Києві?
On Tuesday.	u viw-*to*-rok	У вівторок.
On Sunday.	u ne-*di*-lyu	У неділю.

MONTHS

The names of the months bear no relation to the Latin-based words found in so many European languages. The Ukrainian words are much more closely related to natural phenomena, eg, February is an 'angry' month – that's what *lyu*-ty (лютий) actually means! The juice of the birch tree, be-*re*-za (береза), begins to flow in March – one of the first signs of spring. May is important for grass, tra-*va* (трава). In August farmers would get out their sickle, serp (серп), to harvest the grain. The word for November literally means 'leaf-fall', which is somewhat odd, because all the leaves have fallen by the end of October.

month	*mi*-syats'	місяць

What month is it?
ya-*ky za*-raz *mi*-syats'?   Який зараз місяць?

January the slicing month (the cold seems to slice the body with a knife)	*si*-chen'	січень
February the angry month	*lyu*-ty	лютий
March the month of birches	*be*-re-zen'	березень
April the month of flowers	*kvi*-ten'	квітень
May the month of grasses	*tra*-ven'	травень
June the month of redness (as fruits begin to ripen)	*cher*-ven'	червень
July the month of linden trees	*ly*-pen'	липень
August the month of sickles	*ser*-pen'	серпень
September the month of heather	*ve*-re-sen'	вересень
October the month of yellow colours	*zhow*-ten'	жовтень
November the month of falling leaves	ly-sto-*pad*	листопад
December the month when the soil freezes	*hru*-den'	грудень

SEASONS

seasons	*po*-ry *ro*-ku	пори року
winter	zy-*ma*	зима
in winter	*wzym*-ku	взимку
spring	ve-*sna*	весна
in spring	na-ve-*sni*	навесні
summer	*li*-to	літо
in summer	*wlit*-ku	влітку
autumn	*o*-sin'	осінь
in autumn	vo-se-*ny*	восени

ПОРИ РОКУ

DATES

What's the date today?
> ya-*ke* s'o-*ho*-dni chy-*slo*?   Яке сьогодні число?

It's the fifth.
> *pya*-te   П'яте.

But:

I arrived on the fifth.
> ya pry-*i*-khaw *pya*-to-ho   Я приїхав п'ятого.

It's 1 September.
> *per*-she *ve*-re-snya   Перше вересня.

It's 26 February.
> dva-tsyat' *sho*-ste *lyu*-to-ho   Двадцять шосте лютого.

It's 30 July.
> try-*tsya*-te *lyp*-nya   Тридцяте липня.

My birthday's 20 December.
> miy den' na-*ro*-dzhen-nya   Мій день народження
> dva-*tsya*-to-ho *hru*-dnya   двадцятого грудня.

ДАТИ

Present

today	s'o-*ho*-dni	сьогодні
this year	ts'o-*ho ro*-ku	цього року
this month	ts'o-*ho mi*-sya-tsya	цього місяця
this week	ts'o-*ho ty*-zhnya	цього тижня

Тепер

Past

		Минуле
yesterday	*wcho*-ra	вчора
day before yesterday	po-za-*wcho*-ra	позавчора
last year	my-*nu*-lo-ho *ro*-ku/to-*rik*	минулого року/торік
last month	my-*nu*-lo-ho *mi*-sya-tsya	минулого місяця
last week	my-*nu*-lo-ho *ty*-zhnya	минулого тижня
long ago	da-*wno*	давно

Future

		Майбутнє
tomorrow	*zaw*-tra	завтра
day after tomorrow	pi-slya-*zaw*-tra	післязавтра
next year	na-*stup*-no-ho *ro*-ku	наступного року
next month	na-*stup*-no-ho *mi*-sya-tsya	наступного місяця
next week	na-*stup*-no-ho *ty*-zhnya	наступного тижня
soon	ne-za-*ba*-rom	незабаром
an hour from now	*che*-rez ho-*dy*-nu	через годину

DURING THE DAY

		ПРОТЯГОМ ДНЯ
morning	*ra*-nok	ранок
in the morning	*wran*-tsi	вранці
in the afternoon	u-*den'*	удень
evening	*ve*-chir	вечір
in the evening	u-*ve*-che-ri	увечері
night	nich	ніч
at night	u-no-*chi*	уночі

TIME, DATES & FESTIVALS

USEFUL WORDS

КОРИСНІ СЛОВА

a year ago	rik to-*mu*	рік тому
always	*zaw*-zhdy	завжди
anytime	ko-*ly ne*-bud'	коли-небудь
at the moment	te-*per*/*za*-raz	тепер/зараз
century	sto-*lit*-tya	століття
during	pid chas	під час
earlier/sooner	ra-*ni*-she	раніше
early	*ra*-no	рано
every day	shcho-*dnya*	щодня
every hour	shcho-ho-*dy*-ny	щогодини
every week	shcho-*ty*-zhnya	щотижня
every year	shcho-*ro*-ku	щороку
forever	na-*zaw*-zhdy	назавжди
for the time being	*po*-ky shcho	поки що
from time to time	chas vid *cha*-su	час від часу
immediately	ne-*hay*-no	негайно
just now	*til'*-ky-no/	тільки-но/
	shchoy-no	щойно
late	*pi*-zno	пізно
later on/then	*po*-tim	потім
later	pi-*zni*-she	пізніше
never	ni-*ko*-ly	ніколи
not any more	*bil'*-she ni	більше ні
not yet	shche ni	ще ні
now	*za*-raz	зараз
on time	*wcha*-sno	вчасно
since then	z to-*ho cha*-su	з того часу
sometime	ko-*lys'*	колись
sometimes	*in*-ko-ly	інколи
soon	ne-za-*ba*-rom	незабаром
still	wse shche	все ще
sundown	*za*-khid *son*-tsya	захід сонця
sunrise	skhid *son*-tsya	схід сонця

NATIONAL FESTIVALS

ДЕРЖАВНІ СВЯТА

no-*vy* rik   Новий рік

The New Year is observed by all. Parties begin on the evening of 31 December and continue throughout the next day. A public holiday is celebrated on 1 January.

svyat *ve*-chir i riz-*dvo*   Свят вечір і Різдво

Christmas is observed on 7 January, according to the tradition of the eastern Christian Church. Carols are sung and nativity plays are performed. Christmas Eve (6 January) is celebrated with a ritual meal at which there should be, at least in theory, twelve courses, none of them containing meat. A Christmas food not prepared at any other time is ku-*tya* (кутя), which contains poppy seeds, cracked wheat, honey, nuts and raisins.

sta-*ry* no-*vy* rik   Старий Новий рік

Some families also celebrate the Old New Year on 14 January. They may then go on to take a dip in the (often iced-over) water on the feast of the Epiphany on 19 January.

NIGHT NOTIONS

'Night' is regarded as beginning quite late and corresponding to the period of sleep. So on many occasions 'last night' should be translated in Ukrainian as 'yesterday evening', wcho-ra wve-che-ri (вчора ввечері):

What play did you see last night?
   ya-*ku* pye-su vy ba-chy-ly wcho-ra wve-che-ri?
   Яку п'єсу ви бачили вчора ввечері?

mi-zhna-*ro*-dny zhi-*no*-chi den' Міжнародний Жіночий день
International Women's Day is celebrated on 8 March with a public holiday. At home women are given gifts and flowers by the men, while in the workplace this is done on the preceding day.

pa-skha Пасха
This is the word used for all the holy days of Easter. It derives from the Hebrew for 'Passover'. Easter is a moveable feast, but it always falls in spring. The dates of Easter for Ukrainian Orthodox and Ukrainian Greek Catholics rarely coincide with those celebrated by the Western Christian cultures. Easter Sunday is called ve-*lyk*-den' (Великдень) which literally means 'great day'. Special Easter cakes are baked and brought to church to be blessed. Eggs – real ones, not chocolate – are painted and exchanged as presents. These are called py-san-*ky* (писанки). People greet each other with the words khry-*stos* vo-*skres* (Христос воскрес) which means 'Christ is risen'. The response is vo-*i*-sty-nu vo-*skres* (Воістину воскрес), 'He is risen indeed'.

per-she *traw*-nya Перше травня
May Day, which is part of the Soviet heritage, is celebrated on 1-2 May. However, the underlying ideology has gradually become marginal, and for most people this is just an occasion for short vacations in nice spring weather.

den' kon-sty-*tu*-tsi-yi День Конституції
The Constitution Day is celebrated on 28 June, marking the adoption of the new Ukrainian Constitution in 1996.

den' pe-re-*mo*-hy День перемоги
Victory Day on 9 May marks the anniversary of the victory over Nazi Germany in WWII.

den' ne-za-*le*-zhno-sti   День незалежності
u-kra-*yi*-ny   України

The celebration of Independence Day on 24 August is a comparatively recent introduction.

This last festival is marked by public demonstrations, concerts and special open-air markets; the streets are decorated with flags and banners.

CONGRATULATIONS & BEST WISHES   ПРИВІТАННЯ

If you're in Ukraine during a major festival (or on a friend's birthday) and would like to greet your friends in the Ukrainian way, here are some phrases that may help:

Happy ...	vi-*ta*-yu vas iz ...	Вітаю Вас із ...
Birthday	dnem	днем
	na-*ro*-dzhen-nya	народження
New Year	no-*vym ro*-kom	Новим роком
Christmas	riz-*dvom*	Різдвом
Easter	ve-*ly*-ko-dnem	Великоднем

Or, more formally:

Accept my congratulations on ...		
pry-*mit'* mo-*yi*		Прийміть мої
po-zdo-*row*-len-nya/		поздоровлення/
vi-*tan*-nya z ...		вітання з ...

I wish you ...	ya ba-*zha*-yu vam ...	Я бажаю Вам ...
happiness	*shcha*-stya	щастя
health	zdo-*ro*-wya	здоров'я
success	*u*-spi-khiw	успіхів

ЧИСЛО І КІЛЬКІСТЬ
NUMBERS & AMOUNTS

CARDINAL NUMBERS

КІЛЬКІСНІ ЧИСЛІВНИКИ

The numbers for 'one' and 'two' change according to the gender of the noun they accompany.

How many?	*skil'*-ky?	скільки?
0	nul'	нуль
1	o-*dyn*/o-*dna*/o-*dne* (m/f/neut)	один/одна/одне
2	dva/dvi (m & neut; f)	два/дві
3	try	три
4	cho-*ty*-ry	чотири
5	pyat'	п'ять
6	shist'	шість
7	sim	сім
8	*vi*-sim	вісім
9	*de*-vyat'	дев'ять
10	*de*-syat'	десять
11	o-dy-*na*-tsyat'	одинадцять
12	dva-*na*-tsyat'	дванадцять
13	try-*na*-tsyat'	тринадцять
14	cho-tyr-*na*-tsyat'	чотирнадцять
15	pya-*tna*-tsyat'	п'ятнадцять
16	shi-*sna*-tsyat'	шістнадцять
17	si-*mna*-tsyat'	сімнадцять
18	vi-si-*mna*-tsyat'	вісімнадцять
19	de-vya-*tna*-tsyat'	дев'ятнадцять
20	*dva*-tsyat'	двадцять
21	*dva*-tsyat'	двадцять
	o-*dyn*/o-*dna*/o-*dne* (m/f/neut)	один/одна/одне
30	*try*-tsyat'	тридцять
40	*so*-rok	сорок
50	pya-de-*syat*	п'ятдесят
60	shis-de-*syat*	шістдесят
70	sim-de-*syat*	сімдесят

80	vi-sim-de-*syat*	вісімдесят
90	de-vya-*no*-sto	дев'яносто
100	sto	сто
101	sto o-*dyn*	сто один
200	*dvi*-sti	двісті
246	*dvi*-sti *so*-rok	двісті сорок
	shist'	шість
300	*try*-sta	триста
400	cho-*ty*-ry-sta	чотириста
500	pyat-*sot*	п'ятсот
600	shis-*sot*	шістсот
700	sim-*sot*	сімсот
800	vi-sim-*sot*	вісімсот
900	de-vyat-*sot*	дев'ятсот
1000	*ty*-sya-cha	тисяча
2000	dvi *ty*-sya-chi	дві тисячі
1 million	mil'-*yon*	мільйон
2 million	dva mil'-*yo*-ny	два мільйони
3 million	try mil'-*yo*-ny	три мільйони

WEIGHTS, MEASURES & DISTANCES

How many kilometres to ...?
skil'-ky ki-lo-me-triw do ...? Скільки кілометрів до ...?

kilometre(s)	ki-lo-*metr*/ ki-lo-me-try	кілометр/ кілометри
metre(s)	metr/me-try	метр/метри
centimetre(s)	san-ty-*metr*/ san-ty-me-try	сантиметр/ сантиметри
millimetre(s)	mi-li-*metr*/ mi-li-me-try	міліметр/ міліметри
kilogram(s)	ki-lo-*hram*/ ki-lo-*hra*-my	кілограм/ кілограми
half a kilo	pi-wki-lo-*hra*-ma	півкілограма
gram(s)	hram/*hra*-my	грам/грами
litre(s)	litr/*li*-try	літр/літри
half a litre	piw-*li*-tra	півлітра

NUMBERS & AMOUNTS

ORDINAL NUMBERS

ПОРЯДКОВІ ЧИСЛІВНИКИ

Ordinal numerals are adjectives, which means they change form according to the gender of the following noun. Refer to the Grammar chapter (page 21) to check on the different endings. The numerals are given here in the masculine nominative singular.

Which one?	ko-*try*?	котрий?
1st	*per*-shy	перший
2nd	*dru*-hy	другий
3rd	*tre*-tiy	третій
4th	che-*tver*-ty	четвертий
5th	*pya*-ty	п'ятий
6th	*sho*-sty	шостий
7th	*s'o*-my	сьомий
8th	*vos'*-my	восьмий
9th	de-*vya*-ty	дев'ятий
10th	de-*sya*-ty	десятий
11th	o-dy-*na*-tsya-ty	одинадцятий
20th	dva-*tsya*-ty	двадцятий
21st	*dva*-tsyat' *per*-shy	двадцять перший
30th	try-*tsya*-ty	тридцятий
100th	*so*-ty	сотий
1000th	*ty*-syach-ny	тисячний

FRACTIONS

ДРОБИ

1/4	chvert'	чверть
1/3	tre-*ty*-na	третина
1/2	po-lo-*vy*-na	половина
2/3	dvi tre-*ty*-ny	дві третини
3/4	try *chve*-rti	три чверті

COLLECTIVE NUMERALS
ЗБІРНІ ЧИСЛІВНИКИ

Collective numerals are used to count human beings and nouns that have no singular form. Collective numerals above 4 end in **-ero (-еро)**.

2	*dvo*-ye	двоє		7	*se*-me-ro	семеро
3	*tro*-ye	троє		8	*vos'*-me-ro	восьмеро
4	*che*-tve-ro	четверо		9	*de*-vya-te-ro	дев'ятеро
5	*pya*-te-ro	п'ятеро		10	*de*-sya-te-ro	десятеро
6	*she*-ste-ro	шестеро				

five students	*pya*-te-ro stu-*den*-tiw	п'ятеро студентів
three doors	*tro*-ye dve-*rey*	троє дверей

AMOUNTS
КІЛЬКІСТЬ

How much/many?	*skil'*-ky?	скільки?

Could you please give me (a) ...?	*day*-te, bud' *la*-ska, ...	Дайте, будь ласка, ...
bottle	*plya*-shku	пляшку
carton	pa-*ket*	пакет
half a kilo	piw-ki-lo-*hra*-ma	півкілограма
100 grams	sto *hra*-miw	сто грамів
kilo/kilogram	ki-*lo*/ki-lo-*hram*	кіло/кілограм
packet	*pa*-chku	пачку
tin/jar	*ban*-ku	банку

a little	*tro*-khy/*tro*-shky	трохи/трошки
enough	*do*-syt'	досить
less	*men*-she	менше
many/much/a lot	ba-*ha*-to	багато
more	*bil'*-she	більше
some/several	*kil'*-ka/*de*-kil'-ka	кілька/декілька
too little	za-*ma*-lo	замало
too much	za-ba-*ha*-to	забагато

NUMBERS & AMOUNTS

КРИЗИ

EMERGENCIES

GENERAL

ЗАГАЛЬНЕ

Get lost!	*zny*-kny!	Зникни!
Go away!	het' (*zvid*-sy); i-*dy*/i-*dit*' (*zvid*-sy)! (inf/pol)	Геть (звідси); Іди/Ідіть (звідси)!
Help!	rya-*tuy*-te/ do-po-mo-*zhit*'!	Рятуйте/ Допоможіть!
Police!	mi-*li*-tsi-ya!	Міліція!
Stop it!	pry-py-*ny*/ pry-py-*nit*'! (sg, inf; pl, pol)	Припини/ Припиніть!
Thief!	*zlo*-diy/ hra-*bu*-yut'!	Злодій/ Грабують!
Watch out!	o-be-*re*-zhno!	Обережно!

It's an emergency!
tse *du*-zhe ter-mi-*no*-vo!;
tse kry-*ty*-chna
sy-tu-*a*-tsi-ya!

Це дуже терміново!;
Це критична
ситуація!

I'm lost.
ya za-blu-*kaw*/
za-blu-*ka*-la (m/f)

Я заблукав/
заблукала.

Please help us.
do-po-mo-*zhit*' nam,
bud' *la*-ska

Допоможіть нам,
будь ласка.

Where are the toilets?
de tu-a-*le*-ty?

Де туалети?

237

EMERGENCIES

HEALTH   ЗДОРОВ'Я

Call a doctor!
  (*vy*-klych-te) *li*-ka-rya!   (Викличте) лікаря!
Call an ambulance!
  vy-klych-te shvyd-*ku*   Викличте швидку
  (do-po-*mo*-hu)!   (допомогу)!
I'm ill.
  ya *khvo*-ry/*khvo*-ra (m/f);   Я хворий/хвора;
  me-*ni* po-*ha*-no   Мені погано.
My friend is ill.
  miy druh za-khvo-*riw* (m);   Мій друг захворів;
  mo-ya *po*-dru-ha   моя подруга
  za-khwo-*ri*-la (f)   захворіла.
I have medical insurance.
  u *me*-ne ye me-*dych*-ne   У мене є медичне
  stra-khu-*van*-nya   страхування.

DEALING WITH THE POLICE   МІЛІЦІЯ

Call the police!
  vy-klych-te mi-*li*-tsi-yu!   Викличте міліцію!
Where's the police station?
  de vid-*di*-len-nya mi-*li*-tsi-yi? Де відділення міліції?
We want to report an offence.
  my *kho*-che-mo za-ya-*vy*-ty   Ми хочемо заявити
  pro *zlo*-chyn   про злочин.

I've been ...	me-*ne* ...	Мене ...
beaten up	po-*by*-ly	побили
injured	po-*ra*-ny-ly	поранили
raped	zgval-tu-*va*-ly	зґвалтували
robbed	po-hra-bu-*va*-ly	пограбували

I've lost my ...	ya za-hu-*byw*/	Я загубив/
	za-hu-*by*-la ... (m/f)	загубила ...
My ... has/have been stolen.	u *me*-ne *wkra*-ly ...	У мене вкрали ...
bag	*sum*-ku	сумку
credit card	kre-*dy*-tnu	кредитну
	kart-ku	картку
keys	klyu-*chi*	ключі
money	*hro*-shi	гроші
passport	*pa*-sport	паспорт
travellers cheques	do-*ro*-zhni *che*-ky	дорожні чеки

I'm sorry; I apologise.
  vy-bach-te   Вибачте.
I didn't realise I was doing anything wrong.
  ya ne znaw/*zna*-la, shcho   Я не знав/знала, що
  ro-*blyu* shchos' ne tak (m/f)   роблю щось не так.
I didn't do it.
  ya ts'o-*ho* ne ro-*byw*   Я цього не робив.
We're innocent.
  my ne-*vyn*-ni   Ми невинні.
Is there a fine we can pay to clear this?
  chy *mo*-zhna *za*-mist'   Чи можна замість
  ts'o-ho za-pla-*ty*-ty   цього заплатити
  shtraf?   штраф?
What am I accused of?
  w *cho*-mu me-*ne*   В чому мене
  zvy-nu-*va*-chu-yut'?   звинувачують?

EMERGENCIES

THE POLICE MAY SAY ...

vas *bu*-de zvy-nu-*va*-che-no v ...
Вас буде звинувачено в ...
You'll be charged with ...

yo-*ho*/yi-*yi* *bu*-de zvy-nu-*va*-che-no v ...
Його/Її буде звинувачено в ...
He'll/She'll be charged with ...

an-ty-der-*zha*-wniy di-*yal*'-no-sti
антидержавній діяльності
anti-government activity

zaw-dan-*ni* ti-*les*-nykh u-*shko*-dzhen'
завданні тілесних ушкоджень
assault (causing severe bodily harm)

po-*bo*-yakh
побоях
assault (causing bodily harm)

zlo-mi
зломі
illegal entry

wbyw-stvi
вбивстві
murder

pe-re-bu-*van*-ni w kra-*yi*-ni bez *vi*-zy
перебуванні в країні без візи
not having a visa

pe-re-bu-*van*-ni w kra-*yi*-ni bez *diy*-sno-yi *vi*-zy
перебуванні в країні без дійсної візи
overstaying your visa

zbe-ri-*han*-ni za-bo-ro-ne-nykh re-cho-*vyn*
зберіганні заборонених речовин
possession (of illegal substances)

THE POLICE MAY SAY ...

vzhy-*van*-ni/zbe-ri-*han*-ni/roz-pow-syu-dzhen-ni
nar-*ko*-ty-kiw
вживанні/зберіганні/розповсюдженні наркотиків
taking/storing/distributing drugs

zgval-tu-*van*-ni
зґвалтуванні
rape

kra-*dizh*-tsi
крадіжці
robbery/theft

drib-*no*-mu roz-kra-*dan*-ni *wla*-sno-sti
дрібному розкраданні власності
shoplifting

po-*ru*-shen-ni *pra*-vyl do-ro-zhn'o-ho *ru*-khu
порушенні правил дорожнього руху
traffic violation

vid-*su*-tno-sti *do*-zvo-lu na *pra*-tsyu
відсутності дозволу на працю
working without a permit

Could I use the telephone?
mo-zhna po-dzvo-*ny*-ty?　Можна подзвонити?

May I phone [from here;
from your place]?
mo-zhna [*zvid*-sy; vid vas]　Можна [звідси; від вас]
po-dzvo-*ny*-ty?　подзвонити?

I need a lawyer.
me-*ni* po-*tri*-ben a-dvo-*kat*　Мені потрібен адвокат.

EMERGENCIES

Please, give me a lawyer
who speaks English.

   da-yte, bud' *la*-ska,
   a-dvo-*ka*-ta, ya-*ky*
   ho-*vo*-ryt'
   po-an-*hliy*-s'ky/
   an-*hliy*-s'ko-yu

Дайте, будь ласка,
адвоката, який
говорить
по-англійськи/
англійською.

I want to phone my embassy.

   ya *kho*-chu
   za-te-le-fo-nu-*va*-ty
   do po-*sol*'-stva mo-*ye*-yi
   kra-*yi*-ny

Я хочу
зателефонувати
до посольства моєї
країни.

I have no money.

   u *me*-ne ne-*ma*-ye hro-*shey*

У мене немає грошей.

I need help.

   me-*ni* po-*trib*-na
   do-po-*mo*-ha

Мені потрібна
допомога.

I want to go home!

   ya *kho*-chu do-*do*-mu!

Я хочу додому!

Notations used in this phrasebook are described in full on page 11 of the Introduction. In addition to this, the following notation applies in regard to parts of speech in the dictionary:

Nouns are not indicated. Verbs are preceded by 'to'. This serves to distinguish a verb from its noun counterpart, when applicable, eg, 'to answer' versus 'answer'.

A

to be able	moh-*ty*	могти

> I can.
> ya mo-*zhu*
> Я можу.
>
> I can't.
> ya ne mo-*zhu*
> Я не можу.
>
> Can you please ...?
> vy ne mo-*zhe*-te ...?
> Ви не можете ...?

about (approximately)	*blyz'*-ko • pry-*bly*-zno	близько • приблизно
above (adv)	*vy*-shche	вище
above (prep)	nad	над
abroad	za kor-*do*-nom	за кордоном
to accept	pry-*ma*-ty	приймати

> I accept.
> ya pry-*ma*-yu
> Я приймаю.
>
> Do you accept?
> vy pry-*ma*-ye-te?
> Ви приймаєте?

accident	a-*va*-ri-ya • ne-*shchas*-ny *vy*-pa-dok	аварія • нещасний випадок
accommodation	zhy-*tlo*	житло
addict	nar-ko-*man*	наркоман
addiction	nar-ko-ma-*ni*-ya	наркоманія
address	a-*dre*-sa	адреса
administration	a-dmi-ni-*stra*-tsi-ya	адміністрація
admission (entry)	wkhid	вхід
admission fee	(*pla*-ta za) wkhid	(плата за) вхід
admission (of guilt)	vy-*znan*-nya	визнання
to admit (allow entry)	wpu-*ska*-ty	впускати
to admit (confess)	vy-*zna*-va-ty	визнавати

A

English	Pronunciation	Ukrainian
adult	do-ro-sly/do-ro-sla (m/f)	дорослий/доросла
adventure	pry-ho-da	пригода
advice	po-ra-da	порада
to advise	ra-dy-ty	радити
aeroplane	li-tak	літак
by plane	li-ta-kom	літаком
after	pi-slya	після
again	zno-vu	знову
against	pro-ty	проти
to agree	po-ho-dy-ty-sya	погодитися

I agree.
zho-den/zho-dna (m/f)
згоден/згодна.

Do you agree?
vy zho-dni?
Ви згодні?

Agreed!
do-mo-vy-ly-sya!
Домовилися!

agriculture	sil'-s'ke ho-spo-dar-stvo	сільське господарство
ahead	wpe-red	вперед
aid	do-po-mo-ha	допомога
AIDS	snid (syn-drom na-bu-to-ho i-mu-no-de-fi-tsy-tu)	СНІД (синдром набутого імунодефіциту)
airline	a-vi-a-li-ni-ya	авіалінія
airmail	a-vi-a-po-shta	авіапошта
by airmail	a-vi-a-po-shto-yu	авіапоштою
alarm clock	bu-dyl'-nyk	будильник
all	wsi	всі
allergy	a-ler-hi-ya	алергія
to allow	do-zvo-lya-ty	дозволяти
almost	may-zhe	майже
alone	sam	сам
also	ta-kozh	також
alternative (n)	al'-ter-na-ty-va	альтернатива
always	zaw-zhdy	завжди
amazing	wra-zha-yu-chy	вражаючий
ambassador	po-sol	посол
ambulance	shvyd-ka do-po-mo-ha	швидка допомога
among	se-red	серед
ancient	sta-ro-daw-niy	стародавній
and	i • y • ta	і • й • та

244

B

angry	roz-*hni*-va-ny	розгніваний
answer	vid-po-*vid'*	відповідь
to answer	vid-po-vi-*da*-ty	відповідати
antique (adj)	sta-ro-*daw*-niy	стародавній
any	ya-*kys'*	якийсь
anytime	ko-ly-ne-*bud'*	коли-небудь
apartment	kvar-*ty*-ra	квартира
appointment	zu-*strich*	зустріч
approximately	pry-*bly*-zno	приблизно
archaeological	ar-khe-o-lo-*hich*-ny	археологічний
to argue	spe-re-*cha*-ty-sya	сперечатися
argument	su-pe-*rech*-ka	суперечка
to arrive	pry-bu-*va*-ty	прибувати
art	my-*stets*-tvo	мистецтво
ashtray	po-*pil'*-nych-ka	попільничка
to ask	py-*ta*-ty	питати
at (place)	u • w	у • в
at (time)	o • ob	о • об
automatic	aw-to-ma-*tych*-ny	автоматичний
autumn	o-*sin'*	осінь

B

baby	ne-mow-*lya*	немовля
babysitter	*nya*-nya	няня
back	na-*zad*	назад
backpack	ryug-*zak*	рюкзак
bad	po-*ha*-ny	поганий
bag	*sum*-ka	сумка
baggage	ba-*hazh*	багаж
ball (dance)	bal	бал
ball (object)	*myach*	м'яч
bank	bank	банк
bar	bar	бар
bath	*van*-na	ванна
bathroom	*van*-na (kim-*na*-ta)	ванна (кімната)
battery	ba-ta-*re*-ya	батарея
beach	*plyazh*	пляж
beautiful	*har*-ny	гарний
because	to-*mu* shcho	тому що
bed	*lizh*-ko	ліжко
bedbugs	blo-*shchy*-tsi	блощиці
before (conj)	persh nizh	перш ніж
before (prep)	*pe*-red	перед
beggar	zhe-*brak*	жебрак
begin	po-chy-*na*-ty	починати
beginner	po-cha-*tki*-vets'	початківець
behind	*zza*-du	ззаду
below (adv)	wny-*zu*	внизу
below (prep)	pid	під
berth (train)	po-*ly*-tsya	полиця
beside	*ko*-lo • *po*-ruch iz	коло • поруч із

best	nay-*kra*-shchy	найкращий
better	*kra*-shchy	кращий
between (prep)	mizh	між
Bible	*bi*-bli-ya	біблія
bicycle	ve-lo-sy-*ped*	велосипед
big	ve-*ly*-ky	великий
bill	ra-*khu*-nok	рахунок
birthday	den' na-ro-dzhen-nya	день народження
to bite	ku-*sa*-ty	кусати
bitter	hir-*ky*	гіркий
blanket	ko-*wdra*	ковдра
to bless	bla-ho-slo-*wlya*-ty	благословляти

Bless you!
na zdo-*row*-ya!
На здоров'я!

blind	sli-*py*	сліпий
blood	krow	кров
boat	pa-ro-*plaw* • *cho*-ven	пароплав • човен
body	*ti*-lo	тіло
bomb	*bom*-ba	бомба

Bon appetit!
smach-*no*-ho!
Смачного!

book	*knyzh*-ka	книжка
bookshop	kny-*har*-nya	книгарня
bored, to be	nu-dy-ty-sya	нудитися

I'm bored.
me-*ni* nu-dno • na-*bry*-dlo
мені нудно • набридло

| border | kor-*don* | кордон |
| to borrow | po-zy-*cha*-ty | позичати |

May I borrow this?
mo-zhna, ya tse po-zy-*chu*?
Можна, я це позичу?

boss	shef	шеф
both	o-*by*-dva	обидва
both ... and ...	tak ... yak i ...	так ... як і ...
bottle	*plya*-shka	пляшка
bottle opener	vid-kry-*vach*-ka •	відкривачка •
	kor-ko-*tyah* • *shto*-por	коркотяг • штопор
box	ko-*rob*-ka	коробка
boy	*khlo*-pchyk	хлопчик
brakes	*hal'*-ma (pl)	гальма
brave	kho-*ro*-bry	хоробрий
bread	khlib	хліб
break (pause)	pe-re-*rva*	перерва
break (holiday)	vid-po-*chy*-nok	відпочинок

to break	la-*ma*-ty • ro-zby-*va*-ty	ламати • розбивати
breakfast	sni-*da*-nok	сніданок
to breathe	dy-*kha*-ty	дихати
bribe (n)	kha-*bar*	хабар
to bribe	da-*va*-ty kha-ba-*rya*	давати хабаря
bridge	mist	міст
bright	ya-*skra*-vy	яскравий
to bring	pry-*no*-sy-ty	приносити

Can you bring it?
pry-ne-*sit'*, bud' *la*-ska
Принесіть, будь ласка.

broken	ro-*zby*-ty • po-*la*-ma-ny	розбитий • поламаний
brother	brat	брат
bucket	vi-*dro*	відро
building	bu-*dy*-nok	будинок
to burn	ho-*ri*-ty	горіти
bus	aw-to-bus	автобус
business	*bi*-znes • *spra*-va	бізнес • справа
businessperson	bi-zne-*smen* (m) • di-lo-va *zhin*-ka (f)	бізнесмен • ділова жінка
busy	zay-*nya*-ty	зайнятий
but	a-*le*	але
to buy	ku-pu-*va*-ty	купувати

Where did you buy this?
de vy tse ku-*py*-ly?
Де Ви це купили?

C

cafe	ka-*fe* • ka-*vyar*-nya	кафе • кав'ярня
camera	fo-to-a-pa-*rat*	фотоапарат
camp (n)	*ta*-bir	табір
to camp	ro-zby-*va*-ty *ta*-bir	розбивати табір
campfire	ba-*hat*-tya • *vo*-hny-shche	багаття • вогнище
camp site	*kem*-pinh	кемпінг
can (to be able)	*mo*-zhna	можна

Can I take a photograph?
mo-zhna fo-to-hra-fu-*va*-ty?
Можна фотографувати?

No, you can't.
ni, ne *mo*-zhna
Ні, не можна.

| can | blya-*shan*-ka • (kon-*ser*-vna) *ban*-ka | бляшанка • (консервна) банка |

to cancel	ska-so-vu-va-ty •	скасовувати •
	ska-su-va-ty	скасувати
can opener	vid-kry-va-chka	відкривачка
candle	svi-chka	свіча
candy	tsu-ker-ky	цукерки
capital (city)	sto-ly-tsya	столиця
capitalism	ka-pi-ta-lizm	капіталізм
car	aw-to(-mo-bil') • ma-shy-na	авто(мобіль) • машина
cards (playing)	kar-ty	карти
to care	tur-bu-va-ty-sya	турбуватися

I don't care.
me-ni bay-du-zhe • me-ne tse ne tur-bu-ye
Мені байдуже • Мене це не турбує.

| careful | o-be-re-zhny | обережний |

Careful!
o-be-re-zhno!
Обережно!

| carriage (train) | va-hon | вагон |
| to carry | no-sy-ty • ne-sty | носити • нести |

I'll carry it.
ya bu-du ne-sty
Я буду нести.

cashier	ka-syr	касир
cathedral	so-bor	собор
CD	kom-pakt dysk • si-di	компакт диск • CD
to celebrate	vid-zna-cha-ty •	відзначати •
	svya-tku-va-ty	святкувати
cemetery	tsvyn-tar •	цвинтар •
	kla-do-vy-shche	кладовище
certificate	po-svid-ka • po-svid-chen-nya	посвідка • посвідчення
certain (sure)	u-pew-ne-ny	упевнений

Are you sure?
vy wpew-ne-ni?
Ви впевнені?

| chair | sti-lets' | стілець |
| chance | mo-zhly-vist' • shans | можливість • шанс |

by chance
vy-pad-ko-vo
випадково

change (money)	zda-cha • re-shta	здача • решта
change (transport)	pe-re-sad-ka	пересадка
to change (trains)	ro-by-ty	робити
	pe-re-sad-ku •	пересадку •
	pe-re-si-da-ty	пересідати
cheap	de-she-vy	дешевий
cheaper	de-shew-shy	дешевший
cheese	syr	сир

chemist	a-*pte*-ka	аптека
child	dy-*ty*-na	дитина
chocolate	sho-ko-*lad*	шоколад
to choose	vy-by-*ra*-ty	вибирати
Christmas	riz-*dvo*	Різдво
Christmas Eve	svyat-ve-*chir*	Святвечір
church	*tser*-kva	церква
cigarettes	tsy-har-*ky*	цигарки
cinema	*ki*-no	кіно
circus	tsyrk	цирк
city	*mi*-sto	місто
city centre	tsentr *mi*-sta	центр міста
clean (adj)	*chy*-sty	чистий
cloakroom	har-de-*rob*	гардероб
clock	ho-*dyn*-nyk	годинник
close (nearby)	*blyz'*-ko	близько
to close	za-chy-*nya*-ty	зачиняти

It's closed!
za-*chy*-ne-no!
Зачинено!

clothing	o-*dyah*	одяг
coin	mo-*ne*-ta	монета
cold (adj)	kho-*lo*-dny	холодний
cold	za-*stu*-da	застуда
colour	*ko*-lir	колір
comb	hre-*bin'*	гребінь
to come	i-*ty* • *pry*-ty	іти • прийти

Can we come tomorrow?
mo-zhna *pry*-ty za-*wtra*?
Можна прийти завтра?

Come here!
i-*dit'* syu-*dy*!
Ідіть сюди!

The bus is coming.
yi-de aw-*to*-bus
Їде автобус.

comfortable	zruch-*ny*	зручний
communism	ko-mu-*nizm*	комунізм
company (business)	kom-*pa*-ni-ya	компанія
compartment (train)	ku-*pe*	купе
complex (adj)	skla-*dny*	складний
concert	kon-*tsert*	концерт
condom	pre-zer-va-*tyw* •	презерватив •
	kon-tra-tsep-*tyw*	контрацептив
to confirm	pid-*tver*-dy-ty	підтвердити

Congratulations!
vi-*ta*-yu! • *mo*-yi po-zdo-row-*len*-nya!
Вітаю! • Мої поздоровлення!

constipation	za-por	запор
consulate	kon-sul'-stvo	консульство
contact lens	kon-tak-tna lin-za	контактна лінза
contagious	za-raz-ny • in-fek-tsiy-ny	заразний • інфекційний
contraceptive	pro-ty-za-pli-dny	протизаплідний
	za-sib	засіб
conversation	ro-zmo-va	розмова
to cook	ho-tu-va-ty	готувати
corner (of a room)	ku-tok	куток
corner (of a street)	rih	ріг

at/on the corner
na ro-zi
на розі

corrupt (adj)	ko-rum-po-va-ny •	корумпований •
	pro-da-zhny	продажний
corruption	ko-rup-tsi-ya	корупція
cost	tsi-na	ціна
to cost	ko-shtu-va-ty	коштувати

It costs ...
tse ko-shtu-ye ...
Це коштує ...

How much does ... cost?
skil'-ky ko-shtu-ye ...?
Скільки коштує ...?

cough	ka-shel'	кашель
to count	ra-khu-va-ty	рахувати
courtyard	dvir	двір
crazy	bo-zhe-vil'-ny	божевільний
credit card	kre-dy-tna kar-tka	кредитна картка
crop	u-ro-zhay	урожай
customs office	my-tny-tsya	митниця
to cut	ri-za-ty	різати
to cycle	yi-kha-ty ve-lo-sy-pe-dom	їхати велосипедом

D

dad	ta-to	тато
daily	shcho-den-ny	щоденний
dairy products	mo-loch-ni pro-duk-ty	молочні продукти
damp	vo-lo-hy	вологий
to dance	tan-tsyu-va-ty	танцювати
dangerous	ne-bez-pech-ny	небезпечний
dark	te-mny	темний
date (time)	chy-slo • da-ta	число • дата

date of birth
da-ta na-ro-dzhen-nya
дата народження

daughter	do-chka •	дочка •
	don'-ka	донька

dawn	svi-*ta*-nok	світанок
day	den'	день
dead	*mer*-tvy	мертвий
deaf	hlu-*khy*	глухий
death	smert'	смерть
to decide	vy-ri-shu-va-ty	вирішувати
decision	ri-*shen*-nya	рішення
delay	za-*trym*-ka	затримка
delicious	smach-*ny*	смачний
delightful	chu-*do*-vy	чудовий
democracy	de-mo-*kra*-ti-ya	демократія
demonstration (protest)	de-mon-*stra*-tsi-ya	демонстрація
to depart (leave)	vid-yizh-*dzha*-ty	від'їжджати

The flight departs at …
vy-lit *rey*-su o …
Виліт рейсу о …

What time does it leave?
o ko-*triy* ho-dy-ni vid-*praw*-len-nya?
О котрій годині відправлення?

department store	u-ni-ver-*mah*	універмаг
departure	vid-*praw*-len-nya	відправлення
to destroy	ruy-nu-va-ty • ny-shchy-ty	руйнувати • нищити
development	ro-zvy-tok	розвиток
diabetic	di-a-be-tyk	діабетик
dictatorship	dyk-ta-*tu*-ra	диктатура
dictionary	slow-*nyk*	словник
different	*in*-shy • *ri*-zny	інший • різний
difficult	vazh-ky	важкий

It's difficult!
vazh-ko!
Важко!

dinner	o-*bid*	обід
direct	prya-my	прямий
dirt	brud	бруд
dirty	bru-*dny*	брудний
disabled person	in-va-*lid*	інвалід
discount	znyzh-ka	знижка
discrimination	dy-skry-mi-*na*-tsi-ya	дискримінація
disinfectant	de-zin-fi-*ku*-yu-chy za-sib	дезінфікуючий засіб
distant	vid-*da*-le-ny	віддалений
to do	ro-by-ty	робити

I'll do it.
ya tse zro-*blyu*
Я це зроблю.

Can you do that?
vy tse *mo*-zhe-te zro-by-ty?
Ви це можете зробити?

doctor	*li*-kar	лікар
dog	so-*ba*-ka	собака
dole (unemployment benefits)	fi-*nan*-so-va do-po-*mo*-ha be-zro-*bi*-tnym	фінансова допомога безробітним
doll	*lyal'*-ka	лялька
door	*dve*-ri (pl)	двері
double	po-*dviy*-ny	подвійний

double bed
dvo-*spal'*-ne *lizh*-ko
двоспальне ліжко

double room
no-mer na dvokh
номер на двох

down(stairs) (direction, adv)	wnyz	вниз
down(stairs) (location, adv)	wny-zu	внизу
downtown	tsentr *mi*-sta	центр міста
dream	*mri*-ya • son	мрія • сон
to dress	o-dya-*ha*-ty-sya	одягатися
dried	*su*-she-ny	сушений
drink	na-*piy*	напій
to drink	*py*-ty	пити

I don't drink spirits.
ya ne pyu spyrt-*no*-ho.
Я не п'ю. спиртного.

Do you drink beer?
vy pye-*te py*-vo?
Ви п'єте пиво?

drinkable	*py*-tny • dlya *pyt*-tya	питний • для пиття

drinkable water
py-tna vo-*da*
питна вода

to drive	vo-*dy*-ty (ma-*shy*-nu)	водити (машину)
drivers licence	(vo-*diy*-s'ki) pra-*va*	(водійські) права
drugs (illegal)	nar-ko-ty-ky	наркотики
drunk (inebriated)	*pya*-ny	п'яний
dry (adj)	su-*khy*	сухий
during	pid chas	під час
dust	pyl	пил

E

English	Pronunciation	Ukrainian
each	*ko-zhny*	кожний
early	*ran-*niy	ранній
earn	*za-ro-blya-*ty	заробляти
earnings	*za-ro-bi-*tok	заробіток
Earth	*ze-mlya*	Земля
earthquake	*ze-mle-trus*	землетрус
east	skhid	схід
Easter	ve-*lyk-*den' • *pa-*skha	Великдень • Пасха
Easter Eggs	*py-san-*ky	писанки
easy	leh-*ky*	легкий
eat	*yi-*sty	їсти
economical	e-ko-no-*mich-*ny	економічний
economics	e-ko-no-*mi-*ka	економіка
economy	e-ko-no-*mi-*ka	економіка
economy (thrift)	e-ko-no-*mi-*ya	економія
education	o-*svi-*ta	освіта
elections	*vy-*bo-ry	вибори
electricity	e-*lek-*try-ka	електрика
elevator (lift)	lift	ліфт
email	e-*lek-tron-*na po-shta • i-*meyl*	електронна пошта • імейл
embassy	po-*sol'-*stvo	посольство
emergency exit	za-pa-*sny* vy-*khid*	запасний вихід
employer	pra-tse-*da-*vets'	працедавець
empty	po-*ro-*zhniy	порожній
end	ki-*nets'*	кінець
energy	e-*ner-*hi-ya	енергія
English	an-*hliy-*s'ky	англійський
to enjoy (oneself)	o-*der-zhu-*va-ty za-do-vo-*len-*nya	одержувати задоволення
enough	*do-*syt'	досить
to enter	*wkho-*dy-ty	входити
entrance (to an apartment building)	pid-*yizd*	під'їзд
entry	wkhid	вхід
environment	naw-ko-*ly-*shnye se-re-*do-*vy-shche	навколишнє середовище
equal (adj)	*riw-*ny	рівний
European (adj)	yew-ro-*peys'-*ky	європейський
evening	ve-chir	вечір
event	po-*di-*ya	подія
every	*ko-*zhny	кожний
every day	shcho-*dnya*	щодня
everyone	wsi • *ko-*zhny	всі • кожний
everything	wse	все
example	*pry-*klad	приклад

for example
na-*pry*-klad
наприклад

to exchange   ob-*mi*-nyu-va-ty   обмінювати

Excuse me.
vy-bach-te • pe-re-*pro*-shu-yu
Вибачте. • Перепрошую.

exhausted	zmu-che-ny	змучений
exhibition	vy-staw-ka	виставка
exile	za-slan-nya	заслання
exit	vy-khid	вихід
expensive	do-ro-hy	дорогий
experience	do-svid	досвід
export	ek-sport	експорт
to export	vy-vo-zy-ty	вивозити
eye	o-ko	око

F

false	fal'-shy-vy	фальшивий
family	si-mya	сім'я
family (extended)	ro-dy-na	родина
fan (cooling)	ven-ty-lya-tor	вентилятор
fan (sports)	u-bo-li-val'-nyk	уболівальник
far	da-le-ko	далеко
farm	fer-ma	ферма
fast (adj)	shvyd-ky	швидкий
fast (adv)	shvyd-ko	швидко
to fast	po-sty-ty	постити
fat (adj)	tow-sty	товстий
fat	sa-lo • zhyr	сало • жир
father	bat'-ko	батько
fault	vy-na	вина

It's my fault.
ya vy-nen/vyn-na (m/f)
Я винен/винна.

fault (technical)	po-shko-dzhen-nya	пошкодження
fear	strakh	страх
fee	pla-ta	плата
to feel	po-chu-va-ty se-be	почувати себе
feeling	po-chut-tya	почуття
ferry	po-rom	пором
festival	fe-sty-val'	фестиваль
festival (religious)	svya-to	свято
fever	ha-ryach-ka	гарячка
few	ma-lo • ne-ba-ha-to	мало • небагато

a few
de-kil'-ka
декілька

English	Pronunciation	Ukrainian
fiance(e)	na-re-*che*-ny/ na-re-*che*-na (m/f)	наречений/ наречена
film (movie)	fil'm	фільм
film (roll of)	fo-to-*pliw*-ka	фотоплівка
filtered (water)	fil'-*tro*-va-na (vo-*da*)	фільтрована (вода)
fine (penalty)	shtraf	штраф
fire	po-*zhe*-zha	пожежа
firewood	*dro*-va	дрова
first	*per*-shy/*per*-sha (m/f)	перший/перша
fish	*ry*-ba	риба
flag	*pra*-por	прапор
flashlight (torch)	ky-shen'-*ko*-vy li-*khta*-ryk	кишеньковий ліхтарик
flight	reys	рейс
flood	po-vin'	повінь
floor	pi-*dlo*-ha	підлога
on the floor na pi-*dlo*-zi		на підлозі
flower(s)	*kvi*-tka/*kvi*-ty (sg/pl)	квітка/квіти
to follow	i-*ty* sli-dom	іти слідом

Follow me!
i-*dit'* za mno-yu!
Ідіть за мною!

food	*yi*-zha	їжа
food poisoning	khar-cho-ve o-*tru*-yen-nya	харчове отруєння
football	fut-*bol*	футбол
foreign	i-no-ze-mny	іноземний
forever	na-*zaw*-zhdy	назавжди
to forget	za-bu-*va*-ty	забувати

I forgot.
ya za-*buw*/za-*bu*-la (m/f)
Я забув/забула.

You forgot.
vy za-*bu*-ly
Ви забули.

to forgive	vy-ba-*cha*-ty	вибачати
formal	for-*mal*'-ny	формальний
fragile	lam-*ky*	ламкий
free (gratis)	bez-ko-*shtow*-ny • bez-*pla*-tny	безкоштовний • безплатний
free (not bound)	vil'-ny	вільний
to freeze	mo-ro-*zy*-ty	морозити
fresh	*svi*-zhy	свіжий
friend	druh	друг
friendly	*dru*-zhniy	дружний
full	*pow*-ny	повний
fun	za-*ba*-va • *ra*-dist'	забава • радість
funny	smi-*shny*	смішний

G

game	hra	гра
garbage	smit-*tya*	сміття
garden	sad	сад
garden (vegetable)	ho-*rod*	город
gas (cooking)	haz	газ
gas (petrol)	ben-*zyn*	бензин
gate	vo-*ro*-ta (pl)	ворота
generous	shche-dry	щедрий
gift	po-da-*ru*-nok	подарунок
girl	*diw*-chy-na	дівчина
girlfriend	po-dru-ha	подруга
to give	da-*va*-ty	давати

Give me ...
day-te me-*ni* ...
Дайте мені ...

I'll give you ...
ya dam vam ...
Я дам вам ...

glass (of water)	*sklyan*-ka (vo-*dy*)	склянка (води)
glass (of vodka)	*char*-ka (ho-*ril*-ky)	чарка (горілки)
glasses (spectacles)	o-ku-*lya*-ry	окуляри
to go (on foot)	*i*-ty • kho-*dy*-ty	іти • ходити

I'm going to ... (do something)
ya zby-*ra*-yu-sya ...
Я збираюся ...

I'm going to ... (somewhere)
ya *yi*-du/ydu w/do ...
Я їду/йду в/до ...

Are you going there?
vy *yi*-de-te/yde-*te* tu-*dy*?
Ви їдете/йдете туди?

to go (train/bus/car)	*yi*-kha-ty • *yi*-zdy-ty	їхати • їздити
God	boh	Бог
good	*do*-bry	добрий
government	u-*ryad*	уряд
greedy	*zha*-dib-ny	жадібний
to grow (to increase)	ro-*sty*	рости
to grow (to produce)	vy-ro-shchu-va-ty	вирощувати
to guess	wha-*da*-ty	вгадати
guide	hid	гід
guidebook	pu-tiw-*nyk*	путівник
guilty	*vyn*-ny	винний
guitar	hi-*ta*-ra	гітара

H

hair	vo-*los*-sya	волосся
hairdresser	pe-ru-*kar*	перукар
half	po-lo-*vy*-na	половина
handbag	*sum*-ka	сумка
handicapped person	in-va-*lid*	інвалід
handicrafts	re-*me*-sla	ремесла
handsome	wrod-*ly*-vy • *har*-ny	вродливий • гарний
happy	shcha-*sly*-vy	щасливий

Happy Birthday!
z dnem na-*ro*-dzhen-nya!
З Днем народження!

hard (difficult)	vazh-ky • skla-*dny*	важкий • складний
hard (not soft)	tver-*dy*	твердий
to hate	ne-*na*-vy-di-ty	ненавидіти
to have	*ma*-ty	мати

I have ...
ya *ma*-yu ...
Я маю ...

You have ...
vy *ma*-ye-te ...
Ви маєте ...

Do you have ...?
u vas ye ...?
У вас є ...?

he	vin	він
health	zdo-ro-*vya*	здоров'я
health centre	po-li-*kli*-ni-ka	поліклініка
to hear	*chu*-ty	чути
heat	*spe*-ka	спека
heater	o-bi-hri-*vach*	обігрівач
heavy	tyazh-ky • vazh-ky	тяжкий • важкий

Hello! (inf)
pry-*vit*!
Привіт!

Hello/Goodday!
do-*bry*-den'!
Добридень!

help	do-po-*mo*-ha	допомога
to help	po-moh-*ty* • do-po-*moh*-ty	помогти • допомогти

Can I help (you)?
ya *mo*-zhu (vam) do-po-*moh*-ty?
Я можу (вам) допомогти?

Help!
rya-*tuy*-te!
Рятуйте!

Help yourself!
pry-ho-*shchay*-te-sya!
Пригощайтеся!

here	tut	тут
high	vy-*so*-ky	високий
hill	pa-horb	пагорб
to hire	*bra*-ty na-pro-*kat*	брати напрокат

I'd like to hire it.
ya [kho-*tiw* by; kho-*ti*-la b] *wzya*-ty tse na-pro-*kat* (m/f)
Я [хотів би; хотіла б] взяти це напрокат.

holiday (religious)	*svya*-to	свято
holiday (vacation)	vid-*pus*-tka	відпустка
on holiday	u vid-*pus*-tsi	у відпустці
school holidays	ka-*ni*-ku-ly	канікули
holy	svya-*ty*	святий
home	dim	дім
homeland	bat'-kiw-*shchy*-na	батьківщина
homosexual (adj)	ho-mo-se-ksu-al'-ny	гомосексуальний
homosexual	ho-mo-se-ksu-a-*list*	гомосексуаліст
honest	che-sny	чесний
hope	na-*di*-ya	надія
to hope	spo-di-*va*-ty-sya	сподіватися
hospital	li-*kar*-nya	лікарня
hospitality	ho-*styn*-nist'	гостинність
hot	ha-*rya*-chy	гарячий
hot (weather)	zhar-ky	жаркий
hot (spicy)	ho-stry	гострий
hotel	ho-*tel'*	готель
hotel room	no-mer	номер
house	dim • bu-*dy*-nok	дім • будинок
country house	kha-ta	хата
housework	do-ma-shnya ro-*bo*-ta	домашня робота
how	yak	як

How do I get to ...?
yak do-*yi*-kha-ty do ...?
Як доїхати до ...?

How are you?
yak vy se-*be* po-chu-va-ye-te?
Як ви себе почуваєте?

How much is/are ...?
skil'-ky *ko*-shtu-ye/ko-shtu-*yut'* ...?
Скільки коштує/коштують ...?

hryvnia (Ukrainian currency)	hryw-nya	гривня
human (adj)	lyuds'-*ky*	людський
hungry	ho-lo-dny	голодний

I'm hungry.
ya *kho-chu yi-*sty
Я хочу їсти.

Are you hungry?
vy *kho-che-te yi-*sty?
Ви хочете їсти?

to hurry	po-spi-*sha-*ty	поспішати

I'm in a hurry.
ya po-spi-*sha-*yu
Я поспішаю.

to hurt	bo-*li-*ty	боліти

My ... hurts.
u *me-*ne bo-*lyt'* ...
У мене болить ...

husband	cho-lo-*vik*	чоловік
hypnotism	hi-pno-*tyzm*	гіпнотизм

I

I	ya	я
ice	lid	лід
with ice	z *l'o-*dom	з льодом
without ice	bez *l'o-*du	без льоду
ice cream	mo-ro-zy-vo	морозиво
icon	i-*ko-*na	ікона
idea	i-*de-*ya •	ідея •
	u-*yaw-*len-nya	уявлення
identification	wsta-*now-*len-nya	встановлення
	o-*so-*by	особи
if	yak-*shcho*	якщо
ill	*khvo-*ry	хворий
illegal	ne-za-*kon-*ny •	незаконний •
	ne-le-*hal'-*ny	нелегальний
imagination	u-*ya-*va	уява
imitation	i-mi-*ta-*tsi-ya	імітація
immediately	ne-*hay-*no	негайно
to import	wvo-zy-ty	ввозити
import	wve-*zen-*nya • *im-*port	ввезення • імпорт
important	vazh-*ly-*vy	важливий
impossible	ne-*mozh-*ly-vy	неможливий
imprisonment	u-*vya-*znen-nya	ув'язнення
in	u • w	у • в
included	w*klyu-*che-no	включено
inconvenient	ne-*zruch-*ny	незручний
industry	pro-my-*slo-*vist'	промисловість
infection	za-ra-*zhen-*nya •	зараження •
	in-*fek-*tsi-ya	інфекція
infectious	in-fek-*tsiy-*ny	інфекційний
informal	ne-for-*mal'-*ny	неформальний

J

information	in-for-*ma*-tsi-ya	інформація
injection	u-*kol* • in-*yek*-tsi-ya	укол • ін'єкція
injury	po-*ra*-nen-nya • *traw*-ma	поранення • травма
insect repellent	ri-dy-*na* vid ko-*makh*	рідина від комах
inside	u-se-*re*-dy-ni	усередині
insurance	stra-khu-*van*-nya	страхування
to insure	stra-khu-*va*-ty	страхувати

It's insured.
tse za-stra-*kho*-va-no
Це застраховано.

intelligent	ro-*zu*-mny	розумний
interesting	tsi-*ka*-vy	цікавий
international	mizh-na-*ro*-dny	міжнародний
Internet	in-ter-*net*	Інтернет
Internet cafe	in-ter-net-ka-*fe*	Інтернет-кафе
invite	za-*pro*-shen-nya	запрошувати
invitation	za-*pro*-shu-va-ty	запрошення

J

jail	vya-*zny*-tsya	в'язниця
jazz	dzhaz	джаз
jeans	*dzhyn*-sy	джинси
jewellery	yu-ve-*lir*-ni *vy*-ro-by	ювелірні вироби
job	ro-*bo*-ta	робота
joke	zhart	жарт

I'm joking.
ya zhar-*tu*-yu
Я жартую.

journey	po-do-*rozh*	подорож
juice	sik	сік
justice	spra-ve-*dly*-vist'	справедливість

K

key	klyuch	ключ
to kill	u-by-*va*-ty	убивати
kind (adj)	*do*-bry	добрий
king	ko-*rol'*	король
kiss	po-tsi-*lu*-nok	поцілунок
to kiss	tsi-lu-*va*-ty	цілувати
knapsack	ryug-*zak*	рюкзак
to know (a person)	*zna*-ty	знати

I know him.
ya yo-*ho* *zna*-yu
Я його знаю.

DICTIONARY

| to know (how to do something) | u-*mi*-ty | уміти |

> I know how to get there.
> ya *zna*-yu, yak tu-*dy* di-*sta*-ty-sya
> Я знаю, як туди дістатися.

L

lake	o-*ze*-ro	озеро
land	ze-*mlya*	земля
landslide	zsuw	зсув
language	mo-*va*	мова
large	ve-*ly*-ky	великий
last (in a series)	o-*stan*-niy	останній
last (eg 'last week')	my-*nu*-ly	минулий
late	*pi*-zniy	пізній
to be late	spi-*zny*-ty-sya	спізнитися

> I'm late!
> za-*pi*-znyu-yu-sya!
> Запізнююся!

| later | pi-*zni*-she | пізніше |
| to laugh | smi-*ya*-ty-sya | сміятися |

> Don't laugh!
> ne *smiy*-te-sya!
> Не смійтеся!

laundry	bi-*ly*-zna	білизна
laundry (place)	*pral*'-nya	пральня
law	za-*kon*	закон
lawyer	a-dvo-*kat*	адвокат
lazy	li-*ny*-vy	лінивий
to learn	u-*chy*-ty • vy-*wcha*-ty	учити • вивчати

> I want to learn Ukrainian.
> ya *kho*-chu vy-*wchy*-ty u-*kra*-*yins*'-ku mo-*vu*
> Я хочу вивчити українську мову.

| to leave (depart) | vid-*kho*-dy-ty • vid-*yizh*-*dzha*-ty • vid-*li*-ta-ty | відходити • від'їжджати • відлітати |

> The flight leaves at ...
> li-*tak* vid-li-*ta*-ye o ...
> Літак відлітає о ...

> What time does the train leave?
> ko-*ly* vid-*kho*-dyt' *po*-yizd?
> Коли відходить поїзд?

> We're leaving for Kyiv tonight.
> u-ve-*che*-ri my vid-*yizh*-*dzha*-ye-mo do *ky*-e-va
> Увечері ми від'їжджаємо до Києва.

| to leave (behind) | za-*bu*-ty | забути |

L

lecturer	vy-kla-*dach*	викладач
left (not right)	*li*-vy	лівий
on/to the left	na-*li*-vo • *li*-vo-ruch	наліво • ліворуч
legal	za-*kon*-ny	законний
less	*men*-she	менше
letter	lyst	лист
liar	bre-*khun*	брехун
lice	vo-shi	воші
life	zhyt-*tya*	життя
lift (elevator)	lift	ліфт
light (not heavy, adj)	leh-ky	легкий
light	svi-tlo	світло
lighter	za-pal'-*ny*-chka	запальничка
like (similar)	*skho*-zhy	схожий
to like	po-*do*-ba-ty-sya	подобатися

I like ...
nam po-*do*-ba-yet'-sya ...
Нам подобається ...

Do you like ...?
vam po-*do*-ba-yet'-sya ...?
Вам подобається ...?

line	*li*-ni-ya	лінія
to listen	*slu*-kha-ty	слухати

Listen to me!
po-*slu*-khay-te me-*ne*!
Послухайте мене!

little (dimension)	ma-*len*'-ky	маленький
little (quantity)	*ma*-lo	мало
to live	zhy-ty	жити

I live in ...
ya zhy-*vu* w ...
Я живу в ...

Where do you live?
de vy zhy-ve-*te*?
Де ви живете?

local	mi-*stse*-vy	місцевий
lock	za-*mok*	замок
long	*dow*-hy	довгий
long ago	*daw*-no	давно
to look	dy-*vy*-ty-sya	дивитися
to look for	shu-*ka*-ty	шукати
to lose	za-hu-*by*-ty	загубити

I've lost my money.
ya za-hu-*byw*/za-hu-*by*-la hro-shi (m/f)
Я загубив/загубила гроші.

to lose (one's way)	za-blu-*ka*-ty • za-*blu*-dy-ty-sya	заблукати • заблудитися

262

I'm lost.
ya za-blu-*kaw*/za-blu-*ka*-la • ya za-blu-*dyw*-sya/za-blu-dy-*la*-sya (m/f)
Я заблукав/заблукала • Я заблудився/заблудилася.

lost (adj)	*wtra-che-ny*	втрачений
loud	*ho-lo-sny*	голосний
love	*lyu-bow* • ko-*khan*-nya	любов • кохання
to love (be fond of)	*lyu-by-ty*	любити

I'm fond of ...
ya *du*-zhe lyu-*blyu* ...
Я дуже люблю ...

Are you fond of ...?
vy *lyu*-by-te ...?
Ви любите ...?

to love (relationships)	ko-*kha*-ty	кохати

I love you.
ya te-*be* ko-*kha*-yu
Я тебе кохаю.

lucky	shcha-*sly*-vy	щасливий
to be lucky	*ma*-ty *shcha*-stya	мати щастя
luggage	ba-*hazh*	багаж
lunch	o-*bid*	обід

M

machine	ma-*shy*-na	машина
mad (crazy)	bo-zhe-*vil'*-ny	божевільний
(made of)	(*zro*-ble-ny) z	(зроблений) з
mail	*po*-shta	пошта
main	ho-*low*-ny	головний
majority	*bil'*-shist'	більшість
to make	zro-*by*-ty	зробити

Did you make it?
vy sa-*mi* tse zro-*by*-ly?
Ви самі це зробили?

man	cho-lo-*vik*	чоловік
many	ba-*ha*-to	багато
map	*kar*-ta	карта
market	*ry*-nok	ринок
at the market	na *ryn*-ku	на ринку
marriage	o-*dru*-zhen-nya	одруження
to marry		
	o-*dru*-zhy-ty-sya	одружитися
(woman to a man)	*vy*-ty za-*mizh*	вийти заміж

I got married.
ya o-*dru*-zhyw-sya (m) • ya o-*dru*-zhy-la-sya; ya *vy*-shla za-*mizh* (f)
Я одружився • Я одружилася; Я вийшла заміж.

massage	ma-*sazh*	масаж

matches	sir-ny-ky	сірники
maybe	ma-but'	мабуть
medication	li-ky (pl)	ліки
medicine	li-ky (pl)	ліки
to meet (someone)	zu-stri-ty	зустріти

I'll meet you.
ya vas zu-stri-nu
Я вас зустріну.

| to meet (each other) | zu-stri-ty-sya | зустрітися |

Let's meet!
zu-strin'-mo-sya!
Зустріньмося!

menu	me-nyu	меню
message	po-vi-do-mlen-nya	повідомлення
metro	me-tro	метро
milk	mo-lo-ko	молоко
million	mil'-yon	мільйон
mind	ro-zum	розум
to mind (to object)	za-pe-re-chu-va-ty	заперечувати

Do you mind ...?
mo-zhna me-ni ...? • vy ne za-pe-re-chu-ye-te?
Можна мені ...? • Ви не заперечуєте?

Never mind!
ni-cho-ho!
Нічого!

Mind out!
o-be-re-zhno!
Обережно!

mineral water	mi-ne-ral'-na vo-da	мінеральна вода
minute	khvy-ly-na	хвилина
to miss	sku-cha-yu za ...	скучаю за ...
mistake	po-myl-ka	помилка
to make a mistake	po-my-ly-ty-sya	помилитися

You've made a mistake.
vy po-my-ly-ly-sya
Ви помилилися.

mix	zmi-shu-va-ty	змішувати
modern	su-cha-sny	сучасний
money	hro-shi	гроші
month	mi-syats'	місяць
monument	pa-mya-tnyk	пам'ятник
more	bil'-she	більше
morning	ra-nok	ранок
mountain	ho-ra	гора
mountaineering	al'-pi-nizm	альпінізм
mother	ma-ty	мати
movie	fil'm	фільм

Let's see a movie.
kho-*di*-mo w ki-*no*
Ходімо в кіно.

mum	*ma*-ma	мама
museum	mu-*zey*	музей
music	*mu*-zy-ka	музика
musician	*mu*-zy-kant	музикант

N

name	i-*mya*	ім'я

My name is ...
me-*ne* zvut'/*zva*-ty ...
Мене звуть/звати ...

What's your name?
yak vas/te-*be* zva-ty? (pol/inf)
Як Вас/тебе звати?

national park	za-po-*vi*-dnyk	заповідник
nature	pry-*ro*-da	природа
near (adv)	blyz'-ko	близько
near (prep)	*bi*-lya	біля
nearby	po-*ruch*	поруч
necessary	po-*trib*-ny	потрібний
to need	*tre*-ba • po-*trib*-no	треба • потрібно

I need ...
me-*ni tre*-ba/po-*trib*-no ...
Мені треба/потрібно ...

We need ...
nam *tre*-ba/po-*trib*-no ...
Нам треба/потрібно ...

Do you need anything?
vam shchos' *tre*-ba/po-*trib*-no?
Вам щось треба/потрібно?

neither ... nor	ni ..., ni	ні ..., ні
never	ni-*ko*-ly	ніколи
new	*no*-vy	новий
news	*no*-vy-*na*/	новина/
	no-vy-ny (sg/pl)	новини
newspaper	ha-*ze*-ta	газета
next	na-*stup*-ny	наступний
night	nich	ніч
no	ni	ні
noise	shum	шум
noisy	*shu*-mny	шумний
none	*zho*-dny	жодний
north	*piw*-nich	північ
nothing	ni-*shcho* • ni-*cho*-ho	ніщо • нічого
not yet	shche ni	ще ні

O

We aren't in Lviv yet.
my shche ne u l'vo-vi.
Ми ще не у Львові.

| now | te-*per* • *za*-raz | тепер • зараз |
| nuclear energy | a-*tom*-na e-*ner*-hi-ya | атомна енергія |

O

obvious	o-che-*vy*-dny	очевидний
occupation	za-*nyat*-tya	заняття
ocean	o-ke-*an*	океан
to offend	o-bra-*zha*-ty	ображати
to offer	pro-po-nu-*va*-ty	пропонувати
office	byu-*ro* • kon-*to*-ra • o-*fis*	бюро • контора • офіс
often	*cha*-sto	часто
oil (crude)	*na*-fta	нафта
oil (cooking)	o-*li*-ya	олія
OK (adv)	nor-*mal'*-no	нормально
old	*sta*-ry	старий
Olympic Games	o-lim-*piy*-s'ki *i*-hry	Олімпійські ігри
on (location)	na	на
on (a particular day)	u • w	у • в
once	raz	раз
once more	shche raz	ще раз
once (upon a time)	ko-*lys'*	колись
one	o-*dyn*	один
one way	v o-*dyn* bik	в один бік
only	*til'*-ky	тільки
open (adj)		
(doors, windows)	vid-*chy*-ne-ny	відчинений
(shop)	vid-*kry*-ty	відкритий
to open		
(doors, windows)	vid-chy-*nya*-ty	відчиняти
(shop)	vid-kry-*va*-ty	відкривати
opera	o-*pe*-ra	опера
opera house	o-*per*-ny te-*atr*	оперний театр
opinion	*dum*-ka	думка

in my opinion ...
na mo-*yu dum*-ku ...
на мою думку ...

opportunity	na-*ho*-da	нагода
opposite (adj)	pro-ty-le-*zhny*	протилежний
opposite (prep)	na-*pro*-ty	напроти
or	a-*bo* • chy	або • чи
order (command)	na-*kaz*	наказ
order (something)	za-*mow*-len-nya	замовлення
to order	za-mo-*vy*-ty	замовити
ordinary	zvy-*chay*-ny	звичайний
organisation	or-ha-ni-za-*tsi*-ya	організація

ENGLISH – UKRAINIAN

P

to organise	vla-*shto*-vu-va-ty	влаштовувати
original	o-ry-hi-*nal'*-ny	оригінальний
other	*in*-shy	інший
outside	na-*zow*-ni	назовні
over (prep)	nad	над
to overnight	pe-re-no-chu-*va*-ty	переночувати
overseas	za kor-*do*-nom	за кордоном
to owe	za-*vy*-ny-ty •	завинити •
	bu-ty vyn-nym	бути винним

> I owe you.
> ya vam *vy*-nen
> Я вам винен.
>
> You owe me.
> vy me-*ni vyn*-ni
> Ви мені винні.

owner	*wla*-snyk	власник

P

pack (of cigarettes)	*pa*-chka (tsy-ha-*rok*)	пачка (цигарок)
package	pa-*ku*-nok	пакунок
packet	pa-*ket*	пакет
padlock	vy-*sya*-chy za-*mok*	висячий замок
painful	bo-*lyu*-chy	болючий
painkillers	zne-bo-lyu-val'-ni za-so-by	знеболювальні засоби
painting	kar-*ty*-na	картина
pair	*pa*-ra	пара
palace	pa-*lats*	палац
paper	pa-*pir*	папір
parcel	po-*syl*-ka	посилка
parents	*bat'*-ky	батьки
park	park	парк
parking	sto-*yan*-ka • *par*-kinh	стоянка • паркінг
parliament	par-*la*-ment	парламент
part	cha-sty-na	частина
to participate	*bra*-ty u-*chast'*	брати участь
participation	u-*chast'*	участь
party	ve-*chir*-ka	вечірка
party (political)	*par*-ti-ya	партія
passenger	pa-sa-*zhyr*	пасажир
passport	*pa*-sport	паспорт
path	*stezh*-ka	стежка
to pay	pla-*ty*-ty	платити
peace	myr	мир
people (crowd)	*lyu*-dy	люди
lots of people	ba-*ha*-to lyu-*dey*	багато людей
people (nation)	na-*rod*	народ
perfect (adj)	do-sko-*na*-ly	досконалий
permanent	po-*stiy*-ny	постійний
permission	do-*zvil*	дозвіл

with your permission
z *va-sho-ho do-zvo-lu*
з Вашого дозволу

permit	pe-re-*pus*-tka	перепустка
to permit	do-zvo-*lya*-ty	дозволяти
persecution	pe-re-*sli*-du-van-nya	переслідування
person	o-*so*-ba	особа
personal	o-so-*by*-sty	особистий
personality	o-so-*by*-stist'	особистість
petrol	ben-*zyn*	бензин
pharmacy	a-*pte*-ka	аптека
phone book	te-le-*fon*-na *kny*-ha	телефонна книга
photograph	fo-*to*(-*hra*-fi-ya)	фото(графія)
to photograph	fo-to-hra-fu-*va*-ty	фотографувати

Can I take a photograph?
chy *mo*-zhna fo-to-hra-fu-*va*-ty?
Чи можна фотографувати?

piece	shma-*tok*	шматок
place	*mi*-stse	місце
plant	ro-*sly*-na	рослина
plate	ta-*ril*-ka	тарілка
play (theatre)	*pye*-sa • vy-*sta*-va	п'єса • вистава
to play	*hra*-ty	грати

Please.
bud' *la*-ska.
Будь ласка.

plenty	ba-*ha*-to	багато
poetry	po-e-*zi*-ya	поезія
to point (with one's finger)	po-*ka*-zu-va-ty (*pal'*-tsem)	показувати (пальцем)
police	mi-*li*-tsi-ya	міліція
politics	po-*li*-ty-ka	політика
pollution	za-*bru*-dnen-nya	забруднення
pool (swimming)	ba-*seyn*	басейн
poor	*bi*-dny	бідний
port	port	порт
positive (certain)	u-*pew*-ne-ny	упевнений

I'm positive.
ya *pe*-ven/*pew*-na (m/f)
Я певен/певна.

postage stamp	*mar*-ka	марка
postcard	ly-*stiw*-ka	листівка
post code	po-*shto*-vy *in*-deks	поштовий індекс
post office	*po*-shta	пошта
pottery (items)	fa-*yans* • ke-ra-*mi*-ka	фаянс • кераміка
pottery (place)	hon-*char*-nya	гончарня
poverty	*bi*-dnist'	бідність
power (strength)	*sy*-la	сила
power (political)	*wla*-da	влада

268

D I C T I O N A R Y

P

Q

practical	prak-*tych*-ny	практичний
prayer	mo-*ly*-tva	молитва
to prefer	na-da-*va*-ty pe-re-*va*-hu	надавати перевагу

I prefer ...
ya na-da-*yu* pe-re-*va*-hu ...
Я надаю перевагу ...

pregnant	va-*hit*-na	вагітна
present (adj)	te-pe-*ri*-shniy •	теперішній •
	ny-*ni*-shniy	нинішній
present (gift)	po-da-*ru*-nok	подарунок
president	pre-zy-*dent*	президент
pretty	*har*-ny	гарний
to prevent	pe-re-shko-*dzha*-ty •	перешкоджати •
	za-po-bi-*ha*-ty	запобігати
price	tsi-*na*	ціна
priest	svya-*shche*-nyk	священик
prime minister	pre-*myer*-mi-*nistr*	прем'єр-міністр
prison	vya-*zny*-tsya	в'язниця
prisoner	vya-*zen'*	в'язень
private	pry-*va*-tny	приватний
probably	ymo-*vir*-no	ймовірно
problem	pro-*ble*-ma	проблема
procession	pro-*tse*-si-ya	процесія
produce (v)	vy-ro-*blya*-ty	виробляти
professional	pro-fe-*siy*-ny	професійний
profit	pry-*bu*-tok	прибуток
promise	o-bi-*tsyan*-ka	обіцянка
to promise	o-bi-*tsya*-ty	обіцяти
prostitute	pro-sty-*tu*-tka	проститутка
to protect	za-khy-*shcha*-ty	захищати
protest	pro-*test*	протест
to protest	pro-te-stu-*va*-ty	протестувати
public	pu-*bli*-ka	публіка
public (adj)	pu-*blich*-ny •	публічний •
	hro-*mads'*-ky	громадський
in public	pu-*blich*-no	публічно
to pull	tyah-*ty*	тягти
to push	shtow-*kha*-ty	штовхати
to put	po-*sta*-vy-ty •	поставити •
	po-*kla*-sty	покласти

Q

quality	ya-*kist'*	якість
of good quality	ya-*ki*-sny	якісний
question	py-*tan*-nya	питання
queue	*cher*-ha	черга
quick (adj)	shvyd-*ky*	швидкий
quickly	shvyd-*ko*	швидко
quiet (adj)	spo-*kiy*-ny • *ty*-khy	спокійний • тихий

R

race (contest)	bih	біг
race (horses)	pe-re-ho-ny • skach-ky	перегони • скачки
racist	ra-syst	расист
radio	ra-di-o	радіо
railway	za-li-zny-tsya	залізниця
by railway	za-li-zny-tse-yu	залізницею
to rain	doshch	дощ

It's raining.
i-*de* doshch
Іде дощ.

rape	zgval-tu-*van*-nya	зґвалтування
to rape	gval-tu-*va*-ty	ґвалтувати
rare (unusual)	*rid*-ki-sny	рідкісний
rare (meat)	ne-do-*sma*-zhe-ny	недосмажений
raw	sy-*ry*	сирий
razor blades	*le*-za	леза
to read	chy-*ta*-ty	читати
ready	ho-*to*-vy	готовий
reason	pry-*chy*-na	причина
receipt	kvy-*tan*-tsi-ya	квитанція
recently	ne-shcho-*da*-wno	нещодавно
to recommend	re-ko-men-du-*va*-ty	рекомендувати
refrigerator	kho-lo-*dyl*'-nyk	холодильник
refugee	*bi*-zhe-nets'	біженець
refund	vy-*pla*-ta •	виплата •
	vid-shko-du-*van*-nya	відшкодування
refuse	*smit*-tya	сміття
to refuse	vid-mow-*lya*-ty-sya	відмовлятися
region	ra-*yon*	район
registered letter	re-ko-men-*do*-va-ny	рекомендований
	lyst	лист
regulation	*pra*-vy-lo	правило
relationship	sto-*sun*-ky	стосунки
to relax	roz-sla-*blya*-ty-sya	розслаблятися
religion	re-*li*-hi-ya	релігія
to remember	pa-mya-*ta*-ty	пам'ятати
remote	vid-*da*-le-ny	віддалений
rent (accommodation)	kvar-*tyr*-na *pla*-ta •	квартирна плата •
	o-*ren*-da	оренда
rent (hiring)	pro-*kat*	прокат
to rent	nay-*ma*-ty	наймати
to repeat	po-*wto*-ryu-va-ty	повторювати

Please repeat that.
po-wto-*rit*', bud' *la*-ska
Повторіть, будь ласка.

| representative | pred-staw-*nyk* | представник |
| republic | re-*spu*-bli-ka | республіка |

reservation	(po-pe-*re*-dnye) za-*mow*-len-nya • *bro*-nya	(попереднє) замовлення • броня
reserve	za-po-*vi*-dnyk	заповідник
to reserve	za-mow-*lya*-ty	замовляти
respect	po-va-*ha*	повага
to respect	sha-nu-*va*-ty	шанувати
responsibility	vid-po-vi-*dal'*-nist'	відповідальність
rest	vid-po-*chy*-nok	відпочинок
to rest	vid-po-chy-*va*-ty	відпочивати
restaurant	re-sto-*ran*	ресторан
to return	po-ver-*ta*-ty-sya	повертатися

We'll return on …
my po-ver-*ta*-ye-mo-sya …
Ми повертаємося …

return ticket	zvo-ro-*tny* kvy-*tok*	зворотний квиток
revolution	re-vo-*lyu*-tsi-ya	революція
rich	ba-*ha*-ty	багатий
right (not left)	*pra*-vy	правий
on/to the right	*pra*-vo-ruch • na-*pra*-vo	праворуч • направо
right (correct)	*pra*-vyl'-ny	правильний

I'm right.
ya *ma*-yu *ra*-tsi-yu
Я маю рацію.

risk	*ry*-zyk	ризик
river	*rich*-ka	річка
road	do-*ro*-ha	дорога
robber	hra-*bi*-zhnyk	грабіжник
robbery	po-hra-bu-*van*-nya	пограбування
roof	dakh	дах
room (general)	ki-*mna*-ta	кімната
room (hotel)	no-*mer*	номер
rope	ka-*nat*	канат
round	kru-*hly*	круглий
rubbish	*smit*-tya	сміття

Rubbish!
ni-se-*ni*-tny-tsi!
Нісенітниці!

ruins	ru-*yi*-ny	руїни
rule	*pra*-vy-lo	правило

S

sad	sum-*ny*	сумний
safe (adj)	ne-po-*shko*-dzhe-ny	непошкоджений
safe	seyf	сейф
safely	bez-*pech*-no	безпечно
safety	bez-*pe*-ka	безпека
salty	so-*lo*-ny	солоний

| same | toy sa-my | той самий |
| to say | ho-vo-ry-ty • ska-za-ty | говорити • сказати |

I said ...
ya ska-zaw/ska-za-la ... (m/f)
Я сказав/сказала ...

Can you say that again?
po-wto-rit', bud' la-ska
Повторіть, будь ласка

scenery	pey-zazh	пейзаж
school	shko-la	школа
secret (adj)	ta-ye-mny	таємний
secret	ta-ye-mny-tsya	таємниця
to see	ba-chy-ty	бачити

I see. (understand)
ya ro-zu-mi-yu
Я розумію.

I see (it).
ya ba-chu (tse)
Я бачу (це).

| selfish | e-ho-yi-sty-chny | егоїстичний |
| to sell | pro-da-va-ty | продавати |

Do you sell ...?
vy pro-da-ye-te ...?
Ви продаєте ...?

send	po-sy-la-ty	посилати
sentence (grammar)	re-chen-nya	речення
serious	ser-yo-zny	серйозний
several	kil'-ka • de-kil'-ka	кілька • декілька
shade	tin'	тінь
share	chas-tka	частка
to share	ro-zdi-lya-ty	розділяти
she	vo-na	вона
shoes	vzut-tya	взуття
shop	ma-ha-zyn • kra-mny-tsya	магазин • крамниця
short (length, duration)	ko-ro-tky	короткий
a short time ago	ne-daw-no	недавно
short (height)	nyz'-ky	низький
shortage	ne-do-sta-cha	недостача
to shout	kry-cha-ty	кричати
to show	po-ka-zu-va-ty	показувати
shut (adj)	za-chy-ne-ny	зачинений

Show me, please.
po-ka-zhit', bud' la-ska
Покажіть, будь ласка.

to shut	za-chy-nya-ty	зачиняти
shy	bo-yaz-ky	боязкий
sick	khvo-ry	хворий

sickness	khvo-ro-ba	хвороба
sign	znak	знак
signature	*pid*-pys	підпис
similar	po-*dib*-ny	подібний
since (from that time)	z to-ho cha-su	з того часу
since (because)	o-skil'-ky	оскільки
since	z to-ho cha-su, yak ...	з того часу, як ...
(after that time)		
since (prep)	z • *pi*-slya	з • після
single (unmarried)	ne-o-*dru*-zhe-ny (m) •	неодружений •
	ne-o-*dru*-zhe-na;	неодружена;
	ne-za-*mizh*-nya (f)	незаміжня
sister	se-*stra*	сестра
to sit	si-*da*-ty	сідати

Sit down!
si-*day*-te!
Сідайте!

to sit (be sitting)	sy-*di*-ty	сидіти
situation	sy-tu-a-*tsi*-ya	ситуація
size	*ro*-zmir	розмір
sleep	son	сон
to sleep	*spa*-ty	спати

I'm asleep.
ya splyu.
Я сплю.

He's asleep.
vin spyt'.
Він спить.

Are you asleep?
vy spy-*te*?
Ви спите?

sleepy	*son*-ny	сонний

I'm sleepy.
ya *kho*-chu *spa*-ty.
Я хочу спати.

slow	po-*vil'*-ny	повільний
slowly	po-*vil'*-no	повільно
small	ma-*ly*	малий
smell	za-*pakh*	запах
to smell	vid-chu-va-ty za-*pakh*	відчувати запах
snow	snih	сніг
soap	*my*-lo	мило
socialism	so-tsi-a-*lizm*	соціалізм
solid (adj)	su-*tsil'*-ny	суцільний
some (quantity)	*kil'*-ka • de-*kil'*-ka	кілька • декілька
somebody	khtos'	хтось
something	shchos'	щось

sometimes	*in*-ko-ly	інколи
son	syn	син
song	*pi*-snya	пісня
so-so	po-ma-*len'*-ku	помаленьку
soon	ne-za-*ba*-rom	незабаром

Sorry!
vy-bach-te!
Вибачте!

south	piw-*den'*	південь
souvenir	su-ve-*nir*	сувенір
speak	ho-vo-*ry*-ty	говорити
special	spe-tsi-*al'*-ny	спеціальний
spirits	spyr-*tni* na-po-yi	спиртні напої
sport	sport	спорт
spring (season)	ve-*sna*	весна
square	*plo*-shcha •	площа •
	may-*dan*	майдан
stairway	*skho*-dy	сходи
stamp	*mar*-ka	марка
standard (adj)	stan-*dar*-tny	стандартний
station (railway)	vog-*zal* •	вокзал •
	stan-tsi-ya	станція
stay	pe-re-bu-*van*-nya	перебування
to stay	pro-*bu*-ty	пробути

I'll stay here for two days.
ya pro-*bu*-du tut dva dni
Я пробуду тут два дні.

| to steal | *kra*-sty | красти |

My money has been stolen.
u *me*-ne wkra-de-no *hro*-shi
У мене вкрадено гроші.

| stop | zu-*pyn*-ka | зупинка |
| to stop | zu-py-*ny*-ty | зупинити |

I stopped the car.
ya zu-py-*nyw*/zu-py-*ny*-la ma-*shy*-nu (m/f)
Я зупинив/зупинила машину.

| to stop | zu-py-*ny*-ty-sya | зупинитися |

The car stopped.
ma-*shy*-na zu-py-*ny*-la-sya
Машина зупинилася.

| storey | po-verkh | поверх |

on the ground floor
na *per*-sho-mu po-*ver*-si
на першому поверсі
(lit: on the 1st floor)

| storm | *bu*-rya • ne-*ho*-da | буря • негода |

| story | o-po-vi-*dan*-nya | оповідання |
| straight | prya-*ty* | прямий |

straight ahead
prya-mo
прямо

strange	*dyw*-ny	дивний
stranger	ne-zna-*yo*-mets'	незнайомець
street	*vu*-ly-tsya	вулиця
strike, on	strayk	страйк
strong	*syl*'-ny	сильний
student	stu-*dent*/	студент/
	stu-*den*-tka (m/f)	студентка
stupid	*dur*-ny	дурний
subway	me-*tro*	метро
suddenly	*rap*-tom	раптом
suitcase	che-mo-*dan* •	чемодан •
	va-*li*-za • va-*liz*-ka	валіза • валізка
summer	*li*-to	літо
sun	*son*-tse	сонце
sure (certain)	u-*pew*-ne-ny	упевнений

Are you sure?
vy *wpe*-wne-ni?
Ви впевнені?

surname	*pri*-zvy-shche	прізвище
surprise	ne-spo-*di*-van-ka	несподіванка
sweet	so-*lod*-ky	солодкий
sweets (candy)	tsu-*ker*-ky	цукерки
synagogue	sy-na-*ho*-ha	синагога
to swim	*pla*-va-ty	плавати
swimming trunks (men's)	*plaw*-ky	плавки
swimsuit (women's)	ku-*pal*'-nyk	купальник

T

| table | stil | стіл |
| to take | *bra*-ty • *wzya*-ty | брати • взяти |

I'll take one.
ya *viz*'-mu o-*dyn*
Я візьму один.

Can I take this?
mo-zhna *wzya*-ty tse?
Можна взяти це?

to talk	roz-mow-*lya*-ty	розмовляти
tall	vy-*so*-ky	високий
tasty	*smach*-ny	смачний
tax	po-*da*-tok	податок
taxi	ta-*ksi*	таксі
teacher	u-*chy*-tel'/	учитель/
	u-*chy*-tel'-ka (m/f)	учителька

telephone	te-le-*fon*	телефон
to telephone	te-le-fo-*nu*-va-ty •	телефонувати •
	dzvo-*ny*-ty •	дзвонити •
	po-dzvo-*ny*-ty	подзвонити
telephone book	te-le-*fon*-ny do-*vi*-dnyk	телефонний довідник
temperature	tem-pe-ra-*tu*-ra	температура
tent	na-*met*	намет
to thank	dya-ku-*va*-ty	дякувати

Thank you.
dya-ku-yu.
Дякую.

theatre	te-*atr*	театр
there	tam	там
they	vo-*ny*	вони
thick	hu-*sty*	густий
thief	zlo-*diy*	злодій
thin	ton-*ky*	тонкий
think	du-ma-ty	думати
thirst	*spra*-ha	спрага

I'm thirsty.
ya *kho*-chu *py*-ty
Я хочу пити.

ticket	kvy-*tok*	квиток
time	chas	час

What time is it?
ko-*tra* ho-*dy*-na?
Котра година?

I don't have time.
ya ne *ma*-yu *cha*-su
Я не маю часу.

timetable	roz-klad	розклад
tin opener	vid-kry-*va*-chka	відкривачка
tip (gratuity)	cha-yo-*vi*	чайові

I'm tired.
ya sto-*my*-wsya/sto-*my*-la-sya (m/f)
Я стомився/стомилася.

together	ra-*zom*	разом
toilet	tu-a-*let*	туалет
toilet paper	tu-a-*let*-ny pa-*pir*	туалетний папір
tomorrow	zaw-tra	завтра
tonight	s'o-ho-dni	сьогодні
	u-ve-che-ri	увечері
too (also)	ta-*kozh*	також
too	(za)-*nad*-to	(за)надто
tooth	zub	зуб
torch (flashlight)	li-*khta*-ryk	ліхтарик
to touch	tor-*ka*-ty-sya	торкатися
tour	ek-*skur*-si-ya	екскурсія

I'm touring Ukraine.
ya po-do-ro-*zhu*-yu po u-kra-*yi*-ni
Я подорожую по Україні.

tourist	tu-*ryst*	турист
towards	do	до
towel	ru-*shnyk*	рушник
town	*mi*-sto	місто
track (path)	*stezh*-ka	стежка
track (railway)	ko-*li*-ya	колія
train	po-*yizd*	поїзд
tram	tram-*vay*	трамвай
transit, in	tran-zy-*tom*	транзитом
to translate	pe-re-kla-*da*-ty	перекладати
translation	pe-re-*klad*	переклад
trekking	po-*khid*	похід
trip	po-*yizd*-ka • po-do-*rozh*	поїздка • подорож
trolleybus	tro-*ley*-bus	тролейбус
true	vir-*ny*	вірний
trust (faith)	do-*vi*-ra	довіра
to try (attempt)	spro-bu-*va*-ty	спробувати
to try (taste food)	ku-shtu-*va*-ty	куштувати
to try on (clothing)	pry-mi-*rya*-ty	приміряти
TV	te-le-*ba*-chen-nya	телебачення

U

umbrella	pa-ra-*so*-lya	парасоля
uncomfortable	ne-*zruch*-ny	незручний
under	pid	під
to understand	ro-zu-*mi*-ty	розуміти

I (don't) understand.
ya (ne) ro-zu-*mi*-yu
Я (не) розумію.

Do you understand me?
vy ro-zu-*mi*-ye-te *me*-ne?
Ви розумієте мене?

unemployed	bez-ro-*bi*-tny	безробітний
unemployment	fi-*nan*-so-va	фінансова
benefits	do-po-*mo*-ha bez-ro-*bi*-tnym	допомога безробітним
university	u-ni-ver-sy-*tet*	університет
unsafe	ne-bez-*pech*-ny	небезпечний
until	do	до
up	*who*-ru	вгору
upstairs	na-ho-*ri*	нагорі
urgent	ter-mi-*no*-vy	терміновий
useful	ko-*ry*-sny •	корисний •
	po-*tri*-bny	потрібний
useless	ne-ko-*ry*-sny •	некорисний •
	ne-po-*tri*-bny	непотрібний

V

vacation (holiday)	vid-*pust*-ka	відпустка
on vacation	u vid-*pus*-tsi	у відпустці
school vacations	ka-*ni*-ku-ly	канікули
vaccination	vak-tsy-*na*-tsi-ya •	вакцинація •
	shche-plen-nya	щеплення
vain, in	*mar*-no	марно
valuable	ko-*shtow*-ny	коштовний
value	*var*-tist'	вартість
various	*ri*-zny	різний
vegetable garden	ho-*rod*	город
vegetarian	ve-he-ta-ri-*a*-nets'	вегетаріанець
vegetarian (adj)	ve-he-ta-ri-*ans*'-ky	вегетаріанський
very	*du*-zhe	дуже
video	*vi*-de-o	відео
view	vyd	вид
village	se-*lo*	село
visa	*vi*-za	віза
to visit	vi-*dvi*-du-va-ty	відвідувати
to vomit	blyu-*va*-ty	блювати
to vote	ho-lo-su-*va*-ty	голосувати

W

to wait	che-*ka*-ty	чекати

> Wait a moment!
> (za-che-*kay*-te) khvy-*ly*-noch-ku!
> (Зачекайте) хвилиночку!

waiter	o-fi-tsi-*ant*	офіціант
walk	pro-*hu*-lyan-ka	прогулянка

> Do you want to go for a walk?
> vy *kho*-che-te pi-*ty* po-hu-*lya*-ty?
> Ви хочете піти погуляти?

to walk	hu-*lya*-ty	гуляти
to want	kho-*ti*-ty	хотіти

> I want ...
> ya *kho*-chu ...
> Я хочу ...
>
> We want ...
> my *kho*-che-mo ...
> Ми хочемо ...
>
> Do you want ...?
> vy *kho*-che-te ...?
> Ви хочете ...?

war	viy-*na*	війна
warm	*te*-ply	теплий
to wash (oneself)	*my*-ty-sya	митися

W

I have to wash. me-*ni tre*-ba po-*my*-ty-sya Мені треба помитися.		
to wash (clothes, etc)	*pra*-ty	прати
They need to be washed. yikh *tre*-ba vy-*pra*-ty Їх треба випрати.		
watch to watch	ho-*dyn*-nyk o-hlya-*da*-ty • spo-ste-ri-*ha*-ty	годинник оглядати • спостерігати
Watch out! o-be-*re*-zhno! Обережно!		
water way	vo-*da* do-*ro*-ha	вода дорога
Which way? ya-*ko*-yu do-*ro*-ho-yu? Якою дорогою?		
WC wealthy weather wedding week	tu-a-*let* ba-*ha*-ty po-*ho*-da ve-*sil*-lya *ty*-zhden'	туалет багатий погода весілля тиждень
Welcome! las-*ka*-vo *pro*-sy-mo! Ласкаво просимо!		
well west wet what	kry-*ny*-tsya *za*-khid *mo*-kry shcho	криниця захід мокрий що
What did you say? *shcho* vy ska-*za*-ly? Що ви сказали?		
when where who	ko-*ly* de khto	коли де хто
Who do I ask? ko-*ho* spy-*ta*-ty? Кого спитати?		
whole wife win window winter wise	ves'/wsya/wse (m/f/neut) dru-*zhy*-na *zhin*-ka vy-*hra*-ty vik-*no* zy-*ma* *mu*-dry	весь/вся/все дружина жінка виграти вікно зима мудрий

wish	ba-*zhan*-nya	бажання
to wish	ba-*zha*-ty	бажати
with	z • iz • zi	з • із • зі
within	wse-*re*-dy-ni	всередині
without	bez	без
woman	*zhin*-ka	жінка
wooden	de-re-*vya*-ny	дерев'яний
work	ro-*bo*-ta	робота
to work	pra-tsyu-*va*-ty	працювати
world	svit	світ
worse (adj)	*hir*-shy	гірший
worse (adv)	*hir*-she	гірше
to write	py-*sa*-ty	писати

I'm writing ...
ya py-*shu* ...
Я пишу ...

She's writing ...
vo-*na* py-she ...
Вона пише ...

| wrong | po-myl-*ko*-vy | помилковий |

You are wrong.
vy po-my-*lya*-ye-te-sya
Ви помиляєтеся.

| year | rik | рік |

two years ago
dva *ro*-ky to-*mu*
два роки тому

yes	tak	так
yesterday	u-*cho*-ra	учора
you (inf)	ty	ти
you (pol/pl)	vy	ви
young	mo-lo-*dy*	молодий

zone	*zo*-na	зона
zoo	zo-o-*park*	зоопарк
zodiac	zo-di-*ak*	зодіак

I
N
D
E
X

UKRAINIAN FINDER

SUSTAINABLE TRAVEL

As the climate change debate heats up, the matter of sustainability becomes an important part of the travel vernacular. In practical terms, this means assessing our impact on the environment and local cultures and economies – and acting to make that impact as positive as possible. Here are some basic phrases to get you on your way …

COMMUNICATION & CULTURAL DIFFERENCES

I'd like to learn some of your local dialects.

ya [kho-*tiw* by/kho-*ti*-la b] pi-du-*chy*-ty *de*-kil-ka z *va*-shykh mis-*tse*-vykh di-a-*lek*-tiv (m/f)	Я [хотів би/хотіла б] підучити декілька з ваших місцевих діалектів.

Would you like me to teach you some English?

chy ne [kho-*tiw* by/ kho-*ti*-la b] ty shcho-by ya do-po-*mih*/do-po-moh-*la* to-*bi* z an-*hliys'*-ko-yu *mo*-vo-yu? (m/f)	Чи ти не [хотів би/ хотіла б] ти щоби я допоміг/допомогла тобі з англійською мовою?

Is this a local or national custom?

tse mis-*tse*-va chy na-*rod*-nya tra-*dy*-tsi-ya?	Це місцева чи народня традиція?

I respect your customs.

ya po-va-*zha*-yu *va*-shi tra-*dy*-tsi-yi	Я поважаю ваші традиції.

COMMUNITY BENEFIT & INVOLVEMENT

What sorts of issues is this community facing?

ya-*ki* prob-*le*-my sto-*yat'* *pe*-red tsym sus-*pil'*-stvom?	Які проблеми стоять перед цим суспільством?

corruption	ko-*rup*-tsi-ya	корупція
literacy	ne-*hra*-mot-nist'	неграмотність

media restrictions	ob-*me*-zhe-na in-for-*ma*-tsi-ya v *pre*-si	обмежена інформація в пресі
political unrest	po-li-*tych*-na ne-sta-*bil'*-nist'	політична нестабільність
unemployment	bez-ro-*bit*-tya	безробіття

I'd like to volunteer my skills.

> ya [kho-*tiw* by/kho-*ti*-la b] za-pro-po-nu-*va*-ty mo-*yi* znan-*nya* (m/f)

Я [хотів би/хотіла б] запропонувати мої знання.

Are there any volunteer programs available in the area?

> chu ne is-*nyu*-yut' po-*bly*-zu proh-*ra*-my u ya-*kykh* u-*cha*-stu-yut' do-bro-*vol'*-tsi?

Чи не існють поблизу програми у яких участують добровольці?

ENVIRONMENT

Where can I recycle this?

> de me-*ni* mozh-na o-*tse* zda-ty na re-*saikl*?

Де мені можна оце здати на ресайкл?

TRANSPORT

Can we get there by public transport?

> chy ne moh-*ly* b my do-*bra*-ty-sya tu-*dy* pub-*lich*-nym trans-*por*-tom?

Чи не могли б ми добратися туди публічним транспортом?

Can we get there by bike?

> chy ne *mozh*-na do-*bra*-ty-sya tu-*dy* ro-*ve*-rom?

Чи не можна добратися туди ровером?

I'd prefer to walk there.

> me-*ni* vy-hid-*ni*-she proy-*tu* tu-*dy* *pish*-ky

Мені вигідніше пройти туди пішки.

ACCOMMODATION

I'd like to stay at a locally-run hotel.

ya [kho-*tiw* by/kho-*ti*-la b]	Я [хотів би/хотіла б]
pe-re-*bu*-ty v mis-*tse*-vo-mu	перебути в місцевому
ho-*te*-li (m/f)	готелі.

Are there any ecolodges here?

chy ne na-*kho*-dyat'-sya	Чи не находяться
tut *e*-ko *lod*-zhy?	тут еко лоджи?

Can I turn the air conditioning off and open the window?

chy ne [mih by/moh-*la* b]	Чи не [міг би/могла б]
ya *vyk*-lyu-chy-ty	я виключити
kon-di-tsi-o-*ner* ta	кондиціонер та
vid-*kry*-ty vik-*no*? (m/f)	відкрити вікно?

There's no need to change my sheets.

ne *tre*-ba mi-*nya*-ty *po*-stil	Не треба міняти постіл.

SHOPPING

Where can I buy locally produced goods/souvenirs?

de *mozh*-na ku-*py*-ty	Де можна купити
to-*va*-ry/su-ve-*ni*-ry	товари/сувеніри
pro-du-*ko*-va-ni mis-*tse*-vo?	продуковані місцево?

Do you sell Fair Trade products ?

chy vy pro-da-*ye*-te	Чи ви продаєте
pro-*du*-kty fer treyd?	продукти 'фер трейд'?

FOOD

Do you sell …?	chy vy pro-da-*ye*-te …?	Чи ви продаєте …?
locally produced food	mis-*tse*-vo pry-ho-*tov*-le-nu *yi*-zhu	місцево приготовлену їжу
organic produce	na-tu-*ral'*-ni pro-*duk*-ty	натуральні продукти

Can you tell me which traditional foods I should try?

chy ne *mo*-zhe-te po-*ra*-dy-ty ya-*ki* tra-dy-*tsiy*-ni *stra*-vy *var*-ta po-*pro*-bu-va-ty?	Чи не можете порадити які традиційні страви варта попробувати?

SIGHTSEEING

Are cultural tours available?

ya-*ki* is-nu-*yut'* kul'-*tur*-ni po-*yizd*-ky?	Які існують культурні поїздки?

Does your company ...?	chy *va*-she pid-pry-*yem*-stvo ...?	Чи ваше підприємство ...?
donate money to charity	*zhert*-vu-ye *hro*-shi na do-bro-*diy*-ni *tsi*-li	жертвує гроші на добродійні цілі
hire local guides	en-ha-*zhu*-ye mis-*tse*-vykh pro-*vid*-ny-*kiv*	енгажує місцевих провідників
visit local businesses	vid-*vi*-du-ye mis-*tse*-vi pid-pry-*yem*-stva	відвідує місцеві підприємства

Does the guide speak ...?	chy pro-vid-*nyk* ho-vo-*rit'* ...?	Чи провідник говорить ...?
Crimean Tatar	po ta-*tars'*-ko-mu	по татарському
Galician	po *ha*-lyts'-ko-mu	по галицькому
Surzhyk	*sur*-zhy-kom	суржиком